HUMANISM IN ENGLAND DURING THE
FIFTEENTH CENTURY

Humanism
in England
During the Fifteenth Century

R. WEISS

BASIL BLACKWELL · OXFORD · 1941

Printed in Great Britain for BASIL BLACKWELL & MOTT LTD,
by the KEMP HALL PRESS LTD, in the City of Oxford

To My Wife

NOTE

Dates are given according to the new use. In order to restrict the number of footnotes references to the same work, etc., have been grouped together when continuous, and the same number of the footnote given to its various references in the text. The bibliography includes only works quoted more than once in the notes. Some well-known studies partly dealing with fifteenth century Italian humanism in England will not be found in it, since the information given there was available in other publications used instead. References to volume XIII of the *Calendar of Entries in the Papal Registers, Illustrating the History of Great Britain and Ireland*, are taken from the page proofs of this volume, which are available at the Public Record Office.

CONTENTS

INSTAURATIO BONARUM LITTERARUM

Ecce renascentis doctrinae gloria floret,
Linguarum floret cognitioque trium.
Migrat in Italiam Graecus thesaurus, et artes
Se reparaturum praedicat usque bonas.
Excolit eloquii vivos Hispania fontes,
Gallia nunc studiis tota dicata nitet.
Nutrit honorifice doctos Germania multos,
Quorum sunt orbi nomina nota probe.
Ingeniorum altrix et nostra Britannia, Phraeum,
Tiptotum, Viduum, Flaminiumque tulit.
Lumina doctrinae, Grocinus deinde secutus,
Sellingus, Linacer, Latimarusque pius,
Dunstallus, Phoenix, Stocleius atque Coletus,
Lilius et Paceus, festa corona virum.
Omnes Italiam petierunt sidere fausto :
Et nituit Latiis Musa Britanna scholis.
Omnes inque suam patriam rediere diserti,
Secum thesauros et retulere suos:
Nempe antiquorum scripta exemplaria passim
Graecorum, aeternas quae meruere cedros.
Vivat doctorum felix industria, per quam
Lux, pulsis tenebris, reddita clara nitet.

J. Leland. *Collectanea* (1770 ed.) V, 137.

A I

PREFACE

THE present study attempts to describe the rise and development of humanism in England up to the accession of Henry VII. It aims above all at showing the transition from medieval to Renaissance culture in this country, and the difficulties which had to be overcome to bring about such a change.

Looked at independently the manifestations of early English humanism may appear to be of restricted interest. But when regarded as a whole and as an episode in the history of ideas they assume a considerable rôle, since they were instrumental in conditioning the intellectual structure of England at the eve of the Reformation—Grocin, Linacre, Colet, and More, are to some extent the direct outcome of them.

ACKNOWLEDGEMENTS

THE kindness of several friends has proved invaluable in the preparation of this study. I must above all thank Professor Cesare Foligno and Mr C. A. J. Armstrong, both of whom spared no effort to help me, especially with problems connected with the presentation of this work. I found the encouragement of the late Lord Tweedsmuir and Professor F. M. Powicke and the advice of Mr E. Lobel extremely valuable, and I feel very much indebted to Mr W. A. Pantin and Miss R. J. Mitchell, both of whom put much valuable material at my disposal.

Mr J. D. A. Barnicot, the Rev Daniel Callus, O.P., Dr S. B. Chrimes, Mr Strickland Gibson, Mgr P. Guerrini, Mr D. Hay, Dr R. W. Hunt, Professor E. F. Jacob, Mr Hiroshi Kawai, Mr N. R. Ker, Dr R. Klibansky, Professor L. Lazzarini, Mr R. J. Liddell, the Rev Gervase Mathew, O.P., Mr R. A. B. Mynors, and Mr J. A. Philip are also very much entitled to my gratitude.

To Professor J. Haller of Stuttgart, who very generously placed at my disposal the proofs of his forthcoming edition of Piero del Monte's Letters, to Miss N. D. Hurnard, Miss W. A. Pronger, and Miss J. Otway-Ruthven, each of whom was good enough to lend me a copy of her thesis, I extend my grateful thanks.

The publication of this work has been rendered possible by the receipt of generous grants from the Committee for Advanced Studies of Oxford University and the Publication Fund of London University, to both of which I am naturally greatly indebted, as I feel indebted to Dr C. T. Onions for including this study in the *Medium Aevum Monographs*. My debt to my wife is very great.

University College, University of London.
   July, 1940.

BIBLIOGRAPHY

MANUSCRIPTS

GREAT BRITAIN AND IRELAND

CAMBRIDGE
Corpus Christi College

MS. no. 170 (Anglo-Roman documents).
MS. no. 423 (Greek *Psalter* with notes by J. Farley).

Gonville and Caius College
MS. no. 230 (Extracts from Whethamstede's works).

Trinity College
MS. no. 823 (T. Gaza, *Grammar*).
MS. no. 1420 (Humanistic miscellany).

CANTERBURY
Dean and Chapter Library
Accounts of Canterbury College, Oxford.

DUBLIN
Trinity College
MS. no. 925 (T. Gaza, *Grammar*).

LONDON
British Museum
Additional MSS.

MS. no. 10344 (Doget's commentary on Plato's *Phaedo*).
MS. no. 15386 (P. Griphus, *De Denariis Sancti Petri*).
MS. no. 26764 (Whethamstede's *Palearium*).

Arundel MSS.
MS. no. 11 (Extracts from Whethamstede's *Granarium*).
MS. no. 249 (Surigone's poems).

Cotton MSS.
MS. Julius F. VII (Notebook of William of Worcester).
MS. Tiberius B. VI (Formulary).
MS. Tiberius D. V (Whethamstede's *Granarium*, part II).
MS. Nero C. VI (Whethamstede's *Granarium*, part I).
MS. Nero D. VII (St. Albans Fraternity Book).
MS. Cleopatra E. III (Miscellaneous Anglo-Roman documents).

Egerton MSS.
MS. no. 646 (Whethamstede's *Pabularium Poetarum*).

Harley MSS.

MS. no. 2485 (Gunthorpe's transcript of Seneca's *Tragedies*).
MS. no. 3346 (Hermonymos' translation of Greek gnomic sentences).

Royal MSS.

MS. 10 B. IX (Henry Cranebroke's notebook).
MS. 12 A. XXIX (Carmeliano's *De Vere*).

OXFORD

Bodleian Library

MS. Auct. F.5.26 (Treatises by Del Monte and Da Castiglionchio).
MS. Auct. G.9.3 (Hermonymos' version of Aristotle's *De Virtutibus*).
MS Bodl. 80 (Free's translation of Synesius).
MS. Bodl. 587 (Free's letters, Gunthorpe's orations, etc.).
MS. Gr. class. e.96 (T. Gaza, *Grammar*).
MS. Lat. misc. d.34 (Beccaria's version of Boccaccio's *Corbaccio*).

University Archives

*Register Aa*5.
*Register Ff.*4.

Balliol College

MS. no. 124 (John Free's notebook).

Magdalen College

MS. no. 37 (Humanistic versions from the Greek).

New College

MS. no. 288 (Chaundler's works).

University College

Computus Rolls, 1429–72.

AUSTRIA

VIENNA

National-Bibliothek

MS. no. 2403 (Flemmyng's *Lucubratiunculae Tiburtinae*).
MS. no. 4139 (Sermon by Andrew Holes).

ITALY

FLORENCE

Biblioteca Riccardiana

MS. Ricc. no. 827 (Letter Book of Pier Candido Decembrio).

MILAN

Biblioteca Ambrosiana

MS. I. 104. sup. (Decembrio's version of Plato's *Republic*).
MS. R. 88 sup. (Notebook of Pier Candido Decembrio).

JAPAN

TOKYO

Imperial University Library

MS. A.100.1300 (Formulary).

VATICAN CITY

Biblioteca Apostolica Vaticana

MS. Vat. Lat. no. 2694 (Letter Book of Piero del Monte).

UNPUBLISHED THESES

Hodge, H.: *The Abbey of St. Albans under John Whethamstede.* (Manchester Ph.D. thesis.)[1]

Hurnard, N. D.: *Studies in Intellectual Life in England from the Middle of the Fifteenth Century till the Time of Colet.* (Oxford D.Phil. thesis.)[2]

Liddell, J. R.: *The First Century of the Library of Corpus Christi College, Oxford.* (Oxford B.Litt. thesis.)[2]

PRINTED SOURCES

Agostini, G. degli, *Notizie Istorico-Critiche intorno la vita e le opere degli Scrittori Viniziani*, Venezia, 1752.

Allen, P. S.: Bishop Shirwood of Durham and his Library, *E.H.R.* XXV (1910) pp. 445–56.

Annales Monasterii Sancti Albani a J. Amundesham, ed. H. T. Riley, (R.S.) 2 vols., London, 1870–1.

Bale, J.: *Scriptorum Illustrium Maioris Brytanniae Catalogus*, Basileae, 1559.

Balzani, U.: 'Un' Ambasciata inglese a Roma,' *Archivio della Società Romana di Storia Patria*, III (1880) pp. 175–211.

Baron, H.: *Leonardo Bruni Aretino*, Leipzig, 1928.

Bertalot, L.: 'Forschungen über Leonardo Bruni Aretino,' *Archivium Romanicum*, XV (1931) pp. 284–323.

Bertoni, G.: *Guarino da Verona tra Letterati e Cortigiani a Ferrara*, Ginevra, 1921.

Borsa, M.: 'Pier Candido Decembri e l'Umanesimo in Lombardia,' *A.S.L.*, X (1893) pp. 1–75, 358–441.

Borsa, M.: 'Correspondence of Humphrey, Duke of Gloucester, and Pier Candido Decembrio,' *E.H.R.* XIX (1904) pp. 509–26.

(Der) Briefwechsel des Eneas Silvius Piccolomini, ed. R. Volkan, *Fontes Rerum Austriacarum, Diplomataria et Acta*, vols., LXI–II, LVII, Wien, 1909–12.

Bruni, L.: *Epistolarum Libri VIII*, ed. L. Mehus, 2 vols., Florentiae, 1741.

Burchardus, J.: *Diarium*, ed. L. Thuasne, 2 vols., Paris, 1883.

Burrows, M.: 'Memoir of William Grocin,' *Collectanea*, (O.H.S.) vol. II, Oxford, 1890, pp. 332–79.

[1] A copy of this thesis is in the University Library, Manchester.
[2] A copy of this thesis is in the Bodleian Library, Oxford.

Calendar of French Rolls for the Reign of Henry VI, *48th Report of the Deputy Keeper of the Public Records*, London, 1887, App. pp. 217–450.

Calendar of Entries in the Papal Registers, Illustrating the History of Great Britain and Ireland, Papal Letters, vols., VII–XII, ed. J. A. Twemlow, London, 1906–33.

Calendar of Patent Rolls preserved in the Public Record Office, Henry V—Richard III, 11 vols., London, 1897–1911.

Calendar of State Papers and MSS. existing in the Archives and Collections of Milan, ed. A. B. Hinds, vol. I, London, 1912.

Calendar of State Papers and MSS. relating to English affairs existing in the Archives and Collections of Venice, ed. Rawdon Brown, vol. I, London, 1864.

Calmette, J., et Perinelle, G.: *Louis XI et l'Angleterre*, 1461–83, Paris, 1930.

(*The*) *Cambridge Medieval History*, ed. C. W. Previté-Orton and Z. N. Brooke, vol. VIII, Cambridge, 1936.

Christ Church Letters, ed. J. B. Sheppard, (C.S.) London, 1877.

(*The*) *Chronicles of the White Rose of York*, London, 1845.

Compendium Totius Gramaticae, Davantriae, 1489.

Copinger, W. A.: *Supplement to Hain's Repertorium Bibliographicum*, 3 vols., London, 1895–1902.

Coxe, O.: *Catalogus Codicum MSS. qui in Collegiis Aulisque Oxoniensibus hodie adservantur*, 2 vols., Oxford, 1852.

Craster, H. H. E.: 'Duke Humphrey's Dante, Petrarch, and Boccaccio MSS.,' *T.L.S.*, 13 May, 1920, p. 303.

Creighton, M.: 'Some Literary Correspondence of Humphrey, Duke of Gloucester', *E.H.R.* X (1895) pp. 99–104.

(*The*) *Dictionary of National Biography*, ed. L. Stephen and S. Lee, 63 vols., Oxford, 1885–1900.

Ditt, E.: 'Pier Candido Decembrio: Contributo alla storia dell' umanesimo italiano,' *Reale Istituto Lombardo di Scienze, Lettere e Arti, Memorie*, XXIV (1934) pp. 21–106.

Documents Illustrating the Activities of the General and Provincial Chapters of the English Black Monks, 1215–1540, ed. W. A. Pantin, (C.S.), vol. III, London, 1937.

Duff, E. Gordon: *Fifteenth Century English Books*, Oxford, 1917.

Epistolae Academicae Oxon., ed. H. Anstey, 2 vols., (O.H.S.) Oxford, 1898.

Epistolario di Guarino Veronese, ed. R. Sabbadini, 3 vols., Venezia, 1915–9.

Flynn, V. J.: 'Englishmen in Rome during the Renaissance,' *Modern Philology*, XXXVI (1938) pp. 121–38.

Gaguin, R.: *Epistole et Orationes*, ed. L. Thuasne, 2 vols., Paris, 1903.

Gams, P. B.: *Series Episcoporum Ecclesiae Catholicae*, Ratisbonae, 1873.

Gascoigne, T.: *Loci e Libro Veritatum*, ed. J. E. Thorold Rogers, Oxford, 1881.

Gasquet, F. A.: *The Eve of the Reformation*, London, 1905.

Gesamtkatalog der Wiegendrucke, vols. 1–6, Leipzig, 1925–34.

Gibson, S.: *Early Oxford Bindings*, Oxford, 1903.

Grace Book A, ed. S. M. Leathes, Cambridge, 1897.

Grace Book B, ed. M. Bateson, Part I, Cambridge, 1903.

Gray, H. L.: 'Greek Visitors to England in 1455–6', *Anniversary Essays by Students of Charles Homer Haskins*, Boston, 1929, pp. 81–116.

Guerrini, P.: *Pietro Carmeliano da Brescia Segretario Reale d'Inghilterra*, Brescia, 1918.

Hain, L.: *Repertorium Bibliographicum*, 2 vols., Stuttgart, 1826–31.

Haller, J.: *Concilium Basiliense*, vol. III, Basel, 1900.

Haller, J. 'England und Rom unter Martin V,' *Quellen und Forschungen aus Italienischen Archiven und Bibliotheken*, VIII (1905) pp. 249–304.

Jacob, E. F.: *Florida Verborum Venustas*, Manchester, 1933.

James, M. R.: *A Descriptive Catalogue of the Manuscripts other than Oriental in the Library of King's College, Cambridge*, Cambridge, 1895.

James, M. R.: *A Descriptive Catalogue of the Manuscripts in the Library of Peterhouse, Cambridge*, Cambridge, 1899.

James, M. R.: *The Ancient Libraries of Canterbury and Dover*, Cambridge, 1903.

James, M. R.: 'The Scribe of the Leicester Codex,' *Journal of Theological Studies*, V (1904) pp. 445–7.

James, M. R.: *The Chaundler MSS.* (Roxburghe Club), London, 1916.

James, M. R.: 'Greek MSS. in England before the Renaissance,' *The Library*, VII (1927) pp. 337–53.

Keussen, H.: *Die Matrikel der Universität Köln*, vol. I, Bonn, 1928.

Kingsford, C. L.: *English Historical Literature in the Fifteenth Century*, Oxford, 1913.

Kirby, T. F.: *Winchester Scholars*, London, 1888.

Lathrop, H. B.: 'The Translations of John Tiptoft,' *Modern Language Review*, XLI (1926) pp. 496–501.

Leach, A. F.: *History of Winchester College*, London, 1898.

Legrand, E.: *Bibliographie Hellenique*, vol. I, Paris, 1885.

Leland, J.: *Commentarii De Scriptoribus Britannicis*, ed. A. Hall, Oxonii, 1709.

Leland, J.: *De Rebus Britannicis Collectanea*, ed. T. Hearne, 6 vols., London, 1774.

Le Neve, J.: *Fasti Ecclesiae Anglicanae*, continued by T. Duffus Hardy, 3 vols., Oxford, 1854.

Letters and Papers Illustrative of the Wars of the English in France, ed. J. Stevenson, (R.S.) 3 vols., London, 1861–4.

'Libellus de Laudibus Duarum Civitatum et Sedium Episcopalium, Welliae scilicet et Bathoniae, per Thomam Chaundeler, Cancellarium Wellensem, collectus,' ed. G. Williams, *Somerset Archaeological and Natural History Society Proceedings*, XIX (1873) pp. 99–121.

Literae Cantuarienses, ed. J. B. Sheppard, (R.S.) 3 vols., London, 1887–9.

Little, A. G.: *The Grey Friars in Oxford*, (O.H.S.) Oxford, 1892.

Lobel, E.: 'A 15 cent. MS. in private hands,' *B.Q.R.* V (1926–9) pp. 134–5.

Lucubraciuncularum Tiburtinarum Libri Duo, S.L.N.A. (Rome c.a. 1480).

Luiso, F. P.: 'Studi su l'Epistolario di Lapo da Castiglionchio Juniore,' *Studi Italiani di Filologia Classica*, VII (1899) pp. 205–99.

(*The*) *Magdalen College Register*, ed. J. R. Bloxam, 7 vols., Oxford, 1853–81.

Mai, A.: *Spicilegium Romanum*, vol. X, Romae, 1839.

Mann, W.: *Lateinische Dichtung in England vom Ausgang der Frühhumanismus bis zum Regierungsantritt Elisabeths*, Halle, 1939.

Mansi, G. D.: *Sacrorum Conciliorum Nova et Amplissima Collectio*, vols., XXIX–XXX, Venetiis, 1788–92.

Mazzatinti, G.: *La Biblioteca dei Re d' Aragona*, Rocca San Casciano, 1897.

(*The*) *Medieval Archives of the University of Oxford*, ed. H. E. Salter, (O.H.S.) 2 vols., Oxford, 1928–31.

Medin, A.: 'Il testamento e l'inventario di un' umanista veronese del secolo XV,' *Miscellanea di Studi in Onore di Attilio Hortis*, vol. I, Trieste, 1910, pp. 459–66.

Mercati, A.: *Per la Cronologia della Vita e degli Scritti di Niccolò Perotti*, Roma, 1925.

(*The*) *Middle English Version of Palladius De Re Rustica*, ed. M. Liddel, Part I, Berlin, 1896.

Mitchell, R. J.: 'English Law Students at Bologna in the Fifteenth Century,' *E.H.R.* LI (1936) pp. 270–87.

Mitchell, R. J.: 'English Students at Padua, 1460–75,' *Royal Historical Society Transactions*, Fourth Series, XIX (1936) pp. 101–17.

Mitchell, R. J.: *John Tiptoft*, London, 1938.

Moore, S.: 'Patrons of Letters in Norfolk and Suffolk, c. 1450,' *P.M.L.A.* XXVII (1912) pp. 188–207, XXVIII (1913) pp. 79–105.

Munimenta Academica, ed. H. Anstey, (R.S.) 2 vols., London, 1868.

Newman, W. L.: 'The Correspondence of Humphrey, Duke of Gloucester, and Pier Candido Decembrio' *E.H.R.* XX (1905), pp. 484–93.

Nogara, B.: *Scritti Inediti e Rari di Biondo Flavio*, Roma, 1927.

Nolhac, P. de, *Petrarque et l'Humanisme*, 2 vols., Paris, 1907.

(*The*) *Official Correspondence of Thomas Beckington*, ed. G. Williams, (R.S.) 2 vols., London, 1872.

Omont, H.: *Georges Hermonyme de Sparte Maître de Grec à Paris et Copiste de Manuscrits*, Paris, 1885.

Opera Hactenus Inedita T. Livii de Frulovisiis de Ferrara, ed. C. W. Previté-Orton, Cantabrigiae, 1932.

Otway-Ruthven, J.: *The King's Secretary and the Signet Office in the XVth Century*, Cambridge, 1939.

(The) Paston Letters, ed. J. Gairdner, 6 vols., London, 1904.

Pastor, L. von, *History of the Popes from the Close of the Middle Ages*, vols. I–IV, London, 1891–4.

Perry, G. G.: 'Bishop Beckington and Henry VI,' *E.H.R.*, IX (1894) pp. 261–74.

Phalaris, *Epistolae*, Oxford, 1485.

Pitseus, J.: *Relationum Historicarum de Rebus Anglicis*, Paris, 1619.

Poggii Epistolae, ed. T. de Tonellis, 3 vols., Florentiae, 1832–61.

Proceedings and Ordinances of the Privy Council of England, ed. H. N. Nicholas, vol. V, London, 1835.

Proctor, R.: *Index to the Early Printed Books in the British Museum*, London, 1898.

(The) Prologues and Epilogues of William Caxton, ed. W. J. B. Crotch, (Early English Text Society), London, 1928.

Radford, L. B.: *Henry Beaufort*, London, 1908.

Ramsay, Sir J. H.: *Lancaster and York*, 2 vols., Oxford, 1892.

(The) Register of Magdalen College, Oxford, New Series, ed. W. D. Macray, vol. I, London, 1894.

(The) Register of Thomas Bekynton, ed. H. C. Maxwell-Lyte, and M. C. B. Dawes, 2 vols., (Somerset Record Society), London, 1934.

Register of the University of Oxford, ed. C. W. Boase, (O.H.S.) vol. I, Oxford, 1885.

Registrum Abbatiae J. Whethamstede, ed. M. T. Riley, (R.S.) 2 vols., London, 1872–3.

Registrum Cancellarii, ed. H. E. Salter, (O.H.S.) 2 vols., Oxford, 1932.

Reports of the Historical MSS. Commission, London, 1870–.

Rosmini, F. de, *Idea dell'ottimo precettore nella vita e disciplina di Vittorino da Feltre e de' suoi discepoli*, Milano, 1845.

Ross, J.: *Historia Regum Angliae*, ed. T. Hearne, Oxonii, 1745.

Rymer, T.: *Foedera*, 20 vols., London, 1704–34.

Sabbadini, R.: *Guarino da Verona e il suo epistolario edito e inedito*, Salerno, 1885.

Sabbadini, R.: 'L'Ultimo ventennio della vita di Manuele Crisolora' (1396–1415), *Giornale Ligustico*, XVII (1890) pp. 321–36.

Sabbadini, R.: *La Scuola e gli Studi di Guarino da Verona*, Catania, 1896.

Sabbadini, R.: *Le Scoperte dei Codici Latini e Greci ne' Secoli XIV e XV*, 2 vols., Firenze, 1905–14.

Sabbadini, R.: *Il Metodo degli Umanisti*, Firenze, 1922.

Sabbadini, R.: 'Tito Livio Frulovisio,' *G.S.L.I.* CIII (1934) pp. 55-73.

Saona, L. de, *Rhetorica Nova*, Apud Sanctum Albanum, 1480.

Schirmer, W. F.: *Der Englische Frühhumanismus*, Leipzig, 1931.

Scofield, C. L.: *The Life and Reign of Edward IV*, 2 vols., London, 1923.

(*The*) *St. Albans Chronicle*, ed. V. H. Galbraith, Oxford, 1937.

Somerset Medieval Wills, (1383-1500), ed. F. W. Weaver, (Somerset Record Society), London, 1901.

Spingarn, J. E.: 'Unpublished Letters of an English Humanist,' *Journal of Comparative Literature*, I (1903) pp. 47-65.

Stone, J.: *Chronicle*, ed. W. G. Searle, Cambridge, 1902.

Tait, J.: 'Letters of John Tiptoft, Earl of Worcester, and Archbishop Neville to the University of Oxford,' *E.H.R.* XXV (1920) pp. 570-74.

Tanner, T.: *Bibliotheca Britannico-Hybernica*, London, 1748.

Thomae de Elmham Vita et Gesta Henrici Quinti, ed. T. Hearne, Oxoniae, 1729.

Thompson, A. Hamilton, ' Visitations of Religious Houses,' *Lincolnshire Record Society*, vol. VII (1914).

Titi Livii Forojuliensis Vita Henrici Quinti, ed. T. Hearne, Oxoniae, 1716.

Toynbee, P.: 'Duke Humphrey's Dante, Petrarch and Boccaccio MSS.' *T.L.S.* 22 April, 1920, p. 256.

Ullman, B. L.: 'Manuscripts of Humphrey, Duke of Gloucester,' *E.H.R.* LII (1937) pp. 670-2.

Venn, J. and J. A.: *Alumni Cantabrigienses*, Part I, Cambridge, 1922-4.

Verrua, P.: *Umanisti ed altri studiosi viri italiani e stranieri di qua e di là dalle alpi e dal mare*, Ginevra, 1924.

Vespasiano da Bisticci, *Vite di Uomini Illustri*, ed. A. Bartoli, Firenze, 1859.

Vickers, K. H.: *Humphrey, Duke of Gloucester*, London, 1907.

'Vita Jannotii Manetti . . . auctore Naldo Naldio Florentino,' L. A. Muratori, *Rerum Italicarum Scriptores*, vol. XX, Mediolani, 1731, pp. 521-607.

'(Le) Vite di Paolo II di Gaspare da Verona e Michele Canensi,' ed. G. Zippel, *Rerum Italicarum Scriptores*, (new edition), tom. III, part XVI, Città di Castello, 1904.

Vogel, M. und Gardthausen, V.: 'Die Griechischen Schreiber des Mittelalters und der Renaissance', *Beihefte zum Zentralblatt für Bibliothekswesen*, vol. XXXIII, Leipzig, 1909.

Voigt, G.: *Die Wiederbelebung des Classichen Alterthums*, 2 vols., Berlin, 1893.

Wadding, L.: *Scriptores Ordinis Minorum*, Romae, 1806.

Walser, E.: *Poggius Florentinus*, Leipzig, 1914.

Warkworth, J.: *Chronicle of the first thirteen years of the reign of Edward IV*, ed. J. O. Halliwell, (C.S.) London, 1839.

Weiss, R.: 'A Letter-Preface of John Free to John Tiptoft, Earl of Worcester,' *B.Q.R.* VIII (1935–8) pp. 101–3.

Weiss, R.: 'The Library of John Tiptoft, Earl of Worcester,' *B.Q.R.* VIII (1935–8) pp. 157–64.

Weiss, R.: 'Another Tiptoft Manuscript', *B.Q.R.* VIII (1935–8) pp. 234–5.

Weiss, R.: 'Per la conoscenza di Dante in Inghilterra nel quattrocento,' *G.S.L.I.* CVIII (1936) pp. 357–9.

Weiss, R.: 'Humanism in Oxford,' *T.L.S.*, 9 January, 1937, p. 28.

Weiss, R.: 'The Earliest Account of the Murder of James I of Scotland,' *E.H.R.* LII (1937) pp. 479–91.

Weiss, R.: 'The Earliest Catalogues of the Library of Lincoln College,' *B.Q.R.* VIII (1935–8) pp. 343–59.

Weiss, R.: 'Antonio Beccaria in Inghilterra', *G.S.L.I.* CX (1937) pp. 344–6.

Weiss, R.: 'Some Unpublished Correspondence of Guarino da Verona,' *Italian Studies*, II (1938–9) pp. 110–7.

Weiss, R.: 'Cornelio Vitelli in France and England', *The Journal of the Warburg Institute*, II (1938–9) pp. 219–26.

Wharton, H.: *Anglia Sacra*, 2 vols., London, 1691.

Willmanns, A.: 'Ueber die Briefsammlungen des Poggio Bracciolini,' *Zentralblatt für Bibliothekswesen*, XXX (1913) pp. 289–331, 443–63.

Worcester, W. of, 'Annales Rerum Anglicarum,' *Letters and Papers Illustrative of the Wars of the English in France*, ed. J. Stevenson, (R.S.) vol. III, London, 1864, pp. 743–93.

Worcester, W. of, *Itinerarium*, ed. J. Nasmith, Cantabrigiae, 1778.

Denholm Young, N.: 'Richard de Bury,' *Royal Historical Society Transactions*, Fourth series, XX (1937) pp. 135–68.

Zanelli, A.: 'Piero del Monte,' *A.S.L.* XXXIV (1907) pp. 318–78, 46–115.

Zellfelder, A.: *England und das Basler Konzil*, Berlin, 1913.

Zeno, A.: *Dissertazioni Vossiane*, 2 vols., Venezia, 1752–3.

Zonta, G. e Brotto, C. A.: *Acta Graduum Academicorum ab anno mccccvi ad annum mcccl*, Padova, 1922.

SIGLA

A.S.L.: Archivio Storico Lombardo.
B.A.: Biblioteca Ambrosiana, Milano.
B.L.: Bodleian Library, Oxford.
B.L.F.: Biblioteca Laurenziana, Firenze.
B.M.: British Museum, London.
B.N.: Bibliothèque Nationale, Paris.
B.Q.R.: The Bodleian Quarterly Record.
B.R.F.: Biblioteca Riccardiana, Firenze.
Copinger: Copinger, Supplement to Hain's *Repertorium Bibliographicum*.
C.P.R.: Calendar of Papal Registers.
C.S.: Camden Society.
C.U.: Cambridge University Library.
D.N.B.: The Dictionary of National Biography.
E.H.R.: The English Historical Review.
Gesamtkatalog: Gesamtkatalog der Wiegendrucke.
Gordon Duff: Gordon Duff, *Fifteenth Century English Books*.
G.S.L.I.: Giornale Storico della Letteratura Italiana.
Hain: Hain, *Repertorium Bibliographicum*.
H.M.C.: Historical Manuscripts Commission.
O.H.S.: Oxford Historical Society.
P.R.: Calendar of Patent Rolls.
P.R.O.: Public Record Office, London.
Proctor: Proctor, *Index to the Early Printed Books in the British Museum*.
R.S.: Rolls Series.
S.P.M.: Calendar of State Papers, Milan.
S.P.V.: Calendar of State Papers, Venice.
T.L.S.: The Times Literary Supplement.
V.L.: Biblioteca Apostolica Vaticana, Città del Vaticano.

INTRODUCTION

IF we compare the state of English learning at the beginning and end of the fifteenth century, a very marked difference will be perceptible. While at the beginning of the century English cultural standards were still thoroughly medieval, at its close they conformed to a certain extent with the ideals of the Renaissance, so that even a fastidious critic of the calibre of Erasmus could be favourably impressed by some of the English scholars with whom he came into contact during his visit to England. Naturally such a change in cultural values was not accomplished in a day. On the contrary it was the result of a slow but steady process of evolution begun during the first quarter of the fifteenth century, which was eventually to grow powerful enough to affect the whole intellectual structure of England by the end of the century. It is in the study of this change, in the history of humanism in England during the first three quarters of the fifteenth century, that it is possible to see how this transition from medieval to Renaissance culture was accomplished. In humanism is to be found an explanation of the achievements of a Grocin and a Linacre, a Colet and a More.

Both the meaning and the origins of humanism have been for some time, and especially of late, the subject of academic controversy.[1] It is therefore advisable to state at once the meaning attributed to the term 'humanism' as far as this book is concerned. 'Humanism' will be understood to embrace the whole range of classical studies and activities as conceived by the Italians from the days of Petrarch, and by 'humanist' the scholar who studied the writings of ancient authors without fear of supernatural anticiceronian warnings, searched for manuscripts of lost or rare classical texts, collected the works of classical writers, and attempted to learn Greek and write like the ancient authors of Rome.

Whatever its actual origins, it is undeniable that it was in fourteenth century Italy that humanism begins to be clearly noticeable as a distinct cultural movement. Its manifestations during this period appear in the form of a compromise with medieval culture, and it is only during the fifteenth century that

---

[1] On this cf. especially I. Siciliano, *Medio Evo e Rinascimento*, Milano, 1936, and *Bulletin of the International Committee of Historical Sciences*, XII (1939) p. 139.

Italian humanism became decidedly independent from medieval habits of thought. Even Petrarch with all his consciousness that the foundations of the learning of his day needed revision, and despite the enlightened character of his outlook and studies, was still in part a man of the Middle Ages, as may be seen from some of his works as, for instance, the *De Remediis Utriusque Fortunae*. Boccaccio also belonged partly to the Middle Ages: his encyclopedic conception of knowledge is typically medieval, while his view of history as a series of moralizing anecdotes is characteristic of medieval historiography.

Perhaps the chief attraction of humanism was that it offered several advantages over scholasticism. In its attempt to unify all knowledge within a system of logic, scholasticism lacked flexibility and powers of adaptation, was difficult of application in particular instances, and left no room for romanticism. Humanism on the other hand with its leaning towards Platonism displayed a wider scope, greater elasticity, and less dogmatism and adherence to formulae, so that all this combined with its emergence as a distinct system at a time when scholasticism had practically ceased to produce original speculation, rendered it very attractive to those scholars who came into contact with it.

Already by the end of the fourteenth century humanism as conceived by Petrarch and his friends had crossed the Italian Alps. The presence of the Papal and later of the antipapal Curia at Avignon, as well as the close relations between France and Italy, were instrumental in extending its influence to France, where already during the reign of Charles VI it included such accomplished followers as Gontier Col, Jean de Montreuil, and Nicholas de Clemanges.

England because of its geographical isolation and the conservative characteristics of its culture began to respond to the influence of humanism at a later stage than France. The beginnings and early development of humanism in this country up to the accession of the Tudors to the English throne form the subject of this book.

It is far from easy to decide what should be accepted as early manifestations of humanism in England. To consider as such every activity connected with the study of classical literature would be too wide and also not entirely correct. Some Latin classics had been read assiduously throughout the Middle Ages. Vergil, Statius, Horace, Lucan, and Ovid, had never ceased to be

studied, and imitations of Roman poets, and especially Ovid, are
frequent occurrences in medieval Latin literature. Ancient prose
authors also had their share of popularity and influence; Sallust,
Cicero, Seneca, and Valerius Maximus, held conspicuous positions
in the *curriculum* of medieval schools, and influenced considerably
rhetoric and historiography. During the twelfth century Bernard
of Chartres taught that all culture was based upon the classics,[1]
while a considerable section of Latin prose, epistolography
especially, was dominated by the clauses of the *Cursus* which
could claim, though indirectly, a classical origin.[2] Thus to label
every activity connected with the antique a humanistic manifestation would make humanism begin in classical times, and
identify as such movements like the revival of Roman law in the
twelfth century and the Aristotelian Renaissance of the thirteenth
century. It is above all in the approach and attitude towards the
classics rather than in the actual study of them that the features of
humanism can be detected. Medieval scholarship had regarded
the writings of ancient authors mainly as quarries of information
from which it was possible to derive facts, anecdotes, useful
examples, and fine phrases, or as texts susceptible of an allegorical
interpretation. Moreover, the disapproval of the early Church
towards classical letters was continually latent in medieval
culture, and it was only completely overcome by the growth of
humanism. Consequently it is of much importance when assess-
ing the outlook towards the classics of an English scholar of the
fifteenth century to take into account the amount of his independence from the old prejudices, and to find out whether an ancient
literary work is regarded as a source of facts, or as a work of art
from which inspiration of an aesthetic and stylistic nature could
be derived.

Another point which should not be overlooked is the way in
which the classics were imitated. As Burdach has pointed out,
'each medieval imitation of the classics proceeds according to the
method of the glossator, that is to say it takes details, choice and
beautiful sentences, with a collector's precision; it is a matter of

---

[1] *Dicebat Bernardus Carnotensis nos esse quasi nanos gigantium humeris insidentes ut possimus plura iis et remotiora uidere non utique proprii uisus acumine aut eminentia sed quia in altum subuehimur et extollimur magnitudine gigantea*, (John of Salisbury, *Metalogicus*, III. 4).
[2] A. C. Clark, *The Cursus in Medieval and Vulgar Latin*, Oxford, 1929, pp. 5–6. On the *Cursus* in England cf. N. Denholm Young, 'The Cursus in England,' *Oxford Essays in Medieval History Presented to Herbert Edward Salter*, Oxford, 1934, pp. 68–103, H. G. Richardson, 'An Oxford Teacher of the Fifteenth Century,' *Bulletin of the John Rylands Library, Manchester*, XXIII (1939) pp. 436–57.

indifference to the collector where they came from; and without any thought about the time and personality of their author they are woven with just pride into the writer's Latin, conforming to a linguistic spirit not in the least ancient but quite contemporary.'[1]

This method of imitation underwent a change with the development of neo-classicism, which turned it into an attempt to render the spirit of the original through a grammatical, stylistic, and lexical reproduction, linked to an effort at conforming with the classical outlook.

Besides such points as these, others should be considered in attempting to trace the early progress of humanism in England. Just as the reactions against medievalism varied from country to country, humanistic movements acquired some peculiar traits according to the country in which they were developed, these being mainly due to the economic and social background. The economic element particularly should not be overlooked, since it played a rôle of some importance in the shaping of the main characteristics of humanism in the various European countries which came under its influence.

The absence of professional humanists in England before the very end of the fifteenth century is not, however, to be attributed entirely to economic, social, and political conditions. All intellectual movements are started by amateurs, and their professional adherents only appear once the movement has established itself securely. Thus if we observe humanism in Italy during the fourteenth century, we shall hardly find any persons pursuing it as a profession before the end of the century. So it is only natural that amateurs should dominate humanism in the countries outside Italy practically until the end of the fifteenth century, considering that humanism began to be developed at a later date beyond the Alps.

Local circumstances moulded the characteristics of humanism in the various European countries which came under its influence during the Renaissance. An interesting illustration of its adaptation to local circumstances is, as it was pointed out by Dr. Ritter,[2] to be found in Germany during the fifteenth century. Humanism there appears to have been developed by schoolmen, and there was apparently no hostility between schoolmen and

---

[1] K. Burdach, *Riforma-Rinascimento-Umanesimo*, Firenze, 1935, p. 77.

[2] G. Ritter, 'Die geschichtliche Bedeutung der deutschen Humanismus,' *Historische Zeitschrift*, CXXVII (1923) pp. 393 ff. An abstract of this article is in E. F. Jacob, *The Fifteenth Century, some recent interpretations*, Manchester, 1930, pp. 14–5.

humanists. The difficulties encountered were not of a learned but of an economic nature, while its popularity in conservative circles seems to have been due to its usefulness in theological studies rather than to its intrinsic value.

Therefore in approaching English humanism it is important to consider the possible influence exercised not only by its scholarly, but also by its economic, political, and social backgrounds, and to bear in mind the peculiarities common to intellectual movements in the making. The importance of patronage will have to be appreciated, and contacts with Italy, both direct and indirect, examined from the angle of their influence on the course of English humanism. The state of scholasticism in England during the fifteenth century must also be borne in mind when reaching a final estimate, as its failure to maintain original speculation opened one of the doors through which humanism secured admission into English life.

II

So far the history of humanism in England during the fifteenth century has been very much neglected. Thomas Warton gave a short account of it in his *History of English Poetry*. Voigt and Sandys dedicated a few pages to it; Bishop Creighton made it the subject of his Rede Lecture and Lewis Einstein wrote a short and superficial survey of it in his *Italian Renaissance in England*. In 1916 a Russian scholar, M. Krusman, published in Odessa an imposing looking volume on humanism in England during the fourteenth century,[1] but the next volume, which was to include the fifteenth century, was never printed. Only as late as 1931 with Dr. Schirmer's *Englische Frühhumanismus* did the first scholarly publication on English fifteenth century humanism appear. This work is, however, satisfactory only up to a point. Schirmer's wide knowledge of printed material does not extend to manuscript sources, a serious handicap in a work where much information can only be gathered from manuscripts and other unpublished documents. The principal faults of Schirmer are, the stress he places upon dividing humanistic and medieval learning, thus creating an artificial standard of values, his neglect of evidence afforded by calligraphy, the copying of humanistic manuscripts, and fashions in style, and the repetition of incorrect statements

---

[1] V. E. Krusman, *Early Humanism in England* (in Russian), Odessa, 1916. A long and detailed review of this work by V. Zabughin is in *G.S.L.I.* LXVII (1916) pp. 404–17.

handed on by historians since the days of Leland. But the weakest point of Schirmer's work is its failure to appreciate the peculiar characteristics of early English humanism. As these appear to bear some resemblance to those of German humanism during the same period, such omission is not to be ascribed entirely to a foreigner's difficulty of appreciating typically English characteristics, as one of the reviewers of this work suggested.[1] Besides these works we have Mann's recent study on Latin poetry in England during the Renaissance,[2] and a few articles dealing, partly or entirely, with early English humanism;[3] but none of them really brings new contributions to the subject.

Of much greater value than attempts to survey the whole of early English humanism and its characteristics, are books and articles dealing with some of its aspects. Vickers' *Humphrey Duke of Gloucester* and Mitchell's *John Tiptoft* provide useful material. Professor Previté-Orton's edition of Frulovisi's works and Professor Jacob's *Florida Verborum Venustas* form a valuable contribution to the meagre bibliography of English humanism. A number of publications by the late Dr. M. R. James and the late Professor Sabbadini also afford information, and have earned much gratitude from anyone carrying out research in the field of early English neo-classicism.

The scarcity of original sources in regard to English humanism in its first stages is very much felt. Many documents of first class importance are lost, such as the letter books of Tiptoft, Flemmyng, Gunthorpe, and Chaundler, the oration delivered in Oxford by Cornelio Vitelli, and Chaundler's reply to it, the Latin poems of Free, Gunthorpe, and Shirwood, and some of Flemmyng, the lists of books bequeathed to Oxford by Tiptoft and Adam de Moleyns, to mention only a few. Of the available sources, besides Rymer's *Foedera*, the volumes of the Rolls Series, the publications of the Camden Society and the Oxford

---

[1] Cf. B. E. C. Davis' review of Schirmer's work in *Medium Ævum*, III (1934) pp. 195–8.
[2] Mann, *Lateinische Dichtung in England vom Ausgang der Frühhumanismus bis zum Regierungsantritt Elisabeths*.
[3] These include E. C. Wright, 'Continuity in English Humanism,' *P.M.L.A.*, LI (1936) pp. 370–6; P. Rebora, 'Aspetti dell' Umanesimo in Inghilterra', *La Rinascita*, II (1939) pp. 366–414; H. Hudson, 'John Leland's List of Early English Humanists,' *The Huntington Library Quarterly*, II (1939) pp. 300–4. D. Bush, *The Renaissance and English Humanism*, Toronto, 1939, does not deal with the fifteenth century. The chapter on humanism in H. Maynard Smith, *Pre-Reformation England*, London, 1938, is not free from mistakes. On the other hand L. E. Elliott-Binns, *England and the New Learning*, London, 1937, provides a useful sketch. I have not been able to see R. Garnett, 'English Humanists in Italy in the XV Century,' *Literature*, January–June, 1900.

Historical Society, and the various Public Record Office Calendars, contain useful information, as do also the epistolaries of Poggio, Bruni, Del Monte, Bekynton, Decembrio, and Free, and the letter books of Oxford University and Christ Church, Canterbury. Prefaces to humanistic works dedicated to English patrons proved of some value too, and the Latin writings of Chaundler and Whethamstede, the translations from the Greek by Free and Sellyng, and Robert Flemmyng's *Lucubratiunculae Tiburtinae* furnished important material. Also useful were some fifteenth century catalogues of English libraries, the evidence supplied by classical and humanistic manuscripts imported from Italy or transcribed in England during the fifteenth century, and the biographies of Vespasiano da Bisticci. Of almost equal value as contemporary authorities were the compilations of early antiquaries and bibliographers, and the works of Leland, Bale, Pits, and Tanner, gave several contributions of importance.

III

The aim of the present book is to give a concise survey of humanism in England during the fifteenth century. As such it would have been only logical to cover in it the period from 1400–1500. Instead the narrative begins at the end of 1418 and stops with the accession of Henry VII in 1485. This curtailed period was chosen for the following reasons. Before Poggio came to England in 1418, it is quite impossible to find, despite Krusman's very decided views to the contrary, any humanistic manifestations in this country. Even the most favourable bias can hardly accept as such the early classical pursuits of Thomas Walsingham at St. Albans or John Serguard at Norwich. It is true then to say that humanistic activity begins in England after Poggio had left; but his letters furnish us with a vivid, though perhaps somewhat biased, picture of English culture at the time of his visit, and his stay in England provides an illustration of some of the difficulties facing the beginnings of a native humanism in this country.

The adoption of that most embarrassing of dates, 1485, as a time limit was due to practical considerations. With the change of dynasty we also find a change in the characteristics of English humanism. Humanism becomes recognized in administrative and academic circles, the Latin secretaryship becomes an official post, and a Royal Librarian appears among Court officials. Humanists begin to lecture regularly at the Universities. Altogether English humanism starts to assume new characteristics. Its status is rapidly settling from that of amateur into that of professional. The common front of scholasticism and humanism begins to split, thus leading to future hostility between the two systems. Moreover, it would have been absurd to end a survey of humanism under Henry VII with the end of the century. To do this would have entailed cutting short the accounts of Grocin, Linacre, More, and Colet, while to complete them would have meant carrying on well into the reign of Henry VIII, and would have added perhaps twice as much to the bulk of this work.

Until the Tudor period English humanism consisted of a series of individual endeavours rather than deliberate concerted efforts. There were no humanists establishing teaching traditions, like Guarino da Verona or Vittorino da Feltre, nor was there any continuity in learning from scholar to scholar. With Humphrey, Duke of Gloucester's as a possible exception, there were no literary circles like those of Naples, Rome, Ferrara, and Florence. What were to be found were isolated patrons like Gloucester, Tiptoft, and William Grey, or prelates pursuing literary studies like Bekynton and Moleyns. Considering these features of early humanism in England it was imperative that an account of it should be written on the lines of the well known works of Voigt and Sandys, since any scheme but theirs would have made this work baseless. It would have been possible to write a description of the rise of humanism in England full of generalizations, with no biographical details given, and with the subject matter divided into various sections, as for instance in Sabbadini's *Il Metodo degli Umanisti*; but owing to the lack of uniformity in English humanism it was necessary to give biographical facts, as these are of great importance in displaying the backgrounds, achievements, and most important of all, the rise of the interest of English scholars in neo-classicism. Of course the method chosen has some inevitable shortcomings, such as interruption in continuity. Yet in the present state of our knowledge it was the only possible presentation of English fifteenth century humanism. All the relevant facts had to be given; without them the account would have been incomplete, while some of the conclusions reached would have appeared at least arbitrary.[1]

[1] It will perhaps be noted that hardly any mention is made in this work of translations of Latin authors into English made during the fifteenth century. As these furnish no evidence

IV

Before beginning our survey of English humanism in its early stages, it will not be inopportune to give a short account of the position of classical studies in England from the beginning of the fourteenth century up to the arrival of Poggio in 1418, as this will disclose the cultural background on which English humanism rested, and the efforts that were necessary to establish it in this country.

The revival of classical learning during the twelfth century and the Aristotelian Renaissance of the thirteenth received valuable contributions from Englishmen. The great figures of John of Salisbury and Robert Grosseteste formed the centres of English culture of their respective ages, and through their endeavours the study of ancient authors in this country received a vigorous impulse. John of Salisbury and Grosseteste were, however, exceptional men, and with their passing the development of classical scholarship in England slowed down considerably. Thus when compared with the progress achieved during the two centuries that preceded it, the fourteenth century displays unmistakable symptoms of stagnation. England produced no scholar of particular eminence, and the conditions of classical learning at the end of the century indicate clearly that no advance had been made since the days of Robert Grosseteste and Roger Bacon. Throughout the century no improvements in Latin style are to be found, nor is there any evidence of particular increase of interest in classical literature. All this is obvious when we consider the accomplishments of those who are considered the principal classical scholars of the time in England. Of these Richard de Bury, Bishop of Durham, was essentially a bibliophile to whom knowledge was a weapon for the defence of faith. It is true that his *Philobiblon* discloses extensive reading of Roman authors[1] and a taste for rhythmic Latin prose. But his outlook displays no greater enlightment than that of literary men of the century preceding him, and there are no grounds for suspecting

connected with the development of humanism in England, they have accordingly been omitted. One should, however, mention the English version of part of Claudian's *De Consulatu Stilichonis* addressed to Richard, Duke of York, in 1445, in MS. (B.M.) Add. no. 11814, as an adaptation of a classical work to modern political ends. On this work cf. Moore, *Patrons of Letters in Norfolk and Suffolk*, c. 1450, pp. 93–5. For similar reasons school teaching in fifteenth century England has not been considered.

[1] On De Bury's knowledge of the classics cf. Sabbadini, *Le Scoperte dei Codici Latini e Greci*, vol. II, pp. 4–9.

him of leanings towards humanism as conceived by Petrarch. His alleged knowledge of Greek[1] seems very doubtful, while his views are unquestionably those of a schoolman. Of a similar quality is the scholarship of De Bury's protegé, Walter Burley. Burley's passion for collecting and pigeon-holing knowledge, his conception of biography as a series of anecdotes, his approach to Aristotle, are typical of his environment and suggest a limited outlook. The same approach to the antique appears in the writings of Nicholas Trivet, whose commentaries on ancient texts conform entirely with medieval traditions of classical scholarship.

Richard de Bury, Burley, and Trivet, flourished during the first half of the fourteenth century, and in their works one may see crystallized the main features of contemporary culture. Equally representative of it, in so far as the second half of the century is concerned, are some of the works of Thomas Walsingham, the St. Albans chronicler.[2] Walsingham's writings connected with classical scholarship, and particularly his hitherto unnoticed *Prohemia Poetarum*,[3] show him as a true medieval scholar. His knowledge of Latin authors was doubtless fairly wide: but neither his Latin prose nor his attitude to the classics show any new departure from the medieval standpoint. Besides Walsingham there were, of course, others pursuing classical studies in England during the second half of the century. Some of these, as for instance John Erghome, assembled books, including manuscripts of ancient authors,[4] but none of them appears to have reached particular distinction as a classical scholar. Among these Erghome is to be noted for having possessed a few Greek books, but whether, and if so to what extent, he knew Greek it is not possible to say. The possibility that some Greek may have been known in England during the fourteenth century must not be excluded altogether. Apart from the suggestion that Richard de Bury may have been acquainted with the rudiments of that language, it has been alleged that Cardinal Adam Easton taught it at Norwich.[5] Had the evidence about this been unques-

[1] Denholm Young, *Richard de Bury*, p. 158.
[2] On Walsingham as a classical scholar cf. *infra*, p. 31, n. 2.
[3] Cf. *infra*, loc. cit.
[4] On Erghome's collection cf. M. R. James, 'The Catalogue of the Library of the Augustinian Friars at York,' *Fasciculus Ioanni Willis Clark Dicatum*, Cantabrigiae, 1909, pp. 9–15. On Erghome cf. A. Gwynn, *The English Austin Friars in the Time of Wyclif*, Oxford, 1940, pp. 129–38.
[5] Tanner, *Bibliotheca Britannico-Hybernica*, p. 266. Concerning a possible study of Greek at

tionable it would have been especially important, since the Cretan Peter Philargos, later Pope Alexander V, studied both there and at Oxford around 1370;[1] which might suggest his having alternated his theological studies with some teaching of Greek.[2]

From what may be gathered from contemporary sources, one can perceive that classical learning in England at the end of the fourteenth century was still completely dominated by medieval tradition, and had yet to acquire any of the characteristics introduced by the Italians. This state of affairs persisted during the early decades of the following century. The treatises on metre of John Serguard[3] and Thomas Langley[4] still conform entirely with established tradition, while the attitude towards Latin style to be found in England during the first half of the fifteenth century[5] is very far from being a product of the Renaissance, and can already be detected in the *Philobiblon* of Richard de Bury. The visit of Emanuel Chrysoloras to England in 1409[6] made no difference to the trend of English learning.[6] He came here on a diplomatic mission, and is known to have visited London and to have searched for ancient texts in the library of Salisbury Cathedral.[7] But he obviously found no opportunity of teaching here.

Before the coming of Poggio, even what may at first appear as evidence of humanism in England during the late fourteenth or the early fifteenth century will cease to appear as such when subjected to a critical examination. In the correspondence between Coluccio Salutati and Archbishop Arundel[8] no signs of humanistic interests can be found on the part of the latter, while the Latin works of Petrarch and Boccaccio which were to be

Norwich, it is interesting to know that John Metham claimed in his *Amoryns and Cleopes*, written in 1448 or 1449, to have translated this work from the Greek with the help of a Greek he met in Norwich, (Moore, op. cit. pp. 147–8). According to Leland John Bate, a Carmelite of York (fl. 1429), knew some Greek (Leland, *De Scriptoribus*, p. 435).

[1] Little, *The Grey Friars in Oxford* p. 249. On Philargos cf. *Ibid.*, pp. 249–50.
[2] On the study of Greek in medieval England cf. G. R. Stephens, *The Knowledge of Greek in England in the Middle Ages*, Philadelphia, 1933. As this work is full of incorrect statements it should be used with caution.
[3] Serguard's *Metristenchiridion* is in MS. Merton Coll., Oxford, no. 299. On Serguard cf. Tanner, op. cit., p. 660, and the article on him in the *D.N.B.*
[4] Langley's *De Varietate Carminum* is in MS. (B.L.) Digby, no. 100.
[5] On this attitude towards style cf. Jacob, *Florida Verborum Venustas*. A handbook for students anxious to learn this 'flowery' style is the *Tractatus de modo inueniendi ornata uerba compilatus per Iohannem priorem quintum de Ingham pro nouellis rudibus celeriter instruendis* in MS. (B.M.) Royal, 12.B.XVII, ff. 53ᵛ–57ᵛ. The author of this work was either John de Blakeney who was elected Prior in 1439 or his successor John de Norwich.
[6] Cf. Sabbadini, *L'Ultimo ventennio della vita di Manuele Crisolora*, p. 333.
[7] Cf. *infra*, p. 15.
[8] Printed in *Epistolario di Coluccio Salutati*, ed. F. Novati, vol. III, Roma, 1911, pp. 360–3, 497–501, 618–21.

found in this country from the second half of the fourteenth
century were clearly not approached in such a way as to exert
humane influence. When Poggio reached England in the autumn
of 1418 he found classical scholarship in this country still conducted on medieval lines and completely unaffected by the
Renaissance. Its state was in some ways similar to that of learning
in Italy before Petrarch, and thus the reception that Poggio was
to receive from his English contemporaries can hardly be matter
for surprise.

Chapter I

WHILE at the Council of Constance, the Florentine humanist Poggio Bracciolini, commonly known as Poggio, met the Bishop of Winchester, Henry Beaufort, who was also attending the Council.[1] At Constance Beaufort was in close contact with the Curia which then numbered several prominent humanists in its establishment. Hence it was perhaps a desire of introducing the polished curial style into his chancery, a move which he may have thought would add to his prestige in general as well as proving valuable politically, that prompted him to offer Poggio employment in his household. As Beaufort's invitation was accompanied by promises of generous reward it could hardly be rejected without careful consideration, and Poggio, to whom it implied also possibilities of inspecting the libraries of English monasteries was eventually unable to resist it, especially as he was then disgusted with the Roman Curia, and his friends were pressing him to accept the offer of the Bishop of Winchester.[2]

Thus during the autumn of 1418 Poggio set out for England where he was to spend the next four years.[3] But his arrival in England was closely followed by disappointment, for his prospects looked far less promising in this country than they had appeared from Constance. True he found sufficient leisure to dedicate to literature,[4] but somehow he had failed to reckon with the impossibility of finding suitable books for his literary pursuits, the lack of which forced him to follow less congenial studies. Without classical texts at his disposal he was reduced to spending his spare time studying Church Fathers such as St. Augustine and St. Jerome, and the unsatisfactory medieval translations of Aristotle and St. John Crysostomus.[5] Now the

[1] Walser, *Poggius Florentinus*, pp. 47-8. On Poggio in England cf. *Ibid.*, pp. 71-83 and Schirmer, *Der Englische Frühhumanismus*, pp. 17-24.

[2] *Poggii Epistolae*, vol. I, p. 46. Vespasiano da Bisticci stated that Poggio had been sent to England by Pope Martin V (Da Bisticci, *Vite di Uomini Illustri*, p. 420).

[3] Walser, op. cit. p. 71. Poggio was already back in Rome in February 1423 (*Ibid.*, p. 84). He must have thought his departure temporary when he left England since he left behind some of his books (*Poggii Epistolae*, vol. I, pp. 168, 170). In May 1425, he was not certain yet whether he would return to England or remain in Rome (*Ibid.*, vol. I, p. 88). During 1425-6 he was actually ordered to return to England, but, much to his relief, this mission failed eventually to materialize (Walser, op. cit., p. 87, n. 3).

[4] Willmanns, *Ueber die Briefsammlungen des Poggio Braccioloni*, p. 301; *Poggii Epistolae*, vol. I, p. 39.

[5] Willmanns, op. cit. p. 300. For his study of ecclesiastical authors cf. *Poggii Epistolae*, vol. I, pp. 30-1, 39-40.

Latin Aristotle prepared during the Middle Ages was by no means remarkable as a specimen of the art of translating ; hence Poggio became increasingly aware that Aristotelian thought had suffered considerably at the hands of translators.

It is only natural that a scholar should wish to derive his knowledge directly; thus Poggio's studies aroused in him a strong desire to learn Greek, a language with which he was not yet familiar, in order to acquaint himself with the original text of Aristotle.[1] However, to learn Greek one needs books and teachers or at least books, and as neither of these were available in England, he was forced to renounce the fulfilment of this desire until his return to Italy.

It is very difficult to concentrate on some particular study without being influenced by it, and Poggio himself experienced this. The more he studied the ecclesiastical authors the greater grew his enthusiasm for them. As a direct result of this his interest in classical letters began to wane in favour of the Church Fathers. So strong was their influence upon him that in one of his letters from England to his intimate friend Niccolò Niccoli, he went so far as to declare that there was nothing but vanity to be found in profane literature, and to regret the time spent in classical studies.[2] Alone in a foreign country amongst strangers deeply imbued with scholasticism, with little to read beyond Aristotle and the Fathers, some alteration in his outlook was inevitable. Still this change was neither permanent nor as deep as some of his letters from England might lead one to believe. While studying the Latinized Aristotle he appeared also to be anxious lest the reading of such rude Latin should affect the purity of his own style,[3] while his bibliophile activities, and his craving for news of Italian humanists, also indicate that his former interests were not really in danger of extinction. It is true that throughout his residence in England he was unable to apply himself to classical studies,[3] but this was due to causes beyond his control.

One of the reasons that had induced Poggio to visit England had been the hope of making important finds in English libraries.

---

[1] *Poggii Epistolae*, vol. I, p. 39. On his desire to learn Greek while in England cf. *Ibid.*, vol. I, p. 34. On his Greek studies cf. L. R. Loomis, 'The Greek Studies of Poggio,' *Medieval Studies in Memory of G. S. Loomis*, Paris, 1927, pp. 488–512.

[2] *Poggii Epistolae*, vol. I, p. 63. Such a change in Poggio's outlook can already be perceived in a letter written to Niccoli on 4 February, 1420, in Willmanns, op. cit., pp. 300–1.

[3] *Poggii Epistolae*, vol. I, pp. 55, 79.

After his successful explorations in Imperial territories, he naturally hoped to gather more material here to add to his already remarkable series of discoveries of lost classical texts.[1] With such an end in view he had already inspected by the beginning of March 1420 some library lists of English monasteries.[2] But much to his disappointment he had found nothing of interest in them.[3] The perusal of more catalogues yielded equally discouraging results, and so much disheartened Poggio that he attributed the poor quality of their contents to former barbaric invasions.[4] The plague that ravaged England in 1420 drove Poggio from London, and gave him the opportunity of touring the country and paying a personal visit to several monastic libraries.[5] But this tour met with indifferent success. Among the libraries which he inspected was that of Salisbury Cathedral which had been visited twelve years earlier by Emanuel Chrysoloras; this he searched particularly for a copy of Origen which had apparently been seen there by the Greek scholar, but his quest proved fruitless.[6]

Failure did not dishearten Poggio, who, despite his lack of success, continued to make inquiries about other libraries. Naturally his experiences had made him rather sceptical of finding hidden treasures in them: nevertheless he was resolved to learn as much as he could about their contents lest something valuable escape him. Amongst those who supplied him with information was the Papal Collector, Simone da Teramo, who told him how a great many books were preserved in some ancient monasteries.[7] Simone's details were, however, received by Poggio with some doubt as he was aware that the Papal Collector had not been

[1] On Poggio's 'finds' cf. Sabbadini, *Scoperte*, vol. I, pp. 77-84, II, pp. 191-3.

[2] *Poggii Epistolae*, vol. I, p. 30. He also searched London bookshops (Willmanns, op. cit. p. 301).

[3] Except a few books described by him as *ad religionem pertinentes*, (*Poggii Epistolae*, vol. I, p. 30).

[4] *Ibid.*, vol. I, pp. 38, 61. The monasteries visited by Poggio cannot have included those at Canterbury, St. Albans, Peterborough, Lanthony, or other important ones, since he would have found in them several classical MSS.

[5] *Ibid.*, vol. I, p. 43. He was absent from London for two months during the summer, (*Ibid.*, vol. I, p. 40).

[6] *Ibid.*, vol. I, p. 43. Some Latin translations of Origen were in Salisbury Cathedral Library during the seventeenth century, (E. Bernard, *Catalogus Librorum Manuscriptorum Angliae et Hiberniae*, Oxoniae, 1697, part II, p. 24), and may have been the MSS. seen by Chrysoloras. These MSS. are no longer there.

[7] *Poggii Epistolae*, vol. I, pp. 51-2. The library of another monastery was visited by Poggio in November 1420, (*Ibid.*, vol. I, p. 52). Simone da Teramo had been appointed Papal Collector in England in September 1420, (*C.P.R.* vol. VII, p. 2). On Simone cf. MS. (B.M.) Add. no. 15386, ff. 109ᵛ-110ʳ. A letter of Poggio to Simone is in *Poggii Epistolae*, vol. I, pp. 107-8.

long in England, and was therefore probably repeating hearsay rather than speaking from personal knowledge.[1]

With his master Beaufort Poggio travelled again through England during August and September 1421,[2] but once more his searches proved disheartening. All the libraries examined by him appeared to be well stocked with works of ecclesiastical and medieval learning, but their classical sections produced no novelties for him.[2] Amongst the places which Poggio had intended to visit was Oxford, where he hoped to find something interesting in the library founded by Thomas Cobham, and in the various colleges. But reasons beyond his control prevented him, as far as we know, from visiting the University town,[2] thus incidentally avoiding fresh disappointments, since the contents of Oxford libraries at that time would hardly have aroused his interest. After this second tour Poggio gave up any hopes of renewing his continental successes here. Nevertheless he continued to visit libraries whenever an opportunity arose, and occasionally he transcribed texts found in them.[3] But when we consider that these transcripts included works such as the *Chronicle* of Sigebertus Gemblacensis,[4] we cannot fail to sympathise with the scholar who had brought to light Lucretius and Valerius Flaccus, the *Silvae* of Statius, and several *Orations* of Cicero, to mention only some of Poggio's former finds.

Altogether Poggio's discoveries during his stay in England amounted to a Nonius Marcellus which he found in a London bookshop,[5] a *Historia Tripartita* of Cassiodorus also obtained from a bookseller, and for which he paid three golden crowns,[5] and to these may possibly be added the *Bucolics* of Calpurnius Siculus[6] and Petronius's *Coena Trimalchionis*.[7] Thus Poggio's

---

[1] Cf. *supra*, p. 15, n. 7.

[2] *Poggii Epistolae*, vol. I, pp. 67–8, 70. Also on previous occasions Poggio had been unable to visit Oxford, (*Ibid.*, vol. I, pp. 44, 61). The various references to Oxford in Poggio's letters to Niccoli suggest the latter's anxiety to know about Oxford libraries.

[3] Mai, *Spicilegium Romanum*, vol. X, p. 365.

[4] *Ibid.*, loc. cit., Walser, op. cit. p. 54, n. Poggio's transcript is now MS. National Library, Madrid, X. 81, cf. A. C. Clark's review of Walser, op. cit. in *The Classical Review*, XXIX (1915) p. 249. A 'Sigebertus' was seen by Leland in the London Grey Friars Library (Leland, *Collectanea*, vol. IV, p. 49), and may have been possibly the copy used by Poggio for his transcript.

[5] Willmanns, op. cit. p. 301. Poggio had already found a MS. of Nonius Marcellus while on his way to England, (Walser, op. cit. p. 72). A *Historia Tripartita* appears in the list of Poggio's books, (*Ibid.*, p. 421).

[6] Poggio's sending of this text to Niccoli from England, (*Poggii Epistolae*, vol. I, p. 91), makes it likely that he discovered it in this country.

[7] On Poggio's presumed discovery of the *Coena* in England cf. R. Sabbadini, 'Per la Storia del Codice Traurino di Petronio,' *Rivista di Filologia*, XLVIII (1920) pp. 27–39. Poggio sent a fragment of Petronius to Niccoli from England (*Poggii Epistolae*, vol. I, p. 91).

search for lost classical writings in England failed to produce the rich harvest he had anticipated, the prospect of which had been material in inducing him to accept Beaufort's offers.

Far away from Italy, deprived of personal intercourse with his fellow scholars, Poggio turned to intensive letter writing in order to keep in touch with the Italian literary circles. His chief correspondent during this period was Niccoli, to whom he wrote continually asking for advice and news, discussing learned gossip, and telling him about himself and his hopes for the future.[1] To Niccoli Poggio sent also some of his 'English discoveries,'[2] and there is no doubt that this correspondence helped to make Poggio's life in England more endurable. Besides Niccoli, Poggio's correspondents during this period included Leonardo Bruni, who in one of his letters gave his own version of his fierce quarrel with Niccoli,[3] and Piero Lamberteschi, with whom he exchanged letters on the possibility of employment in Hungary.[4] Through his epistolary activities Poggio was able to receive while here important news as well as current scandal. From Niccoli he heard of Archbishop Capra's discoveries of classical texts in Germany,[5] and the same source notified him with the finding of some lost rhetorical treatises of Cicero by Gerardo Landriani, Bishop of Lodi, in his own Cathedral.[5]

The only person with a real classical training whom Poggio encountered during his four years in England was the Venetian patrician Fantino Zorzi, a former disciple of Guarino da Verona, whom he met in London during the second half of 1420.[6] Mutual tastes made the two Italians friends within a short time, and during Zorzi's stay they saw each other daily,[6] and doubtless often conversed about their common interests. But except for Poggio's references in his letters, we know nothing about Zorzi's visit to England. As he had been one of Guarino's pupils he probably knew some Greek, and from what we know of his later

---

[1] Poggio's extant correspondence with Niccoli from England is in *Poggii Epistolae*, vol. I, pp. 30–84, and Willmanns, op. cit. pp. 300–1. In one of Bruni's Latin dialogues Niccoli is represented criticizing the dialectics of English schoolmen, (T. Klette, *Beiträge zur Geschichte und Litteratur der italienischen Gelehrtenreinassance*, Greifswald, 1889–90, vol. II, p. 53).

[2] *Poggii Epistolae*, vol. I, p. 88.

[3] Bruni's Letter is in Bruni, *Epistolarum Libri Duo*, vol. II, pp. 17–25. On 19 July, 1421, Poggio wrote to Niccoli asking him for Bruni's invective against him (Niccoli) (*Poggii Epistolae*, vol. I, p. 67). (*Laurentius* in the printed text should be read *Leonardus*). This was the '*In Nebulonem Malephicum*' printed in G. Zippel, *Niccolò Niccoli*, Firenze, 1890, pp. 75 ff.

[4] Walser, op. cit. p. 77.

[5] *Poggii Epistolae*, vol. I, pp. 80, 84.

[6] *Ibid.*, vol. I, pp. 57, 60. On Zorzi cf. *Epistolario di Guarino Veronese*, vol. III, p. 84.

C

biography he appears to have been remarkably learned. Considering his accomplishments and that he spent some months in England, it would have been of much interest to know with whom he established contacts, and whether he was able to exercise any intellectual influences however slight.

While Poggio could find intellectual satisfaction from his meetings with Zorzi, his feelings were doubtless different in regard to the Papal Collector, Simone da Teramo, who had furnished him with some information about libraries.[1] But then Simone's learning was that of the average curialist of his time, and although he was able to display when necessary a knowledge of ancient literature and adorn his letters with classical quotations,[2] he could hardly have satisfied Poggio's high standards.

Poggio's visit to England is interesting as showing how he reacted to the English environment and to the various Englishmen he met. His employer does not appear to have taken much interest in Poggio's studies once he had landed in England. During the early period of his stay in Beaufort's household he was often left behind in London while the Bishop was travelling.[3] Later, however, he is known to have accompanied his master occasionally on journeys through England,[4] and in spite of Poggio's complaints it is possible to perceive that Beaufort was anxious to retain him in his service, and was trying to meet his wishes.[5] On the other hand it is not surprising that Beaufort showed few inclinations for Italian culture. When one's interests are centred around a single object, one seldom finds sufficient leisure for other pursuits, and as Beaufort's energies were absorbed by politics, both English and Papal, he could hardly spare time for the patronage of letters.

Like most of the households of great prelates, Beaufort's included several ecclesiastics who served him in capacities requiring some literacy. Such persons were obviously the most likely to come under the influence of Poggio's personality because of their close contact with him and because of their

[1] Cf. *supra*, p. 15.
[2] Cf. for instance his letter to Humphrey of Gloucester in *Official Correspondence of Thomas Beckington*, vol. I, pp. 283–4.
[3] *Poggii Epistolae*, vol. I, p. 31.
[4] Cf. *supra*, p. 16.
[5] Beaufort wished to retain Poggio in his service, as is shown by his refusal to allow him to leave in 1420, (*Poggii Epistolae*, vol. I, p. 45). To please Poggio he went as far as to promise to him before the Papal Collector the first benefice vacant (*Ibid.*, vol. I, p. 69), and eventually gave him the Rectory of Drokensford in the Diocese of Winchester, on which cf. Walser, op. cit. pp. 76–7, 333–4.

literary upbringing, and two of them especially, Nicholas
Bildestone and Richard Petworth, actually do appear to have
become attracted by humanism.

Nicholas Bildestone,[1] whom Poggio described to Niccoli as
homo perhumanus,[2] was Chancellor to Beaufort.[3] During his life he
rose to such high ecclesiastical dignities as Archdeacon of Winton[3] and Dean of Salisbury,[3] and was employed on diplomatic missions to Rome on several occasions.[4] As a fellow official
in Beaufort's household, Bildestone enjoyed close contact with
Poggio during the latter's stay in England, a relationship he
must have found congenial as well as stimulating, since he shared
some of the literary interests of his Italian colleague. Nor was his
intercourse with the Italian scholar completely severed by
Poggio's return to Italy. They were both to meet again in Rome
in 1424, when Poggio proved of assistance to Bildestone who
was then searching unsuccessfully for Petrarch's Latin works.[5]
Bildestone's anxiety to read Petrarch shows his interest in humane
letters, an interest confirmed by a letter addressed to him by
Piero del Monte about 1436–7, which discloses that he was the
owner of a classical library.[6] It is very likely that Bildestone came
across other humanists during his visits to Rome. None the less
his studies appear to have been those of a dilettante, although
one suspects that he may have used his familiarity with polite
letters to improve the standard of his diplomatic language.

Also Richard Petworth, Beaufort's secretary,[7] seems to have
felt Poggio's influence, this being manifested in his activities,
which though limited, show interesting tendencies towards

[1] On Bildestone cf. Schirmer, op. cit. pp. 23–4. A letter from Poggio to him dated 6
February, 1436, is in *Poggii Epistolae*, vol. II, p. 71. Bildestone died on 31 May, 1441, (Le
Neve, *Fasti Ecclesiae Anglicanae*, vol. II, p. 616).

[2] *Poggii Epistolae*, vol. I, p. 170.

[3] He is described as Beaufort's Chancellor in 1427, (*C.P.R.* vol. VII, p. 35) but he doubtless occupied that position long before. He was already Archdeacon of Winton in 1427,
and was still occupying that office in 1435, (*Ibid.*, vol. VIII, pp. 208, 534). He was Dean of
Salisbury from 1435 until his death, (Le Neve, op. cit. vol. II, p. 616).

[4] In 1422 he went to Rome as 'King's Orator', (Schirmer, op. cit. p. 24, n. 47). (The accounts relating to this mission are in P.R.O. *Exchequer, Various Accounts*, 322–10). He
returned there in 1424, 1427, and 1435, (*C.P.R.* vol. VII, pp. 28, 35, 503). He had also been
ordered to go to Rome as 'King's Orator' in 1431, but Robert Fitzhugh, the King's
Proctor in Rome, was eventually sent, (Radford, *Henry Beaufort*, pp. 196–7). Bildestone's
commission is in MS. (B.M.) Cotton, Cleop. E. III, fo. 43ʳ, and is dated 5 January, 1431.
On Bildestone in Rome cf. Haller, *England und Rome unter Martin V*, pp. 258, 291.

[5] *Poggii Epistolae*, vol. I, pp. 149, 170.

[6] MS. (V.L.) Vat. Lat. no. 2694, fo. 117ᵛ. Another letter of Del Monte to Bildestone dated
31 July, 1439 is in *Ibid.*, ff. 183ʳ⁻ᵛ.

[7] On Petworth cf. Hamilton Thompson, *Visitations of Religious Houses*, pp. 205–6, on his
relations with Poggio cf. Schirmer, op. cit. pp. 20–4. He was already Beaufort's secretary in
1415 (H.M.C., *Report on the Manuscripts of Lord Middleton*, London, 1911, pp. 102–3).

Italian culture unfortunately undeveloped by his lack of a proper training. Already in 1415 Petworth was employed as secretary by Beaufort,[1] in whose household he met Poggio, who soon became his friend. From the evidence furnished by Poggio's correspondence with him,[2] it seems doubtful whether Petworth was more attracted by the study of the classics than his fellow countrymen of average learning. On the other hand he took a lively interest in modern writings, as is shown by his request that Poggio should have some of his own works copied for him.[3] He was in contact with persons interested in neo-classicism like Humphrey, Duke of Gloucester,[4] and Aeneas Sylvius' friend, Adam de Moleyns,[4] and thanks to such links he was able to make known in England some of Poggio's treatises. Thus at Poggio's request he showed the *De Varietate Fortunae* to Gloucester,[4] whom he probably also introduced to other writings by his Italian friend. Besides indulging in the study of literature Petworth appears to have been ambitious of acquiring an elegant epistolary style. This is suggested by an extant Latin letter of his which betrays an attempt at writing like a humanist.[5] Although his style appears here to be over-ornate, full of euphuisms, and defective in grammar, it none the less found admirers at Christ Church, Canterbury, for which he translated one of the monastery letters from French into Latin,[6] and where part of his Latin correspondence was almost certainly transcribed during the first half of the fifteenth century.[7] As Petworth exchanged letters with Poggio throughout his life,[8] it would have been interesting to know the Italian's real opinion of Petworth's efforts, and his reactions when reading his Latin. But unfortunately information on this point has been denied to us. The real contribution given by Petworth to the development of English humanism was his

[1] Cf. *supra*, p. 19, n. 7.

[2] Poggio's extant letters to Petworth were written between 1424 and 1448 and are in *Poggii Epistolae*, vols. I–II, *passim*, Mai, op. cit. vol. X, pp. 300–5, and Walser, op. cit. p. 454. It is evident from some of Poggio's letters to Petworth, that Petworth wrote more than once to him attacking the corruption of the Curia, cf. *Poggii Epistolae*, vol. I, p. 139.

[3] Poggio had sent his *De Avaritia* to Petworth and in 1440 stated that he had given his *De Varietate Fortunae* to be transcribed for him, (Mai, op. cit. vol. X, p. 301). The latter was sent to Petworth in 1442 (Walser, op. cit. p. 454) but must have included only books 1–3 since Poggio was offering to have book 4, (*De Rebus Indiae*) copied for Petworth at a later date (Mai, op. cit. vol. X, p. 304). Petworth's appreciation of Poggio's works is also shown in a letter by the latter to Petworth dated 24 May, 1440, (*Ibid.*, vol. X, p. 301).

[4] Walser, op. cit. p. 454. The *De Avaritia* was among the books of Humphrey of Gloucester, cf. *infra*, p. 65, who may have obtained it from Petworth.

[5] Printed in Schirmer, op. cit. p. 23, n. 40.

[6] Cf. *Literae Cantuarienses*, vol. III, p. 189.   [7] Cf. *infra*, p. 129.

[8] Cf. *supra*, n. 2. Petworth died in 1458 (Hamilton Thompson, op. cit, p. 206).

making known the writings of Poggio rather than his unsatisfactory attempts as a stylist.

As far as we know Bildestone and Petworth were the only Englishmen whom Poggio directly influenced during his visit to this country. Even within Beaufort's household he probably failed to impress anyone else with his learning, and though he made other friends,[1] such friendships were of a social rather than a scholarly nature. The slight notice taken of Poggio during his stay in England hardly needs explanation. That one among the leading scholars of his time had failed to stimulate his English contemporaries, has surely to be attributed to apathy on the part of those who came into contact with him, rather than reluctance on Poggio's part to propagate his learning. He was too eager about his intellectual pursuits, not to have helped to improve the state of English classical scholarship had he found opportunities or encouragement. But his studies were far too advanced to find appreciation, and consequently he brought about no changes in the intellectual state of the country that harboured him between 1418 and 1422. The conditions of English learning gave rise to severe judgments on Poggio's part.[2] Perhaps an important cause of the severity of his verdicts against English letters was his homesickness for Italy and his friends, which made him hypercritical of anything English. Still other evidence also shows that the state of learning in England during the time of his residence here was hardly such as to meet with the approval of a person of his exacting standards.[3]

[1] Poggio's English friend 'Toby' to whom Petworth was to show the *De Varietate Fortunae* (Walser, op. cit. p. 454), a fact suggesting an interest in Poggio's writings on his part, may be identified with William Toly, Clerk to the Signet in 1419–22, and Beaufort's secretary after 1422, on whom cf. Otway Ruthven, *The King's Secretary and the Signet Office in the XVth Century*, pp. 139, 184. Other English friends of Poggio were a Thomas 'Guido' (Guy?), (*Poggii Epistolae*, vol. II, p. 168) and Thomas Candour, a Papal Chamberlain, (*Ibid.*, vol. II, p. 318). He also knew Thomas Polton, Bishop of Chichester, with whom he quarrelled in Rome, (Walser, op. cit. p. 86, n. 3). From Italy Poggio sent letters to William Grey, Bishop of Ely, (*infra*, p. 90), John Stafford, Archbishop of Canterbury, (*Poggii Epistolae*, vol. II, p. 318) and to his former master, Beaufort, (Mai, op. cit., vol. X, pp. 250–4).

[2] *Poggii Epistolae*, vol. I, p. 43. He also passed severe judgments on Englishmen, (*Ibid.*, vol. I, p. 64).

[3] Poggio's reputation as a scholar was already established in England during the second quarter of the fifteenth century. One of Petworth's correspondents mentions him (Schirmer, op. cit. p. 25), Gloucester possessed some of his writings (*infra*, p. 65), and some of Poggio's works were submitted to him, (*supra*, p. 20); Poggio's works were possessed by William Grey, Richard Bole, John Free, and Henry Cranebroke (*infra*, pp. 94, 96, 110, 131); Poggio's library was mentioned by Caxton, (*infra*, p. 176), and a printed edition of the *Facetiae* was bound in Oxford towards the end of the fifteenth century (*infra*, p. 175). His letters were used as models of style and found their way into formularies compiled in England during the fifteenth century, cf. *infra*, p. 129 and MSS. Jesus Coll. Cambridge, no. 63, and (B.M.) Cotton, Tib. B. VI.

CHAPTER II

ENGLISH humanism begins only after Poggio had returned to Italy, and the enlightened patronage of Humphrey, Duke of Gloucester, constitutes no doubt one of its earliest as well as one of its most important manifestations.[1] But these were themselves provoked by a series of influences which though not necessarily altogether humanistic, were none the less instrumental in preparing a background for the reception of Italian learning.

Since what one reads constitutes a useful clue to one's intellectual leanings, the presence of Petrarch's and Boccaccio's Latin writings in England from the days of Chaucer[2] forms evidence of interest in some of the productions of early humanists. Caution is, however, necessary when attempting to assess the value of these works as humanistic influences. Some of Petrarch's and Boccaccio's Latin treatises are typically medieval productions; besides, by the end of the fourteenth century both these authors had acquired an authoritative status analogous to that enjoyed by medieval writers as, for instance, John of Salisbury or Walter Burley.[3] It was consequently possible to find persons reading, appreciating, and possessing, some of their works, who were nevertheless completely unaware of the change in standards for which both Petrarch and Boccaccio had stood.

Books alone, moreover, are insufficient to effect a revolution in values, and without personal agencies humanism would in all probability have failed to take root in fifteenth century England. In this Poggio's friends, Petworth and Bildestone, played an important rôle, and even greater and more valuable contributions were made by Papal officials in England and, to a lesser degree, by Englishmen who visited the Roman Court or attended

[1] On Gloucester as a patron of letters cf. *infra*, pp. 39–70.

[2] This is apparent from Chaucer's wide use of Petrarch and Boccaccio. A useful bibliography on his use of these authors is in M. Praz, 'Chaucer and the Great Italian Writers of the Trecento,' *The Monthly Criterion*, VI (1927) pp. 240–2. A MS. of Petrarch's *De Remediis* transcribed in England towards the end of the fourteenth century is now MS. Corpus Christi Coll. Cambridge, no. 40.

[3] This is shown by the way in which these authors were quoted. Petrarch is quoted in a speech delivered before Henry IV in 1408, (*The St. Albans Chronicle*, p. 137). Boccaccio was among the authorities of Jean Petit's apology of tyrannicide, (A. Coville, *Jean Petit*, Paris, 1932, pp. 213, 278). Jean de Montreuil considered Petrarch a '*deuotissimus, catholicus ac celeberrimus philosophus moralis*' (A. Coville, *Gontier et Pierre Col et l'Umanisme en France au Temps de Charles VI*, Paris, 1934, p. 147), a statement reflecting the contemporary attitude to that author. John Lydgate gives a list of Petrarch's Latin writings in one of his works (*Lydgate's Fall of Princes*, ed. H. Bergen (Early English Text Society), pt. II, London, 1924, p. 476).

Italian Universities. The Papal Chancery had moved with the times, and a knowledge of classical Latin was considered as essential in its officials as intimacy with the rules of *dictamen* had been in former days. With the return of the Curia to Rome its establishment had been suddenly depopulated. Part of the officialdom had remained behind in Avignon with the antipope. As a result the gallicized administration had been quickly italianized, and new Italian standards introduced into curial style. The great prestige of the Papal Chancery had attracted several Italian scholars of repute within its ranks, thus conditioning its tone from their conception of values. Besides Poggio, Vergerio, Antonio Loschi, Flavio Biondo, and Leonardo Bruni, had served in it as secretaries or abbreviators,[1] and a set of humanists constituted an inner clique, the occupations of which ranged from the drafting of briefs to the telling of salacious stories in the *bugiale*.[2]

Such a humanistic group within the Papal service was bound to exert its influence when new chancery appointments were being made. It raised the standard of literary qualifications for curial employment, so that during the first half of the fifteenth century the Papal bureaucracy had attained high standards in classical scholarship, and enjoyed a wide reputation for polite letters. Papal officials sent to England during the fifteenth century were generally men of some learning and well disposed towards humanism. Simone da Teramo, whom Poggio met here, though not a professional scholar, possessed some classical learning and a fluent Latin style.[3] Giuliano Cesarini, whom Pope Martin V sent over to England in 1426 to procure the repeal of the *Statute of Provisors*,[4] was equally well equipped with Latin scholarship, and during his visit here spent part of his spare time explaining Trogus Pompeius to the chronicler George Hardyng.[5] During his stay in England Cesarini probably came into touch with the authorities of Oxford University[6] and with Humphrey

---

[1] Poggio for example was employed by the Curia from 1403–18 and from 1423–53 (Walser, op. cit. pp. 19–20, 71, 85, 222). Bruni was in its employment from 1405–15 (*Ibid.*, pp. 22, 42).

[2] On the *bugiale* cf. *Poggii Opera*, Basileae, 1538, p. 491.

[3] Cf. *supra*, p. 18.

[4] A safe conduct to Cesarini going to England was issued in April 1426, (*C.P.R.* vol. VII, p. 16). He was already back in Rome in December 1426, (Haller, *England und Rom unter Martin V*, p. 299).

[5] This he did at the request of Henry Beaufort (C. L. Kingsford, 'The First Version of Hardyng's Chronicle', *E.H.R.* XXVII (1912) p. 464).

[6] To both of whom he had been recommended by the Pope, (*C.P.R.* vol. VII, pp. 32, 36).

of Gloucester,[1] and it is possible that he may have influenced, however slightly, the latter's intellectual pursuits. It was also through a Papal mission that England was visited a little later by the humanist Gaspare da Verona, the future biographer of Pope Paul II, and probably a pupil of Guarino da Verona. This scholar was sent here with the ill-fated Stefano Porcari by Pope Eugenius IV in 1431,[2] and although it is unlikely that he taught in England, it is none the less possible that he influenced some of the Englishmen with whom he established contacts. But a far greater humane influence is to be found in the activities of Piero del Monte, who was Papal Collector in England from 1435 to 1440.[3]

Del Monte, whom Gascoigne pilloried in his *Liber de Veritatibus* for his notorious corruption,[4] was a Venetian who had been educated at the school of Guarino da Verona[5] and at the Universities of Padua[5] and Paris.[5] Besides representing Papal interests in general, Del Monte had been also ordered to do everything in his power while in England to prevent this country siding with the Council of Basle,[6] so that his relations with the English Council were necessarily closer than those of some of his predecessors in the office. In spite of the large amount of Papal business which passed through his hands, his office ensured him sufficient leisure, and this he employed in the pursuit of learning. Thus from a literary point of view his visit proved not barren. While here he composed a controversial pamphlet against the Archbishop of Palermo[6] and a short treatise in the form of a letter addressed to Poggio, in which he wound up the controversy between Guarino and Poggio as to whether Scipio or Caesar had been the greatest general of antiquity.[7] Besides this,

[1] Cf. *supra*, p. 23, n. 6.
[2] *Le Vite di Paolo II di Gaspare da Verona e Michele Canensi*, p. xxiv. Gaspare returned to Rome in January 1432. Later he taught some Englishmen in Rome, (*Ibid.*, pp. xxiv–v). On Gaspare cf. *Ibid.*, pp. xxi–xliii.
[3] On Del Monte cf. especially Zanelli, *Piero del Monte*, Schirmer, op. cit. pp. 44–8, Weiss, *The Earliest Account of the Murder of James I of Scotland*, passim, Degli Agostini, *Notizie Istorico Critiche intorno la Vita e le Opere degli Scrittori Viniziani*, pp. 346–72, and MS. (B.M.) Add. no. 15386, ff. 111ᵛ–113ᵛ. Del Monte was already in London on 10 August, 1435, (Weiss, op. cit. p. 480, n. 4); On 24 October, 1440, Henry VI wrote to the Pope recommending Del Monte who was then leaving England, (*Official Correspondence of Thomas Beckington*, vol. I, pp. 34–6).
[4] Gascoigne, *Loci e Libro Veritatum*, pp. 123, 125–6.
[5] Zanelli, op. cit. pp. 320–3.
[6] *Ibid.*, pp. 94, 338.
[7] Copies of this are in MSS. (B.L.) Bodl. no. 915, (C.U.) Gg. I. 34, Trinity Coll. Cambridge, no. 1420, Bibliothèque de la Sorbonne, Paris, no. 229, Biblioteca Comunale, S. Daniele del Friuli, no. 50. On this controversy cf. Walser, op. cit. pp. 164–76. Del Monte's letters to Poggio from England are in *Ibid.*, pp. 445–53.

he conducted a voluminous correspondence in Latin with friends, curial officials, and English ecclesiastics,[1] and delivered some elegant Latin orations before Henry VI and his Council, in which he defended the Papacy from the charges brought forward by the Council of Basle.[2] But the most important literary work written by Del Monte in this country was his Latin dialogue upon the intrinsic difference between virtues and vices which he wrote in 1438, and in which he introduced as interlocutors his former teacher, Guarino da Verona, and his distinguished contemporaries Francesco Barbaro and Pietro Miani.[3] This dialogue, in which classical and patristic literature is copiously quoted, was dedicated to the Duke of Gloucester, and submitted to Abbot Whethamstede for criticism.[4] Apart from its latinity, which is typical of a cultivated Italian of the fifteenth century, the literary merits of this work are slight, its interest consisting rather in its being the first humanistic treatise written in this country. Yet it appears to have found sufficient favour in England to be copied here several times during the fifteenth century.[5] The work was accompanied by a flattering preface addressed to Gloucester, who was then busy stocking his library with *belles lettres*,[6] and there is no doubt that it was welcomed by him.

In addition, his learned pursuits included an attempt to resume in England the study of Greek which he had relinquished after leaving Guarino's school.[7] Besides searching for manuscripts,[8] and giving advice and encouragement to English friends interested in letters, he requested his friend Ambrogio Traversari to send

[1] Preserved in MS. (V.L.) Vat. Lat. no. 2694. A list of Del Monte's extant letters is in Zanelli, op. cit. pp. 113–5. An edition of this correspondence is being prepared by Professor J. Haller of Stuttgart.

[2] Del Monte's orations are in MSS. (V.L.) Vat. Lat. nn. 2694, 4136.

[3] This treatise is in MSS. (V.L.) Vat. Lat. no. 1048, (C.U.) Ll.I. 7, Corpus Christi Coll. Cambridge, no. 472, (B.L.) Auct. F.5.26, and Lambeth Palace, no. 341. Gloucester presented this treatise to Oxford University in 1444, (*Epistolae Academicae*, vol. I, p. 237). The Bodleian and Lambeth MSS. are copies of the text given to Oxford made in England during the fifteenth century. This work was composed in 1438, (MS. (V.L.) Vat. Lat. no. 2694, fo. 189ʳ).

[4] The letter accompanying a copy of the treatise was written in 1439 (September?) and is in *Ibid.*, ff. 189ʳ⁻ᵛ.

[5] Cf. *supra*, n. 3.

[6] The preface is printed in Creighton, *Some Literary Correspondence of Humphrey, Duke of Gloucester*, pp. 101–3.

[7] MS. (V.L.) Vat. Lat. no. 2694, fo. 164ᵛ.

[8] While here he asked William Wells, Abbot of York, for Alvarus Pelagius' *De Planctu Ecclesiae* (*Ibid.*, fo. 108ᵛ), Vincent Clement for a work of Grosseteste (*Ibid.*, fo. 201ᵛ), Whethamstede for a Josephus (*infra*, p. 27, n. 4), and Bildestone for a Seneca (*supra*, p. 19, n. 6). He had also MSS. transcribed (MS. (V.L.) Vat. Lat. no. 2694, ff. 108ᵛ, 181ᵛ) and intended to search the St. Albans Library (*Ibid.*, fo. 166ᵛ).

some of his works to the Duke of Gloucester and begin a correspondence with him.[1] What had stimulated Del Monte to continue his Greek studies, was mainly the news of the coming of the Greeks to the Council of Ferrara in 1438,[2] and accordingly he began to search for the necessary books. Although he succeeded in finding certain Greek books in London,[2] they were not the ones best suited to his purpose, so that he was compelled to write to Ermolao Barbaro in Italy for some more appropriate Greek texts.[2] Lack of the necessary books was not the only difficulty encountered by Del Monte in his efforts to study Greek in England. After receiving the books from Barbaro he discovered only too soon that no real progress was possible without a master, and as no qualified person was available, his Greek studies made little progress during his stay in this country.[2]

Piero del Monte was just the very man to attract Duke Humphrey, whose friendship he enjoyed throughout his residence in England.[3] In frequent conversations he kept the Duke informed of the latest trend in the Italian world of letters, and acted, perhaps more than any other person, as an adviser to Humphrey in all questions of humane taste.[4] Thus it was on Del Monte's advice that Gloucester decided to take into his service Frulovisi and Beccaria as secretaries,[5] and through him that he acquired several rare manuscripts for his library.[6] Besides Duke Humphrey, Del Monte is known to have been in touch with several other Englishmen of like interests, such as Andrew Holes, Nicholas Bildestone, John Whethamstede, Thomas Bekynton, Adam de Moleyns, and the anglicized Spaniard Vincent Clement.[7] But save in the case of Whethamstede, whom he supplied with texts,[8]

[1] MS. (V.L.) Vat. Lat. no. 2694, fo. 167ʳ. He eventually resumed his Greek studies once back in Italy, where he translated Epiphanius' *Miraculum Eucharistiae*. His version was printed in Rome in 1524.

[2] *Ibid.*, ff. 162ᵛ, 164ᵛ.

[3] Del Monte had been recommended to Gloucester by the Pope (*C.P.R.* vol. VIII, p. 221, n.), saw him often on Papal business (*Ibid.*, vol. VIII, p. 225, MS. (V. L.) Vat. Lat. no. 2694, fo. 172ᵛ), and was apparently liked by the Duke (*Ibid.*, ff. 242ʳ–4ʳ). The translator of Palladius included him among Gloucester's learned friends (*The Middle English Translation of Palladius De Re Rustica*, p. 22).

[4] Del Monte praised Gloucester's conversation (Vickers, *Humphrey, Duke of Gloucester*, p. 371), showed him Poggio's treatise on the Caesar-Scipio controversy (Walser, op. cit. p. 172, n. 2), and advertised Traversari's achievements to him (MS. (V.L.) Vat. Lat. no. 2694, ff. 166ᵛ–7ʳ). On his discussions with him cf. *Ibid.*, loc. cit., and Walser, op. cit. p. 172, n. 2.

[5] Cf. *infra*, pp. 41, 45.

[6] Cf. *infra*, p. 28.

[7] On his contacts with these people cf. *infra*, pp. 34, 73, 76, 79, 81, *supra*, p. 19.

[8] Cf. *infra*, p. 34.

there is no positive evidence that he cultivated an exchange of ideas with any of them, though he certainly corresponded with Bildestone and Clement over manuscripts.[1] Yet, knowing the inclinations of these correspondents, it is not impossible that they availed themselves of the gifted Papal Collector in their midst to acquire something of polite learning, may be their very outlook was conditioned by his influence.

Despite his many friends, Del Monte's visit to England was not a happy one. Like his friend Poggio he suffered from the impossibility of finding persons of the same standard of learning as his own, and this coupled with the strangeness of weather and customs made him look forward eagerly to a return to his native land.[2] Nor would he appear to have entertained a great opinion of the English as classical scholars, for in one of his letters to Traversari written in October 1438 he made a violent indictment of English scholarship which echoes that of Poggio to Niccoli.[3] His encouragement of English humanism was chiefly prompted by ulterior motives; in submitting his treatise on virtues and vices to the judgment of Abbot Whethamstede, Del Monte hoped to cajole him into parting with some books he very much coveted,[4] while it was chiefly opportunism that prompted him to encourage Duke Humphrey in his patronage of letters. Thanks mainly to his petty private designs his influence on English scholarship proved most beneficial. It was through him that several modern works were first introduced into England, through him that two distinguished Italian humanists entered the service of Duke Humphrey, and partly through him that the achievements of the Italians were made known among the Duke's entourage. The fact that he succeeded in exercising a strong influence whereas Poggio, who was far more gifted, failed to arouse interest, may be mainly ascribed to Del Monte's coming seventeen years later, when his predecessors in the Papal Collectorship had in some way prepared the ground for a 'reception' in England, and to his office which placed him in contact with Duke Humphrey and the most important dignitaries of the English church.

[1] Cf. *supra*, p. 19, *infra*, p. 76.
[2] Walser, op. cit. pp. 449, 451, MS. (V.L.) Vat. Lat. no. 2694, fo. 164ᵛ.
[3] *Ibid.*, loc. cit.
[4] This is suggested especially by his writing to Whethamstede in 1439 asking for the loan of an ancient Josephus, (*Ibid.*, fo. 189ᵛ), which may perhaps be identified with the twelfth century Josephus from St. Albans now MSS. (B.M.) Royal, 15.D.VI–VII. Two letters of Del Monte to Whethamstede are in MS. (V.L.) Vat. Lat. no. 2694, ff. 125ʳ, 189ʳ⁻ᵛ.

Del Monte's influence did not end with his departure. From Italy he continued, at any rate for a time, to keep up his connexion with Gloucester, and from there he sent him manuscripts and maintained an exchange of letters.[1]

As we have seen these Legates and Collectors were men of learning; they were in continuous contact with the most educated section of English society, and were prepared to participate in humanistic activities, so that their actual influence upon English culture cannot be denied. Less obvious, and incidentally much less valuable, was the effect of the Englishmen who went to Rome or attended Italian Universities.[2] It is true that the Papal Curia had so many humanists in its permanent establishment that it was easy for English visitors to come into contact with them. Yet it seems unlikely that their contribution amounted to more than bringing books home, and acquainting their friends with some of the accomplishments of the Italians.

These exchanges of Papal bureaucrats and Englishmen in Italy were not in themselves sufficient to cause the acceptance of humanism in England, had it not been for another factor. This was the interest in Latin style which was to be found in England at the beginning of the fifteenth century.

During the first quarter of the fifteenth century there prevailed in this country a taste for writing Latin in an extremely flowery and 'euphuistic' style.[3] This fashion was more a symptom of decadence than a novelty. A recurrence of the phenomenon known as Alexandrianism in Greek and Africanism in Latin literature, it generally heralded a decline in literary values. Obscurity and involution in style, extravagance and over-elaboration in imagery and metaphor, an obvious painstaking care in diction, were its principal characteristics, convenient if not attractive substitutes for lack of original inspiration. With medieval latinity exhausted an acceptance of such rhetorical devices had been inevitable, and their spread and appreciation in literary circles discloses besides a dearth of creative powers a taste ready to acquiesce in the unusual and extravagant. The essence of medieval 'euphuism' as practised in England was drawn from several sources. Besides the general decline of standards in Latin letters, a strong influence had been exerted

[1] Creighton, *Some Literary Correspondence of Humphrey, Duke of Gloucester*, pp. 100–1.
[2] On Englishmen attending Italian Universities during the period cf. especially Mitchell, *English Law Students at Bologna in the Fifteenth Century*.
[3] On this fashion cf. *supra*, p. 11, n. 5.

upon it by the *dictamen* with its stress upon diction, and by rhetoric as expounded by writers like Geoffrey of Vinsauf and Matthew of Vendôme, according to which elaboration and ornament played an important rôle in literary composition.[1]

A love for the 'sensational' and the 'unusual' in expression, an almost 'baroque' sense of values, as will reappear in Elizabethan England with Lilly's *Euphues* and its imitators, and in seventeenth century Italy with 'Marinismo,' are the most obvious features of this stylistic manner. As in Euphuism, Gongorism, and Marinismo, greater emphasis was given to diction than to subject matter. Now Italian humanists also attributed great importance to style. But their literary aims were not to be carried out merely by a painstaking verbal choice. Seeking inspiration from Cicero they tried to reproduce a classical atmosphere rather than just giving a collection of Ciceronian clichés.

However slight the value of the stylistic attitude prevalent in some English literary circles, at least since the days of Richard de Bury, one merit cannot be denied to it: it developed sensibility towards style, to use a colloquial expression, it made scholars 'style conscious.' Although the taste inspiring it was doubtful, it was none the less able to arouse the curiosity of men of letters for other literary ways. Therefore the writings of Italian humanists could not avoid commanding attention once they became available in England.

Late medieval rhetoric was mainly centred upon epistolography. The Latin epistle was conceived as an instrument of power as well as of polite intercourse. Hence the writing of letters had become subjected to elaborate rules. The collecting of epistolaries has a long tradition dating from classical times, but it never proved as popular as during the later Middle Ages. Collections of letters, like those of Peter de Vinea[2] or Peter of Blois, were transcribed innumerable times and formed very much sought after models throughout Europe. This practice was not ended by the Renaissance. From Petrarch onwards the leading Italian humanists published their letters, and stray pieces from their epistolaries were given room in formularies. Copies of these epistolaries and formularies crossed the Italian Alps. Some

---

[1] On their theories cf. E. Faral, *Les Artes Poétiques du XII et du XIII Siècles*, Paris, 1924, *passim*.

[2] On the diffusion of his works in England, cf. E. Kantarowicz, 'Petrus de Vinea in England,' *Mitteilungen des Oesterreiches Instituts für Geschichteforschungen*, LI (1937–8) pp. 44–88.

reached England, and as they displayed an obvious stylistic superiority they aroused interest at once. Though no fine scholars from a classical standpoint, English literary men were nevertheless capable of perceiving in the writings of the Italians a beauty worthy of imitation. Now their outlook made them naturally anxious to include in their collections the choicest specimens of Latin finery. Thus with a view to improving their styles they did not hesitate to accept works of Poggio, Guarino, Bruni, and other Italian scholars, for their formularies,[1] just as they had formerly accepted those of Thomas of Capua and Guido Faba.

It is in this appreciation of polite literature from a stylistic angle, and through the various activities of Papal officialdom in England and Englishmen back from Italy, that one can find the origins of the acceptance of humanism in this country. It is in the amateurish classical pursuits of Simone da Teramo, in the teaching of Cesarini, in the studies of the friends of Poggio, and above all in the influence of Del Monte, in books brought from Italy and including examples of humanistic literature, that the beginnings of English humanism are to be sought. These various activities taken together succeeded in achieving what Poggio had failed to accomplish. But then the task of introducing neo-classicism into England was clearly beyond the strength or capabilities of one man only. To begin any alteration in the characteristics of a culture several centuries old, gradual and indirect methods are perhaps necessary, and Poggio's attempts had constituted nothing less than a direct attack.

If the influences described above eventually led to the establishment of humanism in this country, many were the difficulties facing its beginnings. Perhaps the greatest of these was that its letter was obviously more easy to appreciate than its spirit, and thus the first humanistic manifestations in England naturally suffered from such drawbacks as are constantly present in attempts at assimilating values more subtle than one's own.

The impact of humanism on English medieval tradition is perhaps best studied in the writings of John Whethamstede, Abbot of St. Albans.[2] Besides being chronologically one of the

---

[1] Cf. for instance MSS. (B.M.) Cotton, Tib. B.VI, Jesus Coll. Cambridge, no. 63, Imperial University Library, Tokyo, A.100.1300, (B.L.) Ashm. 789.

[2] On Whethamstede cf. especially Schirmer, op. cit. pp. 82–98, Jacob, *Florida Verborum Venustas*, pp. 5–17. The most complete account of Whethamstede is in the unpublished thesis by Miss H. Hodge, *The Abbey of St. Albans under John Whethamstede*, which includes a criticism of Schirmer's account at pp. 172–5.

first Englishmen who came into direct contact with Italian humanism, Whethamstede's learning gives an illustration of some of the difficulties inherent in the reception of Italian Renaissance culture here. A perusal of his career shows that he was acquainted with Italian scholars and Englishmen interested in the revival of classical learning, that he had access to a considerable number of ancient and modern texts, and that he was both fascinated by and actively interested in the humanist movement. On the other hand a mere glance at his voluminous works will sufficiently dispel any illusion as to the nature of his learning. His Latin style, his conceptions of history and culture, his handling of authorities, the angle from which he approached the classics, are still typically medieval, and only superficial humanistic influences appear in his writings. Dr. Schirmer in his monograph on early English humanism gives Whethamstede a prominent place among the pioneers of neo-classicism in England.[1] There can be no doubt that Whethamstede played a rôle of some importance in its development in this country; but it is impossible to class him in the ranks of humanists, unless we are prepared to label as such everyone who wrote Latin, read the classics, and practised rhetoric, during the Middle Ages. If we compare his classical scholarship with that of Thomas Walsingham,[2] we shall find that Whethamstede, though belonging to a later generation, had made no progress. His standards are neither higher nor more modern than those of the last continuator of the *St. Albans Chronicle*: his erudition is just as medieval. Thus in Whethamstede we find one of the last exponents of a purely medieval outlook, for in spite of his efforts he remained fundamentally unaffected by modern influence. Brought up in an intellectual atmosphere utterly unlike humanism, Whethamstede found his education a permanent bar to acquiring the spirit of the antique.

He belonged to a family closely connected with St. Albans Abbey, and as a child he was sent to school to acquire the necessary knowledge to become a monk.[3] Dates are rather uncertain in so far as his early life is concerned: thus we do not know when he became a monk at St. Albans, or in what year he

---

[1] Cf. Schirmer, op. cit. pp. 82–98.

[2] On Walsingham as a classical scholar cf. *The St. Albans Chronicle*, pp. XLI–V. His *Prohemia Poetarum* is in MS. (B.M.) Harl. no. 2693.

[3] MS. (B.M.) Harl. no. 139, fo. 191ʳ (quoted in Hodge, op. cit. p. 6). Whethamstede's family name was 'Bostok,' 'Whethamstede' being his birthplace (MS. (B.M.) Cotton, Nero, D.VII, fo. 27ʳ).

was sent to the University. At Oxford he attended Gloucester College,[1] and was a contemporary of Thomas Bekynton then at New College.[1] His academic career must have been a distinguished one, for at some period around 1414–1417 he occupied the Priorship of his college,[2] which later during his two abbacies was to be the recipient of several of his benefactions.[3] While he was Prior of Gloucester College he also attended the courses of the faculty of Divinity, in which he incepted in 1417.[4] But shortly after his inception he returned to St. Albans, where in 1420 he was elected to succeed William Heyworth as Abbot.[5] Direct evidence has not come down to us, yet it seems fairly certain that by this time he had already developed that attraction for the classics which never abandoned him throughout his life. The origins of such interests are not very difficult to conjecture: classical scholarship had flourished at St. Albans throughout the later Middle Ages, so that it is hardly to be doubted that the classical tradition there was material in determining the bent of his literary outlook. To this, rather than to his Oxford career, is to be traced the origin of his taste for the antique, which conformed with the fashions which had prevailed at St. Albans at least since the days of Matthew Paris. His journeys in Italy, where he went in 1423 to attend the Councils of Pavia and Siena,[6] brought him into contact with Italian letters and probably added to his classical knowledge. His visit to Italy is mainly known because of his spirited defence at Pavia against Richard Flemmyng's attack on the English abbeys,[7] and his obtaining fresh privileges for St. Albans from Pope Martin V.[7] Yet, as far as his studies are concerned, the importance of his Italian sojourn consists rather in his having met humanists, probably inspected the very important Visconti library at Pavia, which contained Petrarch's collection of manuscripts,[8] and, judging by what we know of his

---

[1] His going to Oxford must have taken place before 1414 when he was already Prior of Gloucester College, Oxford (*infra*, n. 2). On his being Bekynton's contemporary cf. *Registrum Abbatiae J. Whethamstede*, vol. II, p. 397.

[2] The date of his appointment to it is unknown. He was already Prior in 1414–7 and had already ceased to hold this office between 1417–20. (*Documents Illustrating the Activities of the General and Provincial Chapters of the English Black Monks*, vol. III, pp. 177, 185).

[3] These included the building of a chapel, library, and garden wall, (Amundesham, *Annales Monasterii Sancti Albani*, vol. II, p. 264) as well as presents of books, (*infra*, p. 37).

[4] *Documents Illustrating the Activities . . . of the English Black Monks*, vol. III, p. 185.

[5] W. Dugdale, *Monasticon Anglicanum*, vol. II, London, 1819, p. 199.

[6] On which cf. Amundesham, op. cit. vol. I, pp. 130–5, 138–47.

[7] *Ibid.*, vol. I, pp. 73–81, 148–65.

[8] On this library cf. G. D'Adda, *Indagini storiche, artistiche, e bibliografiche sulla libreria Visconteo-Sforzesca del Castello di Pavia*, Milano, 1875. Whethamstede's quotations from a

bibliophile's tastes, in his having made purchases of books. On his return to England[1] Whethamstede continued to rule his abbey, alternating his religious duties with his studies and with patronage until 1440, when he resigned his abbacy on a plea of ill health.[2] By that time he had long been recognized by some of his English contemporaries as one of the leading Latin prose writers of his day. It was because of this that in 1427 he had been asked by Archbishop Chichele to write on his behalf to Pope Martin to justify him for the failure of his attempts to have the Statute of Provisors repealed,[3] and to this he may also have owed his appointment as one of the English envoys to the Diet of Frankfurt in 1442.[4]

In 1452 Whethamstede was torn away from his learned leisure and re-elected abbot.[5] This second tenure without Duke Humphrey's protection and with battles raging more than once around his abbey proved full of troubles and anxieties. Yet amidst the strife of the contending parties he was able to pursue his studies and deplore the horrors of civil war in his abominable Latin verse.[6] He was still abbot when he died in 1465 after a long career, during which his studies had occupied the foremost place amongst his activities.[7]

During his life Whethamstede was in close contact with some of the pioneers of humane learning in England. Amongst these was Humphrey of Gloucester, whom he presented with a Latin Plato[8] and with a Cato,[9] and probably the *Chronicles* of Matthew Paris,[10] besides several of his own writings.[11] Whethamstede

Latin Homer (*infra*, p. 36) suggest his access to the *Iliad* latinized by Leontius Pilatus formerly belonging to Petrarch and preserved there, (De Nolhac, *Petrarque et l'Humanisme*, vol. I, p. 103). Such a view is supported by the extreme rarity of Pilatus' work and by Whethamstede's reference to a commentary on Homer, which can only be identified with Petrarch's *marginalia* on his Latin *Iliad*. The only other Latin *Iliad* existing then was the version by Andrea da Rieti, on which cf. R. Weiss, 'An Unknown Fifteenth Century Version of the *Iliad*', *B.Q.R.* VII (1934) p. 464, but this included only books I–XII while Whethamstede quotes also from book XVIII; therefore his use of it must be excluded.

[1] He was already at St. Albans on 25 February, 1424, (Amundesham, op. cit. vol. I, p. 82).

[2] On his resignation cf. *Ibid.*, vol. II, pp. 233–47. An account of his first abbacy is in MS. (B.M.) Cotton, Nero, D.VII, ff. 27ʳ–35ʳ.

[3] Amundesham, op. cit. vol. I, p. 17.   [4] *Calendar of French Rolls*, p. 353.

[5] On 16 January, 1452. On his re-election cf. *Registrum Abbatiae J. Whethamstede*, vol. I, pp. 9–18. An account of his second abbacy is in MS. (B.M.) Cotton, Nero, D.VII, ff. 37ʳ–43ʳ.

[6] *Registrum Abbatiae J. Whethamstede*, vol. I, pp. 395–6, 399–401.

[7] He died on 20 January, 1465 (*Ibid.*, vol. II, p. 25).

[8] Now MS. Corpus Christi Coll. Oxford, no. 243.

[9] Amundesham, op. cit. vol. II, p. 256. This may have been the *Catonem Comentatum* presented to Oxford by Gloucester in 1444 (*Epistolae Academicae*, vol. I, p. 237).

[10] Now MS. (B.M.) Royal 14.C.VII. About the possibility that Gloucester obtained it from Whethamstede cf. Vickers, op. cit. p. 432.

[11] Cf. *infra*, p. 34, n. 1.

D

appears to have been closely connected with Duke Humphrey up to the time of the latter's tragic death,[1] and doubtless during their frequent meetings they discussed topics connected with learning as well as politics, and increased each other's store of knowledge.[2] It cannot have been only opportunism that made the Abbot seek the Duke's patronage, but also genuine appreciation of his fondness for learning, for Humphrey actually was the very kind of man to inspire Whethamstede's admiration. So close was Whethamstede's connexion with him, that the English translator of Palladius included him among the men of learning grouping around the Duke.[3] Gloucester was, however, as it will be seen later, a patron of letters rather than a scholar, and thus he was hardly in a position to exercise anything but a superficial intellectual influence outside the sphere of patronage. It is therefore to Whethamstede's relations with the Papal Collector, Piero del Monte, who introduced him to Plutarch[4] and perhaps to Bruni's writings,[4] rather than to Humphrey that we have to look in order to establish the neo-classical influence to which he was subjected.

Piero del Monte can hardly have been the only source that provided Whethamstede with Italian books. Whethamstede's knowledge of neo-classical works is much too wide, and consequently it seems very likely that he acquired some also during his visit to Italy,[5] and from other sources unknown to us, but which may possibly have included Duke Humphrey and some of the Italians in his entourage.

A perusal of extant evidence shows that Whethamstede must have possessed, or at least been acquainted with, a considerable number of classical and modern authors. Apart from works given to the monastic and college libraries which he built,[6] he

[1] Amundesham, op. cit. vol. II, p. 256. Whethamstede's *Granarium* was given to Oxford by Gloucester in 1444, (*Epistolae Academicae*, vol. I, p. 235). One of its volumes was seen there by Leland who copied a few passages from it, (Leland, *Collectanea*, vol. IV, p. 58).
[2] On his connexion with Humphrey cf. Vickers, op. cit. pp. 383–4. Leland states that Humphrey often visited Whethamstede (Leland, *De Scriptoribus Britanniae*, p. 437).
[3] *The Middle English Translation of Palladius De Re Rustica*, p. 22.
[4] MS. (V.L.) Vat. Lat. no. 2694, fo. 125ʳ. For Whethamstede's knowledge of Bruni's works cf. *infra*, p. 36, n. 10.
[5] This is possible since he was already interested in humanism at the time of his visit to Italy in 1423, as is shown by his letter to a fellow traveller in Italy whom he later learnt to be a leading Venetian humanist (Guarino?), in Amundesham, op. cit. vol. I, pp. 136–8.
[6] Whethamstede paid for the building of libraries at St. Albans and at Gloucester College, (Amundesham, op. cit. vol. II, p. 258, and *supra*, p. 32, n. 3). On the MSS. given by him to these libraries, cf. *infra*, p. 37, nn. 3, 5. On his benefactions to the St. Albans library cf. also MS. (B.M.) Cotton, Nero, D.VII, fo. 37ᵛ.

almost certainly had a very important collection of manuscripts
at his disposal. Of course it might perhaps be rash to assume that
he possessed everything he quotes: still it is probably a safe
assumption that his library contained a most impressive selection
of classical and humanistic texts.

Whethamstede's literary productions[1] show his preference for
encyclopedias in which he could tabulate under special headings
the limits of his wide reading. His *Granarium*[2] follows the lines
laid down by Isidore of Seville, Vincent of Beauvais, and Boccaccio, as does also his *Palearium*.[3] In his *Pabularium*[4] on the other
hand he collected a *Florilegium* from Latin poets, both classical
and medieval. Besides these voluminous compilations, Whethamstede prepared other encyclopedias,[5] tables to various authors,[6]
a treatise on the Holy Land,[7] Latin verse,[8] and other writings,
some of which are still extant. The extent of the Abbot's reading,
his catholicity in taste, are displayed in his literary remains. How
extensive was his acquaintance with Latin literature is shown by
his use of Roman authors. Especially noteworthy are his allusions
to works very little known in medieval times. Beside writers
familiar throughout the Middle Ages occur rarities such as
Lactantius' commentary on Statius,[9] the *Satyricon* of Petronius,[10]
Martial,[11] Quintilian's *Institutiones*,[12] and the *Bucolics* of Cal-

[1] On Whethamstede's works cf. Schirmer, op. cit. pp. 92–7, Jacob, *Florida Verborum Venustas*, pp. 13–7, and Hodge, op. cit. pp. 170–8.
[2] This was in four parts and was completed during Whethamstede's first abbacy (Amundesham, op. cit. vol. II, p. 270). Portions of part I are in MSS. (B.M.) Arundel, no. 11,
Cotton, Nero, C.VI, and Gonville and Caius Coll. Cambridge, no. 230. Sections of part II
are in MSS. (B.M.) Arundel, no. 391 and Cotton, Tib. D.V. Extracts from the other parts
are in MSS. (B.L.) Bodl. no. 585, and (B.M.) Cotton, Titus, D.XX.
[3] What remains of the *Palearium* is in MS. (B.M.) Add. no. 26764. Also this work was
compiled during Whethamstede's first abbacy, (Hodge, op. cit. p. 39).
[4] The only known copy of this work is now MS. (B.M.) Egerton, no. 646.
[5] These included the *Manipularium* and the *Propinarium*, both of which are now lost, and
on which cf. Hodge, op. cit. pp. 176–7. The *Propinarium* was presented to Oxford University
by the author, cf. *infra*, p. 37, n.1. He also seems to have been the author of a *Florarium* now
lost, (MS. Gonville and Caius, Cambridge, no. 230, fo. 1ʳ).
[6] On his *Tabulae* cf. Amundesham, op. cit. vol. II, p. 270, and Bale, *Scriptorum Illustrium
Maioris Brytanniae Catalogus*, p. 584. His *Tabula* of Valerius Maximus is in MS. (B.L.) Auct.
F. *inf.* I. I.
[7] Leland, *De Scriptoribus*, p. 438.
[8] For his verse cf. Amundesham, op. cit. vol. II, p. lvi. His Latin letters are in *Registrum
Abbatiae J. Whethamstede*, vol. II, pp. 365–476.
[9] MS. (B.M.) Add. no. 26764, ff. 10ᵛ, 12ʳ, 13ʳ⁻ᵛ, 17ʳ, etc.
[10] MS. (B.M.) Egerton, no. 646, ff, 36ᵛ, 48ʳ, 108ʳ, 112ʳ, 113ᵛ. The quotations are from
Satyricon, 14, 80, 109, 137, and are almost certainly derived from Vincent of Beauvais, on
whose use of Petronius cf. B. L. Ullman, 'Petronius in Medieval Florilegia,' *Classical
Philology*, XXV (1930) pp. 11–21.
[11] MSS. (B.M.) Cotton, Tib. D.V. pt. I, fo. 135ᵛ, Egerton, no. 646, ff. 25ᵛ, 43ʳ, etc.
[12] MS. (B.M.) Cotton, Tib. D.V. pt. I, fo. 64ᵛ. His article on Quintilian, (*Ibid.*, ff. 149ʳ⁻

purnius.[1] That Whethamstede possessed no Greek is clearly
demonstrated by his etymologies. Yet the literature, history, and
mythology, of the ancient Greek world must have appealed
powerfully to him, for part of the contents of his encyclopedias
was taken up by Greek subjects. A part of Greek literature was
known to him from translations, which included versions of
Homer,[2] Plato,[3] Aristotle,[4] and Xenophon,[5] and several modern
translations of Plutarch's *Lives*,[6] of which he everywhere made
lavish use. Versions of Greek authors were not the only humanistic works to attract his attention; apparently he was also acquainted with some of the Latin writings of Petrarch,[7] Boccaccio,[8]
Coluccio Salutati,[9] Leonardo Bruni,[10] and Andrea Fiocchi.[11]
Further, he would appear to have known something of Dante[12] and
to have had a particular fondness for Leonardo Bruni, to whom
he dedicated one of the biographical articles of his *Granarium*.[13]
But his favourite modern author was Boccaccio, whose Latin
treatises offered him models of style[14] and copious information.

50ᵛ) shows that he only knew books I–VIII of the *Institutiones Oratoriae* and not the complete
text discovered by Nicholas de Clemanges at the end of the fourteenth century, on which cf.
Sabbadini, *Scoperte*, vol. II, pp. 84–5.

[1] MS. (B.M.) Egerton, no. 646, fo. 110ʳ. This quotation was probably derived from
Vincent of Beauvais, on whose quotations from Calpurnius cf. B. L. Ullman, 'Classical
Authors in Certain Medieval Florilegia', *Classical Philology*, XXVII (1932) pp. 7–10.

[2] Quotations from a Latin *Iliad* and a commentary on it are in MSS. (B.M.) Add. no.
26764, fo. 128ʳ, Egerton, no. 646, fo. 74ʳ. On this version and commentary cf. *supra*, p. 32,
n. 8. The *Odyssey* is quoted in MS. (B.M.) Add. no. 26764, ff. 3ᵛ, 5ᵛ, 139ʳ; the *Odyssey*
quotations are derived from Boccaccio.

[3] MS. (B.M.) Cotton, Tib. D.V. pt. I, fo. 82ᵛ (quotation from the *Timaeus*). An article on
Plato is in *Ibid.*, ff. 138ᵛ–40ʳ. A Plato was presented by Whethamstede to Gloucester, (*supra*,
p. 33).

[4] He appears to have only known the medieval translations of this author. It is, however,
possible that he saw Bruni's versions owned by Gloucester.

[5] MS. (B.M.) Cotton, Tib. D.V. pt. I, fo. 169ᵛ (Bruni's version of the *De Tyranno*).

[6] MS. (B.M.) Cotton, Tib. D.V. pt. I, ff. 138ᵛ, 142ᵛ, 146ᵛ, 157ʳ, 159ʳ, 168ʳ, etc. Whethamstede's article on Plutarch is in *Ibid.*, ff. 140ʳ–ᵛ. Some of Plutarch's *Lives* had been
given to Whethamstede by Piero del Monte in 1437, (MS. (V.L.) Vat. Lat. no. 2694, fo.
125ʳ).

[7] Of Petrarch he knew the *De Viris Illustribus* (MSS. (B.M.) Cotton, Tib. D.V. pt. I, ff.
27ʳ, 39ᵛ, 164ᵛ, Nero, C.VI, fo. 175ᵛ).

[8] Of Boccaccio he quotes the *De Genealogiis Deorum* (MS. (B.M.) Cotton, Nero, C.VI.ff.
33ʳ, 46ᵛ, etc.) and the *De Claris Mulieribus*, (MS. (B.M.) Cotton, Tib. D.V. pt. I, fo. 6ʳ).

[9] He quotes Salutati's *De Fato et Fortuna* in MS. (B.M.) Cotton, Tib. D.V. pt. I, fo. 159ʳ.

[10] Besides several of Bruni's latinized Plutarch's *Lives* he knew his version of Xenophon's
De Tyranno, (*supra*, n. 5), the *Cicero Novus*, (MS. (B.M.) Cotton, Tib. D.V. pt. I, fo. 146ᵛ)
and the *De Bello Punico*, (MS. (B.M.) Arundel, no. 11, ff, 92ʳ–99ᵛ).

[11] Of whom he knew the *De Romanorum Magistratibus* commonly attributed to Fenestella
(MSS. (B.M.) Cotton, Tib. D.V. pt. I, fo. 68ᵛ, Add. no. 26764, fo. 111ᵛ).

[12] On his knowledge of Dante and Giovanni da Serravalle's commentary on the *Commedia*
cf. Weiss, *Per la Conoscenza di Dante in Inghilterra nel Quattrocento*, pp. 358–9.

[13] MS. (B.M.) Arundel, no. 11, ff, 92ʳ–99ᵛ.

[14] This is particularly evident in the *Palearium* which is obviously modelled on Boccaccio'
De Genealogiis Deorum.

Whethamstede was scarcely niggardly with his books since Oxford University,[1] Humphrey, Duke of Gloucester,[2] St. Albans Abbey,[3] John, Duke of Bedford,[4] and Gloucester College,[5] were among the recipients of his valuable manuscripts. But whether he exercised much intellectual influence outside his own monastery must remain doubtful. The poor quality of his Latin scholarship did not escape those of his contemporaries who were qualified judges.[6] As his Latin prose reveals, his conception of an elegant style consisted in an almost Alexandrian choice of appropriate images and expressions. This, however, he carried to such excess that his flowery Latin, especially in his letters, is indeed almost a caricature of late medieval finery. His sentences are inflated and contorted, his metaphors often so extravagant, that it is not easy to grasp the meaning he intended to convey. His subject matter is usually sacrificed on the altar of form while the abundance of allegories gives to his productions a highly artificial character. Yet this turgidity impressed several contemporaries, Archbishop Chichele among them.[7]

As a whole Whethamstede's prose resulted in a collection of medieval commonplaces developed into an exaggerated 'euphuism.' His style has no trace of Ciceronianism, and his allegories are those one would expect of a man trained in the schools. Whethamstede's achievement hardly justifies Dr. Schirmer's statement that he 'garbed the literary activity of his monastery in the formal aesthetic spirit of the Renaissance.'[8] That he was interested in Italian humanism is beyond doubt, but the question whether it influenced him must be answered negatively. His conception of history under the form of encyclopedia, and biography as a collection of anecdotes, is typically medieval,[9] equally so his lack of critical faculties. His works are those of a

[1] He presented his *Propinarium* to Oxford about 1463 (*Epistolae Academicae*, vol. II, p. 373).
[2] Cf. *supra*, p. 33.
[3] A list of MSS. given by him to St. Albans is in Amundesham, op. cit. vol. II, pp. 268–71. A badly charred list of books probably given to St. Albans by him is in MS. (B.M.) Cotton, Otho. B.IV, fo. 13ᵛ.
[4] To whom he presented a treatise on astronomy, (Amundesham, op. cit. vol. II, p. 256).
[5] MSS. (B.M.) Royal 8.G.X, (B.L.) Auct. F. inf. I. I, and the former MSS. Merton Coll. Oxford, nn. 251, 318 (now the property of Worcester Coll. Oxford) were presented to Gloucester College by Whethamstede. The half burnt list in MS. (B.M.) Cotton, Otho, B.IV, fo. 12ᵛ was probably a catalogue of the MSS. he gave to Gloucester College.
[6] For instance Thomas Bekynton who criticized his style most mercilessly, cf. *infra*, p. 73.
[7] Cf. *supra*, p. 33. On his style cf. Jacob, *Florida Verborum Venustas*, pp. 9–12.
[8] Schirmer, op. cit, p. 82.
[9] Whethamstede's conception of history does not differ much from that of Benzo d'Alessandria and Petrarch, on which cf. Sabbadini, *Il Metodo degli Umanisti*, pp. 75–6.

thoroughly medieval mind with strong Christian prejudices, a love for pigeon-holing knowledge, and an estimation of the classics chiefly as warehouses of information, such as the *Encyclopedia Britannica* might be considered to-day. To him knowledge was a means, not an end. A humanist would hardly have thought of the ancient gods as daemons,[1] or employed his arguments to defend the Donation of Constantine.[2] Whethamstede was one of the last of the English medieval polygraphers rather than one of the early English humanists. Throughout his career he failed to capture the spirit of humanism although opportunities had been plentiful during his lifetime. Doubtless his rich collection of classical and modern texts, and the ample store of information provided in his works, may have been instrumental in developing humane interests in others. But as far as his writings are concerned, they are chiefly interesting as an illustration of the difficulties facing the growth of humanism in this country, and as an example of classical materials adapted to other than humanist ends. It is possible to learn from them that diligence and zeal were not enough to make a humanist, and that it would have been impossible for neo-classicism to flourish in this country without greater dependence on the Italians. The best summary judgment of John Whethamstede is perhaps to be found in the lines he had written under his stained glass representation in the St. Albans' Library[3]:—

> *Doctor eram minimus, docui magis ipse docendus;*
> *Pastor et exiguus rexi, magis ymo regendus;*
> *Mitram deposui, libro studioque vacavi;*
> *Rursus eam sumpsi, loca libris hecque paravi.*

[1] Cf. MS. (B.M.) Cotton, Tib. D.V. pt. I, ff. 115ᵛ-6ᵛ (article on *Miracula Deorum*). The article begins *Mirabilia sunt demonorum* . . . Before proceeding to give examples Whethamstede warns the reader against the fallacious nature of these miracles.

[2] MS. (B.M.) Cotton, Nero, C.VI, ff. 53ᵛ-56ʳ.

[3] M. R. James, 'On the glass in the windows of the library of St. Albans Abbey,' *Cambridge Antiquarian Society Publications, Reports and Communications*, VIII (1893-5) p. 220.

CHAPTER III

In the previous chapters some endeavour has been made to describe the background against which the rise of English humanism took place. Clearly a revision of established values was necessary if humane standards were to be adopted in this country, and as the subsequent change in fifteenth century English culture shows, such revision did actually occur. Much of the credit for this change is due to the patronage and taste of Humphrey, Duke of Gloucester,[1] thanks to whom Italian values began to affect English intellectual life.

The origins of Duke Humphrey's interest in neo-classicism must remain a matter for conjecture, since what has come down to us about his early life and education gives no certainty on this point. It is true that love of books existed in his family, that his father King Henry IV[2] and his brothers King Henry V[3] and John, Duke of Bedford,[4] were keen bibliophiles. But although this may perhaps assist us in establishing the sources of his attitude towards learning, it is of no avail so far as the origins of his intellectual interests are concerned. His alleged education at Balliol College, Oxford,[5] is equally of no help, for even if we were sure that he was educated there, it would hardly be possible in the light of what is known about Oxford in the early fifteenth century, to assume that his fondness for classical and modern authors originated there. A more likely origin for Humphrey's interest in humanism may, on the other hand, be found in his contacts with Collectors and envoys sent to England by the Roman Curia. These were generally men with classical learning, and one of them, Piero del Monte, as we saw, played a distinguished rôle in the history of humanism, while Giuliano Cesarini taught Latin during his visit to England:[6] it seems very

[1] On Gloucester's learned activities cf. Vickers, op. cit. pp. 340–82, Schirmer, op. cit. pp. 26–59, Borsa, *Correspondence of Humphrey, Duke of Gloucester, and Pier Candido Decembrio.*
[2] Besides having MSS. prepared for him he was a benefactor of the Oxford University Library (*Munimenta Academica*, vol. I, p. 266).
[3] On Henry V as a bibliophile cf. Vickers, op. cit. p. 343. After the capture of Caen Henry V reserved for himself a MS. of French chronicles out of the spoils of the town (*The First English Life of Henry V*, ed. C. L. Kingsford, Oxford, 1911, p. 92), and at his death he bequeathed books to Oxford (*Epistolae Academicae*, vol. I, p. 151).
[4] On Bedford's love of books cf. Vickers, op. cit. pp. 345–6, and E. F. Bosanquet, 'The Personal Prayer-Book of John of Lancaster Duke of Bedford, K.G.' *The Library*, 4th series, XIII (1932–3) pp. 148–54.
[5] On Gloucester's education cf. Vickers, op. cit. pp. 8–9.
[6] Cf. *supra*, p. 23.

likely therefore that Humphrey's curiosity in polite letters dated
from his relations with Papal officials whom he met in virtue of
his position. Perhaps Simone da Teramo, Cesarini, and Gerardo
Landriani,[1] all of whom knew Humphrey, and certainly Del
Monte, were partly responsible for developing his intellectual
outlook. Some support to this conjecture is lent not only by Del
Monte's activities in England, but also by a letter written by
Simone da Teramo to Gloucester in 1424 to exculpate himself
from some charges.[2] The abundance of classical quotations
throughout this letter hints that its writer was familiar with the
Duke's tastes, and the circumstances suggest that he knew the
right chord to strike to regain his favour.

Besides these Papal representatives, friends like the Italian
born Bishop of Bayeux, Zenone da Castiglione,[3] who had been
educated by humanists, and John Whethamstede, Abbot of St.
Albans, were also instrumental in aiding the development of
the Duke's literary interests. Books played a certain part also in
shaping his tastes. With the growing of humanism in Italy neo-
classical writings, and especially Latin translations of Greek
authors, were beginning to flood the international book trade,
and some of these reached Duke Humphrey through gift and
purchase,[4] and acquainted him with the 'New Learning.'

The Italian scholars had sedulously fostered a belief that their
art and it alone could confer immediate honour and an undying
reputation on the patrons in whose service it was employed.[5]
At a time when rhetoric and hyperbole were serious arguments,
and men were grown so solicitous of fame, especially pos-
thumous fame, the protestations of a few literary specialists were
seized upon at their face value by ambitious and competing
princes. The possession of a chancery where correspondence was

---

[1] Landriani, then Bishop of Lodi, was sent to England by the Council of Basle in 1432
(R. Sabbadini,'Niccolò da Cusa e i conciliari di Basilea alla ricerca dei codici,' *Accademia dei
Lincei, Rendiconti, (Scienze Morali)*, XX (1911) p. 5, n. 3). He met Gloucester (Mansi, *Conciliorum Nova et Amplissima Collectio*, vol. XXX, cols. 165–6), to whom he also wrote later
from Basle (*Official Correspondence of Thomas Beckington*, vol. II, p. 144). An *Oratio Gerardi
Landriani ad Regem Angliae et Episcopos* is in Mansi, op. cit. vol. XXIX, cols. 463–8. On
Landriani in England cf. also Zellfelder, *England und das Basler Konzil*, pp. 54–9. The letters
written by Gloucester to the Council of Basle in 1432 and 1435 in Mansi, op. cit. vol. XXX,
cols. 165–6, 919, are interesting also because of their classical style. As Gloucester had no
Italian scholar in his service at the time, they may possibly be the work of Bekynton who was
then his Chancellor, cf., *infra*, p. 71.
[2] Cf. *supra*, p. 18, n. 2.
[3] On his connexion with Gloucester cf. *infra*, pp. 49–53.
[4] Already in 1433 he possessed Bruni's Latin text of Aristotle's *Ethics*, (*infra*, p. 47).
[5] On the humanists as dispensers of glory cf. V. Rossi, *Il Quattrocento*, Milano, 1933, p. 43.

conducted in accordance with the canons of classical Latin was
no small material asset, and indeed was coming to be regarded
as an indisputable mark of grandeur and power. It was therefore
a decisive step, alike in the history of English taste and in the
intellectual career of Duke Humphrey, when, ceding to current
notions of fame or in imitation of Italian princes, he began to cast
about for a humanist of some distinction who might become his
secretary. There always remains the possibility that Duke
Humphrey was prompted to this decision not merely by an
uncritical appetite for prestige and panegyric, but as a result
of a very subtle estimate of his political prospects. His quarrels
with opponents in the Council turned around nothing so much
as his insistence on an implacable prosecution of the war. If the
French war could be represented in an idealized form as the
heroic exploit that Henry V had bequeathed to his countrymen,
and if an attractive and entirely novel presentation of the war
could be imposed on the minds of even a limited number of
prominent Englishmen, then Duke Humphrey might yet have
his way. Significantly enough Humphrey first invited Leonardo
Bruni to come to England in 1433.[1] But the position of Bruni in
Italy was so elevated and so secure that he declined the invitation.
It was left to the obsequious Del Monte to recommend a former
acquaintance to Duke Humphrey.[2] This was none other than
Tito Livio Frulovisi,[3] a native of Ferrara but brought up in
Venice, where he probably attended the school of Guarino da
Verona.[4] After finishing his University education,[4] Frulovisi had
earned a livelihood by keeping a school in Venice patronized
mainly by the local middle classes, the routine of his school-
mastering being enlivened by violent quarrels with rivals and
critics.[5] Perhaps the main reason which induced Frulovisi to
leave Venice was, besides the unpopularity earned by a malicious
tongue, the outburst against him caused by the performance of
one of his Latin comedies, the *Oratoria*.[6]

Why Frulovisi came to England we do not know: that he came

[1] Cf. *infra*, p. 47.
[2] Sabbadini, *Tito Livio Frulovisio*, p. 59.
[3] On Frulovisi cf. *Opera Hactenus Inedita T. Livii de Frulovisiis de Ferrara*, Sabbadini,
Tito Livio Frulovisio, Kingsford, *English Historical Literature of the Fifteenth Century*, pp.
50–6.
[4] Sabbadini, *Tito Livio Frulovisio*, p. 57. Sabbadini suggests that he attended the University of Padua.
[5] *Opera T. Livii de Frulovisiis*, pp. xi–xii.
[6] The performance of this comedy took place between November 1434 and August 1435
(*Ibid.*, p. xiii).

attracted by the fame of Henry V and Duke Humphrey, as he declared,[1] may be discounted as flattery: positive evidence is limited to his securing his appointment with the Duke through the offices of Piero del Monte. As Del Monte was a Venetian who had attended the school of Guarino da Verona in Venice and the University of Padua,[2] it is very likely that they first met at one of these seats of learning, and that it was on account of their old friendship that Del Monte recommended him.

Gloucester engaged Frulovisi as his 'poet and orator,'[3] and shortly after the Italian had settled in his household, he secured letters of denization for him, which were granted on March 7th, 1437.[3] Frulovisi's principal duties appear to have consisted in conducting part of Humphrey's correspondence,[4] and in preparing a biography of his dead brother, King Henry V.[5] From a passage in one of Frulovisi's comedies, the *Eugenius*, which was written during his sojourn in England,[6] it may be inferred that his appointment was not permanent, but he naturally hoped that it might become so. At least two Latin comedies, the *Peregrinatio* and the *Eugenius*,[6] were composed by Frulovisi at this time. These were possibly performed in his master's household, and though hardly original in plot and style are worthy of attention being the first Renaissance comedies composed in this country. But the capital work that he undertook as Gloucester's 'poet and orator' was the *Vita Henrici Quinti*. A biography of Humphrey's brother, King Henry V, it was in no less degree a characterization, almost a dramatization, of the French war, and one in which Humphrey was well cast if not without justification. The better to serve the ends of his patron who at the moment of its composition was clamouring for war, this time against Burgundy, Frulovisi relegated events in England to the background, so as

---

[1] *Vita Henrici Quinti*, p. 2.

[2] Cf. *supra*, p. 24.

[3] He is described thus in his grant of denization printed in Rymer, *Feodera*, vol. x, pp. 661–2. The exact date of Gloucester's engagement of Frulovisi is not known, but he was already in the Duke's service in 1437. Professor Previté-Orton rightly suggests that Humphrey met Frulovisi in 1436 (*Opera T. Livii de Frulovisiis*, pp. xiii–iv).

[4] This is suggested by Frulovisi's writing to Bruni on Gloucester's behalf on 22 August 1437 (Sabbadini, *Tito Livio Frulovisio* pp. 73–4).

[5] The only edition of it is Hearne's. On the MSS. of this work cf. *Opera T. Livii de Frulovisiis*, pp. xviii–ix. On its importance cf. Kingsford, op. cit. pp. 52–5. *The Vita Henrici Quinti* was dedicated to Henry VI (Frulovisi's preface addressed to the King is in *Vita Henrici Quinti*, pp. 1–3), and in 1463 it was translated into Italian by Decembrio who dedicated it to Francesco Sforza, Duke of Milan. (On this version cf. J. H. Wylie, 'Decembri's version of the *Vita Henrici Quinti* by Tito Livio,' *E.H.R.* XXIV (1909), pp. 84–9). Frulovisi had sent a MS. of the *Vita* to Decembrio (*Opera T. Livii de Frulovisiis*, p. xiv).

[6] *Ibid.*, p. xiv.

to focus attention on the heroic appeal of the campaigns. In all but name it was a pamphlet to glorify Gloucester in his loyalty to his dead brother's cause, and an attempt on behalf of Gloucester's policy to inspire enthusiasm for a war that was turning inevitably to defeat. As a piece of historical writing and as the first 'official' life of an English King, Frulovisi's work could not fail to exercise a remarkable influence upon English historiography, and, as has been rightly pointed out, it anticipates Polydore Vergil in the combining of national feeling with foreign culture,[1] and like Polydore's *Historia Anglica* later, it furnished a useful pattern for future historians.

Alongside with the performance of literary tasks, Frulovisi was instrumental in increasing the library of his English employer; a copy of his *De Republica* was among the books given to Oxford by the Duke in 1444.[2] On the other hand he prepared no translations from the Greek for his master, possibly owing to his being too busy with his life of Henry V, his comedies, and his duties as a secretary, to find time for translating. As Beccaria, who succeeded Frulovisi in Humphrey's employment, prepared several translations, it is probable that Frulovisi would have applied himself to a similar task had his appointment lasted longer. Professor Previté-Orton suggests that the reasons for the termination of Frulovisi's appointment with Gloucester were perhaps that his employer found his Latin too colloquial and his Greek too superficial, and because Frulovisi was apt to fall out with all his neighbours.[3] Probably this latter reason rather than the former was material in terminating his career in Humphrey's household, as it seems doubtful whether the Duke was a good enough scholar to realize the weakness of Frulovisi's qualifications.

Frulovisi was still with Humphrey in August 1437,[4] but perhaps during the following year he was already preparing to cross the Channel.[5] It is not certain whether he was dismissed, but since before leaving England he appealed for help to a well known enemy of Gloucester's, the Chancellor John Stafford,[6] he obviously could no longer rely on the protection of his former employer. Frulovisi appears again in Venice in 1439, when his

---

[1] Kingsford, op. cit., p. 8.
[2] *Epistolae Academicae*, vol. I, p. 236.
[3] *Opera T. Livii de Frulovisiis*, p. xiv.
[4] When he wrote to Bruni on Gloucester's behalf. Cf *supra*, p. 42, n. 4.
[5] *Opera T. Livii de Frulovisiis*, p. xiv.
[6] A poem in which he asks Stafford for help is in *Ibid.*, pp. 390–2.

sharp tongue once more caused him trouble, so that from there he attempted to secure a new appointment in England through his old friend Piero del Monte.[1] This appeal did not prove useless: Del Monte came to his friend's rescue and actually secured for him a Papal Sub-Collectorship[1]; but while on his way to England to take up his new duties, Frulovisi was arrested, as it seems, and not improbably from what we know of his antecedents, on a charge of defamation at the instance of John Gele, an Englishman by denization holding a canonry at Lübeck.[2] As a result of this Frulovisi lost his opportunity of returning to England, a country which he, unlike Poggio and Del Monte, appears to have found particularly congenial.

In spite of what had passed between him and Humphrey, we find Frulovisi even in later years still alluding to him as his master.[3] But to imply from this a connexion, or even a hope on Frulovisi's part of re-entering the Duke's service, would be far fetched. What probably induced him to continue to style Humphrey his master was that the Duke's name was well known in Italian circles and among princes, so that the suggestion of a link with him would doubtless constitute a useful advertisement.

Subject to certain limitations, Frulovisi had been endowed with a very original mind and an unusual grasp of reality. This may be perceived in his writings, which contain several acute observations and striking suggestions. His Latin Comedies and his *Vita Henrici Quinti* show his versatility as an author, while his *De Republica* indicates his readiness to theorize from contemporary conditions and events.[4]

Contact with such a versatile character could scarcely fail to arouse further Humphrey's interest in humanism, but Frulovisi's employment in the Duke's household precluded him from exercising any but a negligible influence outside it. The only field in which he contributed to the cultural development of England was that of historiography: as far as other humane studies were concerned he hardly went beyond bringing Duke Humphrey's contacts with the literary world of Italy closer. Had he, as he

[1] Sabbadini, *Tito Livio Frulovisio*, p. 60.
[2] *Ibid.*, loc. cit. Gele was a Canon of Lübeck (*C.P.R.*, vol. IX, p. 349) who obtained denization on 12 July, 1439, when he was also licensed to hold the benefice of Humberton, (P.R. 1436–41, p. 302).
[3] Borsa, *Pier Candido Decembri e l'umanesimo in Lombardia*, p. 432.
[4] Frulovisi's works, the *Vita* excepted, were published in *Opera T. Livii de Frulovisiis*. The *De Ortographia* printed in Cologne about 1480 under his name is not by him (Sabbadini, *Tito Livio Frulovisio*, p. 56). On the *De Republica* cf. especially *Ibid.*, pp. 61–4.

intended, returned to this country, he would perhaps have made some contribution to the development of humanism in England, almost as valuable as his services to English historiography.[1]

The departure of Frulovisi did not induce Duke Humphrey to give up his intention of having a resident Italian humanist in his household. Instead, the vacancy created by the departure or dismissal of the Ferrarese, was soon filled by another Italian of more or less similar distinction. Also in this case the advice of the obliging Del Monte had been sought and followed, and an appointment made accordingly.[2] Frulovisi's successor was the Antonio Beccaria,[3] who alongside with Del Monte, Whetham-stede, and Frulovisi, is mentioned by the translator of Palladius among the scholars that gathered around Humphrey of Glou-cester.[4] This native of Verona, where he was born about the year 1400,[5] was one of the many pupils of the famous Vittorino da Feltre to attain some distinction in scholarship.[5] His coming to England probably took place during the last quarter of 1438 or the first quarter of 1439,[6] and immediately on arrival he took up his secretarial duties in the Duke's household. Although he was engaged as a secretary,[7] Beccaria's duties were not rigidly confined to chancery routine, but as in the case of Frulovisi, literary activities were also expected of him. Thus besides con-ducting his master's Latin correspondence, for it is practically certain that the Duke's letters to Pier Candido Decembrio came from the pen of Beccaria,[8] he was set to turn into Latin some

[1] Frulovisi's *Vita* was the basis of the biography of Henry V formerly attributed to Thomas Elmham printed in *Thomae de Elmham Vita et Gesta Henrici Quinti*. According to Kingsford, op. cit. p. 59, this work was influenced by Italian learning. Actually all it dis-closes is that its writer was conforming with the over ornate style fashionable in England at the time. Kingsford, op. cit. loc. cit., suggests also that John Somerset, to whom the work is dedicated, had some connexion with humanism. That Somerset was friendly to learning is undoubted, but there is no evidence that he came under Italian influence. A Latin elegy by him in *Thomae de Elmham Vita et Gesta Henrici Quinti*, pp. 347–50, suggests no contacts with the Renaissance.

[2] Weiss, *Antonio Beccaria in Inghilterra*, p. 345. Beccaria dedicated his version of Plutarch's *Pelopidas* to Del Monte (Degli Agostini, op. cit. p. 357). A letter from Del Monte to Beccaria is in MS. (V.L.) Vat. Lat. no. 2694, ff. 190ᵛ–91ʳ.

[3] On Beccaria cf. especially G. C. Giuliari, *Della Letteratura Veronese al cadere del secolo XV e delle sue opere a stampa*, Bologna, 1876, pp. 459–66, De Rosmini, *Idea dell'ottimo precettore nella vita e disciplina di Vittorino da Feltre e de' suoi discepoli*, pp. 234–8, Schirmer, op. cit. pp. 43–4, Vickers, op. cit. pp. 377–9, Medin, *Il testamento e l'inventario di un' umanista veronese del secolo XV*, Weiss, *Antonio Beccaria in Inghilterra*.

[4] *The Middle English Translation of Palladius De Re Rustica*, p. 22.

[5] Medin, op. cit. p. 461; De Rosmini, op. cit. p. 235.

[6] Weiss, *Antonio Beccaria in Inghilterra*, p. 344.

[7] Cf. Gloucester's note in MS. (B.M.) Royal, 5.F.II, fo. 131ᵛ: *Cest liure est a moy Homfrey duc de Gloucestre lequel Jay fait translater de grec en latyn par un de mes secretaires Antoyne de Beccara . . .*

[8] Weiss, *Antonio Beccaria in Inghilterra*, pp. 345–6.

Greek works[1] and Boccaccio's *Corbaccio*.[2] All these versions, which included some treatises by St. Athanasius,[3] an author whose uncompromising orthodoxy must have had a particular appeal for Humphrey, were transcribed in a pleasant round hand by Beccaria himself,[4] and duly placed in the Duke's library.[4]

Unlike Frulovisi and Signorelli, Humphrey's Italian-born physician, Beccaria did not obtain denization, nor is his name to be found in any contemporary English official records. The date of his return to Italy is uncertain, although there is some evidence that he left England in 1445 or 1446.[5] He was certainly not dismissed, for he maintained cordial relations with his former employer after returning to Italy and sent him more Latin versions of St. Athanasius's works.[5]

It is hard to know how much Beccaria influenced the English attitude towards the classical revival. But from the nature of his employment it is reasonable to suppose that he can have done but little teaching while in England. Whether he had any occasion to exercise his remarkable knowledge of Greek must remain more than doubtful. Traces of his action are to be sought rather in the inspiration which his complex personality may have exercised on his patron and the latter's friends.

The employment of Italian secretaries was only a part of Duke Humphrey's extensive patronage, which led him to write to scholars in Italy asking them to prepare new translations from the Greek and to procure books for his library. The first professional Italian humanist approached by Duke Humphrey was the famous Leonardo Bruni, generally known as Leonardo Aretino.[6] It is not known exactly how Bruni first attracted the Duke's

---

[1] Cf. *supra*, p. 45, n. 7 and *infra*, n. 3.

[2] A MS. of this translation is now MS. (B.L.) Lat. misc. d. 34, on which cf. Craster, *Duke Humphrey's Dante, Petrarch, and Boccaccio, MSS.*, p. 303. On this version cf. Vickers, op. cit. pp. 378–9. As the first lines of the title page of the Bodleian MS. are written in the same peculiar script as one of the title pages of MS. (B.M.) Royal 5.F.II, (Gloucester's copy of Beccaria's *Athanasius*), it is obvious that this MS. (which is undoubtedly of English execution) is a copy of Gloucester's own MS.

[3] These translations are in MSS. (B.M.) Royal, 5.F.II, and King's College, Cambridge, no. 27. Both MSS. include dedications to Gloucester and were his own copies of the texts.

[4] Weiss, *Antonio Beccaria in Inghilterra*, p. 346, n. 2. Some of Beccaria's works were presented by Gloucester to Oxford and included Athanasius, the *Corbaccio*, and perhaps Plutarch's *Pelopidas*. (*Epistolae Academicae*, vol. I, pp. 180, 233, Craster, op. cit. p. 303). The Athanasius presented to Oxford in 1444 is now part of MS. (B.M.) Royal 5.F.II.

[5] Weiss, *Antonio Beccaria in Inghilterra*, p. 346, Vickers, op. cit. p. 377.

[6] On Bruni cf. especially Baron, *Leonardo Bruni Aretino*, Bertalot, *Forschungen über Leonardo Bruni Aretino*, L. Bertalot, 'Zur Bibliographie des Leonardus Brunus Aretinus' *Quellen und Forschungen aus Italienischen Archiven und Bibliotheken*, XXVIII (1937–8) pp. 268–85, and the bibliography at the end of the article on Bruni in the *Enciclopedia Italiana*. On Bruni and Gloucester cf. Vickers, op. cit. pp. 352–4, Schirmer, op. cit. pp. 27–28, 33–4.

attention but it is possible to suggest how this may have taken place. In order to explain this it is necessary to bear in mind that already during the earlier decades of the fifteenth century Bruni's reputation as a scholar had spread across the Alps and was by no means unknown in England.[1] Apart from the fact that during his early career Bruni had befriended a 'Thomas of England,'[2] several of his writings were to be found in England during the first half of the fifteenth century, and Abbot Whethamstede held them in sufficient esteem to quote from them copiously, and to include their author in his biographies of famous men.[3] Some works of Bruni's were in the possession of the Bishop of Bayeux, Zenone da Castiglione,[4] a close friend of Humphrey's,[5] so that either Whethamstede or Castiglione may have brought them to the notice of the Duke. It was Bruni's Latin version of Aristotle's *Ethics*, dating from 1416–17,[6] that first attracted Gloucester.[6] The manifest superiority of this translation over the clumsy medieval renderings of the *Ethics* then current made such an impression on him, that he wrote to the translator asking him to visit England. Although the exact date of the beginning of their correspondence is not known, it is very likely that Humphrey's first letter to Bruni was written in 1433.[7] In this letter besides inviting him to England, he asked him to prepare a Latin text of Aristotle's *Politics*, expressing at the same time his admiration for the version of the *Ethics*.[8] Except for the invitation to come to England, which was politely but firmly declined on account of age and other reasons, among which very probably weighed the knowledge of Poggio's experiences in this country, the Duke's

[1] '*aveva grandissima riputazione in Inghilterra*' (Da Bisticci, op. cit. p. 436). An *Oratio in laudem Regis Angliae* in G. Donzellini, *Epistolae Principum, Rerumpublicarum ac Sapientium Virorum*, Venetiis, 1574, pp. 391 ff., has been attributed to Guarino, Bruni, and Frulovisi. Its contents are, however, too vague to suggest a definite authorship, and there are no serious grounds for attributing it to any of these scholars. Possibly it was written as a rhetorical exercise and never delivered.

[2] Bruni, op. cit. vol. I, p. 55. On Thomas cf. Schirmer, op. cit. pp. 11–2.

[3] Cf. *supra*, p. 36.

[4] MS. (V.L.) Regin. no. 1321, fo. 193ʳ.

[5] On his relations with Gloucester cf. *infra*, pp. 49–53.

[6] Cf. Bruni's letters to Gloucester (Baron, op. cit. pp. 138–40) and to Pizzolpasso (on which cf. *infra*, p. 49, n. 1). The date of the letter to Gloucester is *III id. Martias* (Bertalot, *Forschungen über Leonardo Bruni Aretino*, p. 313); its year is 1434 since Bruni started to translate the *Politics* in that year (this being evident from Bruni's statement to Flavio Biondo, on which cf. *infra*, p. 48, n. 8, made in March 1437, in which Bruni declared to have finished the *Politics* after three years' work) and his letter to Gloucester shows his intention to start to translate without delay. On the date of Bruni's *Ethics* cf. Baron, op. cit. p. 164.

[7] Since Bruni's reply to it is of March 1434 (*supra*, n. 6).

[8] Gloucester's letter is lost, but some of its contents may be inferred from Bruni's reply to it.

demands were complied with. In his answer Bruni declared his readiness to begin work on the *Politics*, and enclosed a list of his translations with an offer to send any of them which the Duke might care to possess.[1] During 1434 Bruni started to translate the *Politics*,[2] and already by the beginning of 1437 it was ready and a presentation copy of it was consigned eventually to the Borromei for conveyance to England.[3] Some delay in the actual delivery of this book appears, however, to have intervened, and hence enquiries about it to Bruni from Frulovisi writing on Duke Humphrey's behalf in August 1437. To these Bruni replied that the copy in question had been duly tendered for delivery to the Borromei, but that difficulties had arisen about its transmission, and observed rather pointedly that he had neither asked for, nor so far received any financial benefits from the whole transaction.[4] Eventually the *Politics* reached Duke Humphrey during the first half of 1438,[5] followed by a letter from Bruni to Gloucester expressing his pleasure at the news that the version had reached him, but at the same time reproaching Humphrey for his suspicions and for his conduct.[6]

The connexion between Gloucester and Leonardo Bruni ended with the sending of the *Politics* to England.[7] But even before despatching it Bruni must have despaired of securing an adequate reward from the Duke, for shortly after completing the version he wrote to Flavio Biondo, then one of the Papal secretaries, asking him to offer the translation to Pope Eugenius IV, and forwarding at the same time a copy with a new preface addressed to the Pope.[8] The offer was instantly accepted by Biondo on behalf of the Pope with whom it found much favour.[9]

[1] Baron, op. cit. p. 140.   [2] Cf. *supra*, p. 47, n. 6.

[3] Cf. Bruni's letter to Frulovisi in Sabbadini, *Tito Livio Frulovisio*, pp. 73–4. This letter was written on 13 December, 1437.

[4] Cf. *supra*, n. 3.

[5] That the *Politics* eventually reached Gloucester is evident from Bruni's letter to him of 1 November, 1438, on which cf. *infra*, n. 6. This text had not been sent yet on 13 December, 1437 (cf. Bruni's letter to Frulovisi on which cf. *supra*, n. 3), but must have been sent not later than the summer of 1438, since its reaching the Duke is referred to in Bruni's letter to him of 1 November, 1438.

[6] This letter is printed in H. W. Chandler, *A Catalogue of Editions of Aristotle's Nicomachean Ethics*, Oxford, 1868, pp. 41–4, and is dated 1 November, (1438).

[7] On Bruni's rupture with Gloucester cf. especially Da Bisticci, op. cit. pp. 436–7 and his letter to Pizzolpasso (on which cf. *infra*, p. 49, n. 1). The quarrel was doubtless due to lack of remuneration.

[8] Bruni's letter is dated 1 March, 1437, and is in Bruni, op. cit. vol. II, pp. 180–1. Bruni stated in this to have just accomplished the *Politics* after three years' work. The dedication to the Pope is in Nogara, *Scritti inediti e rari di Biondo Flavio*, pp. 96–7. Neither this nor the letter to Biondo state that the *Politics* had been translated for Gloucester.

[9] Biondo's reply was written on 15 March, 1437, and is in Nogara, op. cit. pp. 93–4.

But Bruni's conduct towards his English patron did not fail to arouse criticism within Italian humanistic circles. Both Decembrio and his patron Archbishop Pizzolpasso openly commented on his behaviour,[1] though doubtless in their case their attitude was inspired by a desire to find favour with the Duke, and establish Decembrio in the vacancy in his patronage caused by the quarrel with Bruni.

Bruni's rupture with Humphrey did not prejudice his reputation in England. A comparatively large number of his works were both copied in this country and imported from abroad during the century,[2] and the manuscripts of his writings presented by Humphrey to Oxford were more than once transcribed by members of the University during the same period.[2] His *Ethics* rapidly replaced the inferior medieval texts to such an extent as to justify the printing of an edition at Oxford during the fifteenth century.[2] Among the humanists of his time, Bruni was doubtless the one whose works were best known in England, a fact due in no small measure to his Latin Aristotle which attracted orthodox schoolmen as well as those drawn to humanism.

Duke Humphrey's break with Bruni was soon followed by connexions with other Italian scholars. In the establishing of these links the chief intermediary was the Bishop of Bayeux,[3] who, during his stay in Italy at the Roman Curia, missed no opportunity of praising Humphrey, his studies, and his patronage, to those humanists whom he met.

A nephew of the great Cardinal Branda and a pupil of Gasparino Barzizza,[3] Zenone da Castiglione had become Bishop of Lisieux while still a young man on his uncle's resignation in his favour.[4] Eight years later in 1432 he was translated from Lisieux to the more important Bayeux,[4] and it was during his tenure of this see that he was able to help Humphrey in his humane pursuits. Castiglione, who had probably met the Duke in Normandy, appears to have interspersed his spiritual duties with

---

[1] Borsa, *Correspondence of Humphrey, Duke of Gloucester*, pp. 513, 525; Newman, *The Correspondence of Humphrey, Duke of Gloucester*, p. 496. Bruni eventually accused Pizzolpasso of defaming him with Gloucester. Cf. Bruni's letter to the former in *Bruni*, op. cit. vol. II, pp. 119–22 in which he also gives his own version of the facts.

[2] Cf. *infra*, pp. 175 and *passim*. MS. (B.L.) Lat. misc. d. 34, which is a transcript of one of Gloucester's MSS. includes a work by Bruni.

[3] He may be identified with one of the nephews of Cardinal Branda who attended the school of Barzizza (Sabbadini, *La Scuola e gli Studi di Guarino da Verona*, pp. 26–7). On Castiglione cf. Borsa, *Pier Candido Decembri e l'Umanesimo in Lombardia*, pp. 57–61, Schirmer, op. cit. pp. 29–32, Vickers, op. cit. pp. 351–2.

[4] Gams, *Series Episcoporum Ecclesiae Catholicae*, pp. 507, 566.

E

literary distractions. He befriended men of letters and collected their writings:[1] also his secretary, the Milanese Rolando Talenti, was a classical scholar of some ability, educated like his master at the school of the Barzizzas.[2] Thus when Castiglione went to the Council of Basle as one of Henry VI's envoys,[3] he was doubtless commissioned by Gloucester to acquire books, and asked to encourage Italian humanists to send him works, more especially versions from the Greek.[4] At Basle he met the Archbishop of Milan, Francesco II Pizzolpasso,[5] a well-known discoverer and collector of classical manuscripts, who at that time enjoyed great authority among Italian men of letters, and thanks to him Zenone was enabled to establish contacts with leading scholars including the secretary of the Duke of Milan, Pier Candido Decembrio.[5]

When the Council of Basle broke with Pope Eugenius, Castiglione sided with the papalist party and left for Italy, where he joined the Papal court in Bologna probably in 1437.[6] Here he remained until the beginning of 1438, when he went to Ferrara for the Council. In Bologna Castiglione met the humanist Lapo da Castiglionchio the younger, then living there,[7] to whom he praised Duke Humphrey for his patronage.[8] Castiglione's praises proved successful with Lapo. Their outcome was that the latter

[1] Cf. *supra*, p. 47, *infra*, pp. 50–2.

[2] On Talenti cf. J. Laffetay, 'Notice sur la vie et les écrits de Roland des Talents Chanoine de Bayeux,' *Bulletin de la Société d'agriculture, sciences, arts etc. de Bayeux*, 1852, pp. 13–57. His education by the Barzizzas is suggested not only by his Milanese extraction and classical education, but also by his cordial relations with both Gasparino and Guiniforte Barzizza (MS. Bibliothèque du Chapitre, Bayeux, no. 5, fo. 37ᵛ).

[3] He was already in Basle on 21 March, 1434, when he petitioned the Council (Haller, *Concilium Basiliense*, vol. III, pp. 101–2). In the following December he was one of the ambassadors of Henry VI as King of France to Basle (*Ibid.*, vol. III, pp. 272–3). He and other envoys were empowered to treat for the reform of the Church and peace with France on 10 February, 1435 (Rymer, op. cit. vol. X, p. 603).

[4] As he was later in Bologna, where he received a letter from Gloucester asking him to procure translations from Greek authors, especially by Guarino and Bruni (MS. (B.R.F.) Ricc. no. 827 fo. 31ᵛ).

[5] Borsa, *Pier Candido Decembri e l'umanesimo in Lombardia*, pp. 57, 59–60. On Pizzolpasso cf. *infra*, p. 54, n. 6.

[6] Castiglione cannot have reached Bologna later than 1437 since Lapo da Castiglionchio, whom he met there, sent a translation to Gloucester during that year acting on Castiglione's advice (*infra*, p. 51). A letter of Henry VI to the Marquess of Ferrara of 5 July, 1438 (*Official Correspondence of Thomas Beckington*, vol. I, pp. 58–60) shows that Castiglione went to Ferrara.

[7] Lapo was in Bologna from July-August 1436 to January 1438, (Luiso, *Studi sull' Epistolario di Lapo da Castiglionchio juniore*, pp. 246, n. 2, 257, 275). On Lapo cf. *Ibid.* On his contacts with Castiglione cf. *Ibid.*, p. 274, MS. (B.L.) Auct. F.5. 26, fo. 58ᵛ.

[8] Luiso, op. cit. p. 274, MS. (B.L.) Auct. F.5.26, fo. 58ᵛ.

sent to the Duke a Latin treatise comparing scholarship with the art of war accompanied by a flattering dedication,[1] together with his translation of some of Isocrates' orations,[2] obviously in order to advertise his skill as a translator as well as to curry favour. Lapo must have been anxious to impress Duke Humphrey since these were soon followed by other works. Thus in December 1437 he dedicated to the Duke a Latin version of Plutarch's *Life of Artaxerxes*,[3] which he despatched accompanied by other Plutarchian biographies which he had latinized.[4]

But Lapo was not to derive any advantages from his presents to Duke Humphrey, for he died shortly afterwards,[5] thus ending what had promised to become a useful connexion for the Duke's learned hobby.

From Bologna Zenone da Castiglione had also corresponded with the humanist Pier Candido Decembrio on matters linked with humanism. Castiglione, who had then read Decembrio's translation of the fifth book of Plato's *Republic*,[6] had forwarded a request to him for the Latin text of the *Republic* prepared by Emanuel Chrysoloras with the help of Uberto Decembrio at the beginning of the fifteenth century,[7] a demand which was interpreted by Decembrio to mean that Castiglione thought that his version of the fifth book was copied from the older translation. In order to repel such a suspicion he sent to Castiglione a manuscript of the fifth book of the older version so that, as he stated in the accompanying letter, he should be able to compare the two renderings. Besides this, he announced to the Bishop that he had decided to turn into Latin the whole of the *Republic* and dedicate it to Gloucester, to whom, he added, he had already sent a letter,

[1] Copies of this work are in MSS. (C.U.) Ll.I. 7, (B.L.) Auct. F.5.26, Lambeth Palace, no. 341. The last two MSS. were transcribed in England during the fifteenth century from Gloucester's copy. Gloucester gave this treatise to Oxford in 1444, (*Epistolae Academicae*, vol. I, p. 235).

[2] MS. (B.L.) Auct. F.5.26, fo. 58ᵛ. Also these orations were transcribed in *Ibid.*, and in the Lambeth MS. from Gloucester's copy.

[3] The dedication to Gloucester is in Luiso, op. cit. pp. 273–5, and is dated *Ex Bononia II non. decemb.* 1437. Copies of this version are in MSS. (B.L.F.) Plut. LXIII, (V.L.) Vat. Lat. nn. 1876, 1880, (B.N.) Lat. nn. 5826, 5828, 5830, 5831, 5836, 6141, etc.

[4] These were the lives of Theseus, Romulus, Solon, Publicola, Pericles, Fabius Maximus, Themistocles, Camillus, and Aratus. (Luiso, op. cit. p. 275). MSS. containing the lives of Camillus and Romolus by Lapo were presented to Oxford by Gloucester in 1444 (*Epistolae Academicae*, vol. I, pp. 235–6).

[5] Of plague at Ferrara, where he had followed the Roman Court, in 1438 (Da Bisticci, op. cit. p. 509).

[6] MS. (B.R.F.) Ricc. no. 827, fo. 13ᵛ. Castiglione had received the translation in Bologna in 1437 from Zenone Amidano who had been entrusted with the conveying of it by Decembrio, (*Ibid.*, fo. 24ᵛ).

[7] *Ibid.*, fo. 13ᵛ. A MS. of this version is now MS. (B.A.) A. 96. *inf.*

a copy of which was enclosed, asking for his opinion of the matter.[1] After some delay Castiglione answered Decembrio's letter stating his reasons for asking for Chrysoloras' work; but at the same time he encouraged Pier Candido to prosecute his task for the Duke.[2]

When the plague and the threats of the Condottiere Niccolò Piccinino moved the Council from Ferrara,[3] Castiglione followed it to Florence, where he was one of the signatories of the Union between the Greek and Latin Churches on 29 May, 1439.[4]

It was almost certainly in Florence[5] that Antonio Pacino of Todi[5] fell under the spell of Castiglione's eulogies of Humphrey. Pacino, a mediocre scholar whose learning was often criticized,[6] encouraged by the Bishop of Bayeux to dedicate a work to Gloucester, sent him a translation of Plutarch's *Marius* with a preface in which an explanation of how he had been induced to dedicate a work to him was added to the conventional pane-gyrics.[7] Unfortunately nothing else is known of the relations of Duke Humphrey and Pacino. But we know that the *Marius* reached the Duke and that he possessed also other translations by this scholar.[8]

After the Council closed Castiglione came to England where he warmly recommended Decembrio to Gloucester,[9] and probably

---

[1] MS. (B.R.F.) Ricc. no. 827, ff. 13ᵛ–14ᵛ. This letter was written in 1437.

[2] *Ibid.*, ff. 31ᵛ–32ʳ. This letter was written from Bologna in 1437.

[3] The Council was transferred to Florence on 10 January, 1439, (F. Gregorovius, *History of the City of Rome in the Middle Ages*, vol. VII, pt. I, London, 1900, p. 69).

[4] Castiglione's own copy of the *Act of Union* is still at Bayeux; on it cf. H. Omont, *Catalogue des MSS. Grecs des Departments*, Paris 1886, pp. 10–1.

[5] On Pacino cf. Zeno, *Dissertazioni Vossiane*, vol. I, pp. 358–60. Pacino's Florentine domicile is suggested by his dedicating several works to well known Florentines, such as Cosimo de Medici and Piero de Pazzi. Cf. MSS. New Coll. Oxford, no. 286, ff. 52ᵛ ff. (this MS. includes also an oration in praise of Florence by him at ff. 234ᵛ ff.), National-Bibliothek, Vienna, no. 3229, ff. 153ʳ ff.

[6] Zeno, op. cit. vol. I, p. 359.

[7] Gloucester's copy of this is now MS. Magdalen Coll. Oxford, no. 37. The dedication is at ff. 1ʳ–ᵛ.

[8] On the other hand the dedicating of this work also to the Archbishop of Florence (MS. New Coll. Oxford, no. 286, ff. 216ʳ ff.) suggests that Gloucester did not respond to Pacino's expectations. But it is of course possible that Pacino sent to England a work already dedicated to another patron, a practice this far from uncommon amongst humanists. The Duke possessed also Plutarch's *Pelopidas* and Gregory of Nazianzus's *De Virtute* latinized by Pacino (both these texts are in MS. Magdalen Coll. Oxford, no. 37) as well as his version of Plutarch's *Agis et Cleomenes* (*infra*, p. 64, n. 7).

[9] Borsa, *Correspondence of Humphrey, Duke of Gloucester*, p. 520. On his coming to England cf. also *Official Correspondence of Thomas Beckington*, vol. I, p. 37. He was in England in 1440–1 and spent the Christmas festivities at Christ Church, Canterbury (Schirmer, op. cit. p. 29, n. 71). The Cicero given to Gloucester is now MS. (B.N.) Lat. no. 8537. On this MS. cf. Vickers, op. cit. p. 436. As the Duke gave this MS. to Oxford in 1439 (*infra*, p. 62, n. 6) it is highly probable that Castiglione had sent it to him from Italy.

presented to him a fair number of classical and humanistic manuscripts which did not, however, include the still extant copy of Cicero's *Letters* which he is known to have given him.[1]

With Castiglione's departure from Italy ended so far as is known his endeavours on behalf of Duke Humphrey. He appears to have acted mainly as a 'publicity agent' for Gloucester in Italy, and as such he made known the Duke's name and tastes among Italian humanists. What he did for Humphrey in Italy forms a counterpart to what Del Monte performed in England, for while he advertised his name among the Italian humanists, the latter made their names known to the Duke.

[1] Cf. *supra*, p. 52, n. 9.

CHAPTER IV

ALREADY in 1437 Pier Candido Decembrio had decided to dedicate a Latin translation of Plato's *Republic* to Duke Humphrey,[1]
whose reputation as a patron was by then established, thanks to
his exchanges with Leonardo Bruni and others, and to the skilful
propaganda of Zenone da Castiglione. These were the considerations that induced Decembrio to dedicate a work to the
Duke and thereby attract his favour. As he was as yet unacquainted with the hoped for Maecenas, Decembrio had recourse
to a fellow citizen, Rolando Talenti, who was then Castiglione's
secretary,[2] to whom he wrote in 1437 enclosing a letter addressed
to the Duke with instructions that it should be forwarded to
him.[2] Decembrio's letter to Humphrey, in which he declared that
his intended dedication of the *Republic* had its origins in Castiglione's praises of his patronage, was eventually forwarded to
England in January 1438 accompanied by an introduction from
Talenti.[3] This was followed by another letter from Talenti to
the Duke[4] who eventually answered accepting the offer with
enthusiasm, and enclosing a reply to Decembrio, in which he
expressed gratification at his proposal.[5]

Besides Talenti, Decembrio also sought to attract Gloucester
by means of the Archbishop of Milan, Pizzolpasso, who doubtless at his instigation wrote to the Duke warmly praising the
Milanese humanist, and begging for Decembrio the place in his
patronage vacated by Bruni.[6] Together with this letter Pizzolpasso sent to Humphrey the fifth book of the *Republic* latinized

---

[1] On Gloucester and Decembrio cf. Vickers, op. cit. pp. 354–68, Schirmer, op. cit. pp.
34–7, Borsa, *Pier Candido Decembri e l'umanesimo in Lombardia*, pp. 62–8, Borsa, *Correspondence
of Humphrey, Duke of Gloucester, and Pier Candido Decembrio*, Newman, *The Correspondence of
Humphrey, Duke of Gloucester, and Pier Candido Decembrio*. On Decembrio cf. especially Ditt,
Pier Candido Decembrio.
[2] On Talenti cf. *supra*, p. 50. Decembrio's letter to him is in MS. (B.R.F.) Ricc. 827,
ff. 55ʳ-ᵛ. Decembrio's letter to Gloucester is in Borsa, *Correspondence of Humphrey, Duke of
Gloucester*, pp. 512–3. In it the writer stated also that he had been moved to offer a version
to him because of Bruni's dedication of the *Politics* to the Pope.
[3] MS. (B.R.F.) Ricc. no. 827, fo. 58ᵛ. Talenti's 'covering' letter to Gloucester is in *Ibid.*,
ff. 57ᵛ–58ʳ.
[4] *Ibid.*, fo. 58ᵛ.
[5] The letter to Talenti is in *Ibid.*, ff. 58ʳ–59ʳ. Gloucester's reply to Decembrio is in Borsa,
Correspondence of Humphrey, Duke of Gloucester, pp. 513–4, and is dated 6 February (1439).
Both letters reached Talenti in April 1439 (MS. (B.R.F.) Ricc. no. 827, fo. 59ʳ). Talenti's
letter to Decembrio forwarding Gloucester's is in *Ibid.*, ff. 59ʳ-ᵛ. In another letter Talenti
asked Decembrio to entrust him with the eventual delivery of the *Republic* to Gloucester
(*Ibid.*, fo. 60ʳ).
[6] This letter is probably of the summer 1439 and is in Newman, op. cit. pp. 496–8. On
Pizzolpasso cf. R. Sabbadini, 'Spogli Ambrosiani Latini,' *Studi Italiani di Filologia Classica*,
XI (1903) pp. 377–83. As he was Bishop of Dax in Gascony from 1423–7 he may have met
Gloucester there. Decembrio's dedication to Amadeo is in MS. (B.A.) I. 104. *sup.* ff. 95ʳ-ᵛ.

by Decembrio and dedicated by him to Giovanni Amadeo.[1]
His intention was to provide Gloucester with a sample from
which he could draw reasonable conclusions as to the scope of
the completed work, and acquaint himself with Decembrio's
talents. Nor did the specimen fail in its purpose, for on reading it
Humphrey grew more than ever desirous of possessing the
entire *Republic* in Decembrio's translation, though it be somewhat wounding to his pride that the fifth book at least had been
dedicated to one other than himself. Accordingly he took the
matter up with Decembrio, complaining that he had been led to
suppose by his letters that he himself should receive the dedication of the entire work, which judging from the specimen would
be of no small merit, and asking how this could be so.[2] Although
pleased that he had met with approval, Decembrio was embar-
rassed lest his prospective patron should suspect him of an
attempt to pass on a work the dedication of which he had already
promised elsewhere. Obviously he could scarcely suppress his
dedication of the fifth book and withdraw his promises of
dedicating other books without the loss of valuable patrons.[3]
As a solution to this dilemma Decembrio chose to compromise,
and replied to Duke Humphrey assuring him that the whole work
would be especially dedicated to his name, as also seven out of
ten books. The other three books, he declared, would be
dedicated to other illustrious men, the presence of whose names
would add to the Duke's glory as planets to the sun.[4] Such
flattery so adroitly derived from astronomy satisfied Duke
Humphrey as to Decembrio's intentions, and made him look
forward to the day when he would receive the complete version.
In the meantime Decembrio, encouraged by his new patron, was
proceeding as quickly as possible, so that during the earlier part
of 1440 he was able to send a draft of the first five books to
the Duke. In the accompanying letter Decembrio stated in self
advertisement that there was already a considerable demand for
his *Republic*, the first half of which was being eagerly read in
Italy and Spain thanks to the Duke's wide reputation.[5] Whether

---

[1] Cf. *supra*, p. 54, n. 6.

[2] Borsa, *Correspondence of Humphrey, Duke of Gloucester*, p. 514. This letter was written on
12 or 13 October, 1439.

[3] Besides book 5 which he dedicated to Amadeo, he dedicated book 6 to the Bishop of
Burgos and book 10 to Pizzolpasso (MS. (B.A.) I. 104. *sup.* ff. 118ʳ, 190ʳ).

[4] Borsa, *Correspondence of Humphrey, Duke of Gloucester*, pp. 514-5 (this letter was probably
written in December 1439).

[5] *Ibid.*, p. 515. Later when announcing that the MS. of the *Republic* would soon be sent,

or not such a statement made any impression on the Duke must be left to the imagination.

Decembrio's draft of the first five books was as enthusiastically received as his rendering of book five, and in his acknowledgment written on 23 March, 1440, Duke Humphrey urged the translator for a speedy completion of the work which he was most anxious to possess.[1] The Duke's desire was apparently met without undue pressure, for shortly after this Decembrio wrote that his text was now finished, that a transcript of the remaining five books would be sent very soon, and that all ten books would be properly transcribed into one volume.[2] This communication, which reached him in the middle of September 1440, was highly pleasing to the Duke. In replying to the welcome news he was full of praise for Decembrio's achievement, and although his protestations might be somewhat exaggerated, yet there is no denying his evident delight at the prospect of receiving the long awaited version of the *Republic*.[2] True it is scarcely credible that this manuscript and it alone was the subject of his thoughts, as might be inferred from a purely verbal interpretation of his correspondence with Decembrio, yet it would not be far from the truth to assume that his feelings were very similar to those of a scholar waiting for a much desired book seen in a bookseller's catalogue.

Despite Decembrio's promises a certain time elapsed before he despatched the complete text to his patron. Naturally Decembrio blamed his scribes, who according to him were entirely responsible for the delay'.[3] But in the meanwhile the Duke was growing impatient. He was glad, he wrote to Decembrio, that the *Republic* was finished, but he made it quite plain that the waiting irritated him.[4] At last, probably during the spring of 1443, a sumptuous copy of the *Republic* beautifully written in a clear Italian hand was presented to Duke Humphrey by the ambassador of the Duke of Milan, Scaramuccia Balbo, to whom Decembrio had entrusted it for delivery.[5] Besides the *Republic* the presentation

---

Decembrio told Gloucester that copies of it were then being asked for by the King of Castile and the Marquess of Ferrara, (*Ibid.*, p. 517). The first five books were sent to the Duke through Talenti who had them transcribed, (Vickers, op. cit. pp. 359–60).

[1] Borsa, *Correspondence of Humphrey, Duke of Gloucester*, pp. 515–6. For the date of this letter cf. Vickers, op. cit. p. 361, n. 1.

[2] Borsa, *Correspondence of Humphrey, Duke of Gloucester*, pp. 516–7.

[3] *Ibid.*, p. 517. (Letter written at the beginning of 1442.)

[4] *Ibid.*, p. 518. (Letter probably written in March 1442.)

[5] *Ibid.*, p. 524.

manuscript contained a general dedication to Humphrey,[1] and each of the ten books had also prefixed a short introduction: seven of these introductions were addressed to Humphrey, and in each explanations of the text alternated with the most lavish praises of the Duke, his patronage, and his scholarship.[1] In accordance with current conventions the Duke is considered as a quasi-divine being, and addressed with the most flattering expressions which could be devised by humanistic ingenuity, while in the letter which accompanied his gift Decembrio brazenly assured Gloucester that his chief ambition was to please him and nothing more.[2]

The *Republic* proved very welcome to Humphrey, who wrote to the translator expressing his gratitude and praising him for the successful execution of his task.[3] That his feelings were genuine is amply proved, since several transcripts of this translation were executed for him in England. Its use by English scholars and the number of copies made here during the second half of the fifteenth century indicate that Decembrio's work did not lack appreciation in this country.[4]

In translating the *Republic* Decembrio had under his eyes the work of Chrysoloras.[5] In fact his version was practically a paraphrase of the older translation in which the Latinity was brought closer to the ideals of Ciceronianism. It is therefore not surprising that Duke Humphrey, brought up on the medieval Plato, should feel enthusiastic when confronted with a text which, though by

[1] The dedication to Gloucester is in Borsa, *Correspondence of Humphrey, Duke of Gloucester*, pp. 525–6, the other introductions are in MS. (B.A.) I. 104. *sup.* ff. 13ʳ–ᵛ, 32ᵛ–3ʳ, 52ᵛ–3ᵛ, 75ᵛ–6ᵛ, 95ʳ–ᵛ, 118ʳ–9ᵛ, 138ʳ–ᵛ, 157ʳ–8ᵛ, 175ᵛ–7ʳ, 190ʳ–ᵛ. A *De omnibus platonice politie libris brevis annotatio* also addressed to Gloucester is at ff. 117ʳ–8ʳ. The MS. of the *Republic* sent to Gloucester is now MS (B.M.) Harl. no. 1705.
[2] Borsa, *Correspondence of Humphrey, Duke of Gloucester*, p. 519.
[3] *Ibid.*, p. 524. This letter was probably written on 1 July, 1443 (Newman op. cit. p. 489).
[4] Gloucester possessed at least three MSS. of the *Republic*. One of these he presented to Oxford in 1444 (*Epistolae Academicae*, vol. I, p. 237), the other two are entered in the 1452 catalogue of the library of King's College, Cambridge, (James, *A descriptive Catalogue . . . of the Manuscripts . . . in the Library of King's College, Cambridge*, p. 75). Decembrio's version was used by Chaundler and Doget (*infra*, pp. 135, 166). A fifteenth century copy of it written in England is now MS. Cathedral Library, Durham, C.IV. 3. Other copies of this text are now MSS. (B.L.) Harl. no. 1705, (V.L.) Vat. Lat. no. 10379, (B.A.) I. 104. *sup.*, Bayerisches Staatsbibliothek, Munich, no. 225. A MS. including the Greek text and Decembrio's version is in the University Library of Salamanca, (Vogel und Gardthausen, *Die Griechischen Schreiber des Mittelalters und der Renaissance*, p. 457).
[5] On this translation cf. *supra*, p. 51. Guarino considered Pier Candido's version a mere revision of the former one, so that the latter regretted that the old version ever came to light, (MS. (B.R.F.) Ricc. no. 827, fo. 86ʳ). The *Republic* was also translated by Antonio Cassarino, who intended to compete with Decembrio, in 1438–47. (R. Sabbadini, *Classici e Umanisti da Codici Ambrosiani*, Firenze, 1933, pp. 91–4). On Pier Candido's method of translation cf. Ditt, op. cit. p. 30–1.

no means perfect, conveyed a satisfactory idea of the original, and could display an attractive Latin garb.

The relations between Humphrey and Decembrio were not confined to the translation of the *Republic*. The Duke's name as a bibliophile was well known, so that while at work on the *Republic* Decembrio had undertaken to procure for him manuscripts of classical authors which were not available in England, and to assist him in building up a library. How far the humanist clique had established a title to be regarded as a body of literary experts and arbiters of taste is nowhere better exemplified than in the recourse commonly had to their advice by Italian princes when forming a library. Cosimo de Medici is known to have relied on Tommaso Parentucelli, later Pope Nicholas V, when reorganizing the library of San Marco, Florence,[1] while Federico da Montefeltro, Duke of Urbino, followed the suggestions of his Florentine bookseller, Vespasiano da Bisticci, when assembling his famous library.[2] Thus in taking advice from a recognized authority Humphrey was conforming with the most enlightened practice of the times. It must remain uncertain whether it was Decembrio who began by offering to purchase books for Duke Humphrey, or whether the latter first asked for books and advice. None the less, as early as the first half of 1440 Gloucester had written to Decembrio enumerating his principal 'desiderata'.[3] He had also sent a catalogue of his library requesting Decembrio to note any works of importance not to be found there, and to offer suggestions on the matter. Decembrio's verdict was that at least one hundred volumes of great importance, of which he enclosed a list,[4] were not included, and he accordingly advised him to fill these gaps. At the same time he was cautious enough to state, lest the large number of indispensable works be interpreted as evidence of a design to profit from the Duke's bibliophily, that he intended to derive no gain from the transaction, and, being familiar with Humphrey's dislike of delay, he warned him that it would be impossible, doubtless for technical reasons, to obtain all the volumes simultaneously.[5]

---

[1] Sabbadini, *Scoperte*, vol. I, pp. 200–1.   [2] Da Bisticci, op. cit. pp. 95–9.
[3] Borsa, *Correspondence of Humphrey, Duke of Gloucester*, p. 517. Decembrio stimulated Gloucester to order MSS. by mentioning rare texts available in Italy. (*Ibid.*, loc. cit.). As early as March 1440 Gloucester had told Decembrio that he possessed Cicero and Livy, asking at the same time for details about books available, (*Ibid.*, p. 516).
[4] This was probably a list similar to Decembrio's catalogue of necessary Latin authors in MS. (B.A.) R.88. *sup.* ff. 172ᵛ–3ʳ, if not actually a copy of it.
[5] Borsa, *Correspondence of Humphrey, Duke of Gloucester*, pp. 517, 518–20, 524.

The list sent by Decembrio with his reply did not fail to stimulate Humphrey's curiosity since it included several classical works only recently brought to light by the Italians. Little wonder then that he instantly ordered several of the works suggested by Decembrio.[1] Naturally enough the Duke was anxious to receive the volumes he had commissioned quickly, and in order to hasten their execution he sent together with the order a note to Decembrio's master, the Duke of Milan, Filippo Maria Visconti, requesting him to allow Decembrio to borrow some texts from the Ducal Library of Pavia so as to place them at the disposal of the scribes engaged upon the task.[1]

As early as 1441 some of the books ordered had been sent by Decembrio to Gloucester, but as in the case of the *Republic* some of them were delayed in transit, with the result that complaints again reached Decembrio, and another copy of the 'desiderata' was sent to him at Milan.[1] Nevertheless by July 1441 at least nine volumes had reached Duke Humphrey,[1] while those due to arrive included the Ciceronian version of Plato's *Timaeus*, a complete Aulus Gellius, the *Libellus Dignitatum*, Censorinus' *De Natali Die*, Apuleius' *De Magia* and *Florida*, the botanical treatise by the Pseudo Apuleius, and the works of Vitruvius, Ptolemy, Hyginus, Columella, Pomponius Mela, and Festus.[1] As far as is known part of the desired volumes eventually reached Humphrey, amongst which were the works of Cato, Varro, Florus' *Epitomae*, the *Physics* by the Pseudo Pliny, and some writings by Decembrio.[2] More books were sent by the Borromei in 1443.[3]

The translation of the *Republic* and the procuring of classical texts appear to have constituted all the transactions that passed between Gloucester and Decembrio. As already noted the latter had been particularly anxious to succeed to the place formerly held by Bruni in the Duke's patronage:[4] in this he was successful,

[1] Cf. *supra*, p. 58, n. 5.
[2] Some delay in the arrival of these MSS. is known to have taken place (Borsa, *Correspondence of Humphrey, Duke of Gloucester*, pp. 522–3). But their presence in Gloucester's library (*Infra*, p. 63) shows that they reached him. Vickers, op. cit. p. 366, suggests that Decembrio's *Declamationes* which were sent to Gloucester by their author were probably two volumes of letters about the *Republic* (Vickers prints *Ethics* meaning *Republic*). It seems hardly likely that *Declamationes* should mean ordinary Latin letters, and they may perhaps be identified with a MS. of *epistolas declamatorias* given by Gloucester to Oxford in 1444 (*Epistolae Academicae* vol. I, p. 236).
[3] Borsa, *Correspondence of Humphrey, Duke of Gloucester*, p. 523. For the date of this letter cf. Newman, op. cit. p. 489. Later Gloucester told Decembrio not to send books through merchants (Borsa, *Correspondence of Humphrey, Duke of Gloucester*, p. 523). In his reply Decembrio stated that he had MSS. of Apuleius and Columella ready to be sent but that he did not know how to despatch them as he did not have messengers to whom he could entrust them (*Ibid.*, p. 521).   [4] Cf. *supra*, p. 54.

but like his predecessor he also terminated relations with his
English patron after a few years. Like Bruni also he was invited
by Duke Humphrey, if a statement made by Decembrio a few
years after the Duke's death is to be believed, to come to England in his employment,[1] but like Bruni he declined, preferring to
remain in the employment of the Duke of Milan rather than
occupy a less secure position in a strange land with a foreign
prince. Probably the reasons which finally led to a breach in the
Decembrio-Gloucester connexion were similar to those which
ended the Duke's relations with Bruni. Obviously it had not been
purely disinterested admiration for Humphrey which had
prompted Decembrio to place himself at his disposal, but rather
hopes of material gain, and the useful advertisement to be
derived from his links with a prince so favourably known in the
learned world. Now no perusal of the extant correspondence
between the Duke and the humanist can fail to disclose a certain
reticence on the part of the former whenever the question of
compensation arises. Promises he lavishes, he pays indeed for the
actual books he receives, but when the question of remuneration
for Decembrio's labours was to be settled, excuses were invariably offered. In addition there was a reasonable fear of offending
the Duke of Milan, in whose employ Decembrio stood, and other
justifications of a similar nature.[2] Decembrio, whatever his
motives, had done a considerable amount of work for Duke
Humphrey, and naturally expected adequate remuneration.
When therefore he realized that settlement was continually being
delayed, his former enthusiasm for his patron cooled off until
their relations ceased.[3] Altogether, it may perhaps be put forward
in Humphrey's defence that his many political anxieties prevented
him from paying too much attention to Decembrio's claims. But
then the former episode with Bruni has also to be taken into
account, and in the light of such a precedent it is not improbable
that Humphrey tried to drive a bargain with Decembrio, as he
had done before with Bruni. The greed of some of the fifteenth
century Italian humanists is notorious, but in this case the blame
can hardly be ascribed to Decembrio. When all is said, Duke

[1] Borsa, *Pier Candido Decembri e l'umanesimo in Lombardia*, p. 432.
[2] Borsa, *Correspondence of Humphrey, Duke of Gloucester*, pp. 523–4.
[3] Among the reasons for Decembrio's rupture with Gloucester there may have been the
latter's refusal to buy him Petrarch's country house at Garignano which Decembrio had
asked for (*Ibid.*, p. 521). Decembrio's last letter to Gloucester is dated 1 June, 1444, and is in
Ibid., pp. 520–22. Its real year is probably 1443 (Newman, op. cit. p. 490). On the ceasing of
the Gloucester-Decembrio connexion cf. Vickers, op. cit. pp. 367–8.

Humphrey's correspondence with Decembrio is of great importance because it brought into England a large number of classical works hitherto unknown, thus enlarging the material on which native humanism could develop.

Duke Humphrey's library,[1] and especially the books he presented to Oxford, were the subject of admiration to his learned contemporaries.[2] His collection of manuscripts was representative of classical, humanistic, and medieval learning, so that if quality is to prevail over quantity, there is hardly any doubt that his collection was the most important in England at his time. Other libraries, such as Christ Church, Canterbury, St. Albans, or Peterborough, may have exceeded it in numbers, but Duke Humphrey's books could display a greater variety of subjects, and included many works to be found nowhere else in the country.

Though chiefly acquired by purchase, Humphrey obtained for his collection several books as gifts from relatives and friends, and he also employed scribes.[3] Amongst those who presented him with books were his wife, probably Jacqueline of Hainault,[4] his brother, John, Duke of Bedford,[4] Zenone da Castiglione, Bishop of Bayeux,[5] John Whethamstede, Abbot of St. Albans,[5] Richard Beauchamp, Earl of Warwick,[6] Lord Carew,[7] Sir John Stanley,[8] Sir Robert Roos,[8] and others.[8] Several books he obtained because their English authors were seeking his patronage,[8] others for the same reason from Italians.

But Humphrey, not content with the books he received as presents from Italy, took active steps to secure others. While the Bishop of Bayeux was in Bologna, Duke Humphrey asked him to secure several translations from the Greek by Guarino and Leonardo Bruni,[9] and when Piero del Monte returned to

[1] On Gloucester's library cf. especially Vickers, op. cit. pp. 426–38, H. H. E. Craster, 'Index to Duke Humphrey's Gifts to the Old Library of the University in 1439, 1441, and 1444,' B.Q.R., I (1914–6) pp. 131–5, Ullman, Manuscripts of Humphrey, Duke of Gloucester.

[2] This is evident from the number of contemporary references. Cf. Epistolae Academicae, vol. I, passim, Kingsford, op. cit. p. 344, The Middle English Translation of Palladius De Re Rustica, p. 22, MSS. Lincoln Coll. Oxford, no. 106, last flyleaf, no. 117, fo. 586ᵛ.

[3] This is deduced from his having owned more than one copy of some of the works sent to him from Italy (Supra, p. 57 n. 4). Among his scribes there were members of his household like Beccaria, and others were engaged for him abroad (Supra, pp. 46, 56, 59).

[4] Vickers, op. cit. pp. 434, 438.

[5] Cf. supra, pp. 33, 53.

[6] Vickers, op. cit. p. 437.

[7] E. J. F. Arnould, 'Henry of Lancaster and his Livre Des Seintes Medicines' Bulletin of the John Rylands Library, Manchester, XXI (1937) p. 353.

[8] Vickers, op. cit. pp. 426, 428, 435, 437.

[9] Cf. supra, pp. 28, 42–3, 46, 50, 58–9.

Italy in 1440, he was instructed to procure books as yet un-represented in the ducal library.[1] Humanists like Frulovisi and Beccaria were set to compose or translate works during their stay in his household,[1] and their copies destined for his shelves were transcribed in an elegant Italian hand.[1] Duke Humphrey's connexion with Decembrio brought, as previously noticed, several important accessions to his collection,[1] while the classical section was re-organized according to the advice of this distin-guished scholar.[1]

Besides increasing his library through purchase and presenta-tion, Duke Humphrey is known to have borrowed books which he particularly wanted to read and presumably could not get in other ways.[2] Unlike the average bibliophile, he appears to have been extremely generous and ready to part with his own volumes. Alfonso V of Aragon, King of Sicily, was presented by him with a French translation of Livy,[3] while a large and important part of his collection he gave during his lifetime to Oxford University.[4]

A perusal of the lists of manuscripts given to Oxford[5] bears out the catholicity of his tastes but suggests a certain predilection for medicine and astrology. These last two subjects, and works of medieval learning, theological and otherwise, formed perhaps the majority of his books. Still classical works and the neo-classical writings of his contemporaries were so far from being negligible that, apart from other evidence, they would suffice in themselves to show the strong bent of his mind towards classicism. Naturally the most interesting part of his library consisted of the manuscripts of ancient authors, some of which had only been brought to light by humanists, or had been very rare throughout the Middle Ages. Of these Humphrey is known to have possessed Cicero's *Epistolae Familiares*,[6] and a manuscript with the letters *Ad Quintum Fratrem*,[7] the *Verrines*,[7] the *Philip-pics*,[7] a volume of orations,[7] and another one containing twenty-

[1] Cf. *supra*, p. 61, n. 9.
[2] For instance in 1446 he borrowed Bruni's version of the *Phaedrus* from Oxford (*Epis-tolae Academicae*, vol. I, p. 246). On this MS. containing the *Phaedrus*, and not the *Phaedo* cf. Vickers, op. cit. p. 415, n. 1.
[3] *Ibid.*, pp. 375–6. This Livy may be possibly identified with MS. Bibliothèque de Sainte Genevieve, Paris, Fr. no. 777 (*Ibid.*, p. 438).   [4] Cf. *infra*, pp. 66–7.
[5] Printed in *Epistolae Academicae* vol. I, pp. 179–83, 232–7.
[6] Now MS. (B.N.) Lat. no. 8537. This MS. was presented by Gloucester to Oxford in 1439 (Vickers, op. cit. p. 436).
[7] *Epistolae Academicae* vol. I, p. 183. As Gloucester wrote to Decembrio in 1440 stating that he owned Cicero, (*supra*, p. 58, n. 3) the Cicero MSS. given by him to Oxford in 1439 must have been duplicates. He also possessed the *Rhetorica ad Herennium*, (*Epistolae Acade-micae*, vol. I, p. 183).

two works by the same author.[1] Among the historians he had all that was known of Livy,[1] and Livy's *Epitomae* by Florus,[1] Caesar's *De Bello Gallico*,[2] and Suetonius' *De Vita Caesarum*.[3] He also owned the *Panegyrici Veteres*,[4] Pliny's *Panegyric to Trajan*,[5] his *Epistles*,[6] and the pseudo-Plinian *Physics*.[7] The Latin polygraphers included Aulus Gellius[8] and Nonius Marcellus,[8] and along with these he possessed Cato's treatise on Agriculture,[8] Palladius,[8] Celsus,[9] Quintilian's *Institutiones*,[10] Apuleius' *Golden Ass*,[10] Varro's *De Lingua Latina*,[10] and Vitruvius on Architecture.[11]

As Humphrey knew no Greek it is not to be wondered at that no text in that language should appear among his books. The nearest approach to an interest in the Greek language on his part is the presence of a Graeco-Latin dictionary among the books he presented to Oxford in 1444.[12] But this was probably one of those medieval etymological compilations which were almost as far removed from Greek scholarship as Humphrey himself was. Ignorance of Greek did not, however, debar him from some of the Greek authors, and as the contents of his library show, he was interested in Latin translations from that language. Plato, Aristotle, and Plutarch, were actually among Humphrey's favourite authors, and modern versions of these and other Greek writers found their way into his library. Of Plato, besides the medieval translations and commentaries

[1] *Epistolae Academicae*, vol. I, pp. 183, 235. Gloucester possessed Livy already in 1440 (*supra*, p. 58, n. 3).

[2] Gloucester possessed at least two MSS. of Caesar, (*Epistolae Academicae*, vol. I, p. 235, James, *A Catalogue of the Manuscripts . . . of King's College, Cambridge*, p. 82).

[3] *Epistolae Academicae*, vol. I, p. 235.

[4] Now MS. (B.N.) Lat. no. 7805. This MS. was transcribed in Italy for Gloucester who presented it to Oxford in 1444 (Vickers, op. cit. p. 436).

[5] *Epistolae Academicae*, vol. I, p. 236. Gloucester had asked Decembrio for this work, (Borsa, *Correspondence of Humphrey, Duke of Gloucester*, p. 517).

[6] Now MS. (B.L.) Duke Humphrey, d. 1. Gloucester presented this MS. to Oxford in 1444 (Vickers, op. cit. p. 426).

[7] *Epistolae Academicae*, vol. I, p. 236. Decembrio had also been asked for this work (Borsa, *Correspondence of Humphrey, Duke of Gloucester*, p. 517).

[8] Epistolae Academicae, vol. I, pp. 183, 236-7. The Cato was obtained from Decembrio (Borsa, *Correspondence of Humphrey, Duke of Gloucester*, p. 522).

[9] James, *A Catalogue of the Manuscripts . . . of King's College, Cambridge*, p. 80. This MS. had the Greek passages transliterated. Celsus was obtained from Decembrio, (Borsa, *Pier Candido Decembri e l'umanesimo in Lombardia*, p. 428).

[10] *Epistolae Academicae*, vol. I, pp. 183, 236.

[11] Gloucester possessed at least two MSS. of Vitruvius, (*Ibid.*, vol. I, p. 236, James, *A Catalogue of the Manuscripts . . . of King's College, Cambridge*, p. 74). Vitruvius did also come from Decembrio, (Borsa, *Correspondence of Humphrey, Duke of Gloucester*, p. 524).

[12] *Epistolae Academicae*, vol. I, p. 236; James, *A Catalogue of the Manuscripts of King's College, Cambridge*, p. 83, registers a *Tabula Greci et Latini* doubtless from Gloucester's library.

obtained from Whethamstede,[1] he possessed Decembrio's Latin *Republic*,[2] and Bruni's *Phaedrus*,[3] and possibly some other versions of Platonic dialogues, also by Bruni. Of Aristotle he had both the *Ethics* and *Politics* in Bruni's Latin text,[4] besides several medieval Aristotelian translations.[5] In addition to these his library possessed some orations by Aeschines also translated by Bruni,[5] three orations of Isocrates by Lapo da Castiglionchio,[6] several of Plutarch's *Parallel Lives* latinized by various humanists,[7] Angelo da Pescheria's Latin Ptolemy,[8] and several versions of St. Athanasius by his own secretary, Antonio Beccaria.[9]

The modern neo-classical authors' treatises and epistolaries found as much favour with Duke Humphrey as their translations, and would appear to have been collected by him. Amongst epistolaries owned by him were to be found those of Nicholas of Clemanges,[10] Coluccio Salutati,[11] and Petrarch.[11] Of Petrarch he possessed also the *De Vita Solitaria*,[12] the *Rerum Memorandarum*,[12] the *De Remediis Utriusque Fortunae*,[12] and other Latin writings, the titles of which cannot be gathered from the lists of his donations to Oxford.[12] Boccaccio was represented by the *De Genealogiis Deorum*,[13] the *De Casibus Virorum Illustrium*,[13] the *De Claris Mulieribus*,[13] and the *De Montibus*,[13] besides Beccaria's

[1] Cf. *supra*, p. 33.

[2] Cf. *supra*, p. 57.

[3] James, *A Catalogue of the Manuscripts . . . of King's College, Cambridge*, p. 75. Gloucester had also borrowed this translation from Oxford in 1446, (*supra*, p. 62 n. 2).

[4] *Epistolae Academicae*, vol. I, p. 181, James, *A Catalogue of the Manuscripts . . . of King's College, Cambridge*, p. 74. He possessed also Bruni's *Oratio in Hypocritas* and his versions of Xenophon's *De Tyranno* and St. Basil, since both appear in MS. (B.L.) Auct. F.5.26, which was copied from a MS. formerly owned by Gloucester, and an unidentified work entered as *Libri Leonardi* in the 1444 list of Gloucester's donations (*Epistolae Academicae*, vol. I, p. 235).

[5] *Ibid.*, vol. I, pp. 181–2, 236.

[6] Cf. *supra*, p. 51.

[7] *Epistolae Academicae*, vol. I, pp. 235–6, James, *A Catalogue of the Manuscripts . . . of King's College, Cambridge*, p. 82. He must have also owned Guarino's version of Plutarch's *De Assentatoris et Amici Differentia* as also this appears in MS. (B.L.) Auct. F.5.26.

[8] Gloucester's copy is now part of MS. Magdalen Coll., Oxford, no. 37. He presented this MS. to Oxford in 1444 (Vickers, op. cit. p. 428). This MS must have come from Decembrio, (Borsa, *Correspondence of Humphrey, Duke of Gloucester*, p. 524).

[9] Cf. *supra*, p. 46.

[10] Gloucester presented MSS. of this text to Oxford in 1439 and 1444 (*Epistolae Academicae* vol. I, pp. 183, 235). The 1444 MS. is now MS. (B.L.) Hatton, no. 36. On this MS. cf. K. Chesney, 'Nicholas de Clemanges,' *Medium Aevum*, VII (1938) pp. 102–4.

[11] *Epistolae Academicae*, vol. I, p. 183, Toynbee, *Duke Humphrey's Dante, Petrarch and Boccaccio MSS.*, p. 256.

[12] *Epistolae Academicae*, vol. I, pp. 180–1, 235, Toynbee, op. cit. p. 256.

[13] *Epistolae Academicae*, vol. I, pp. 183, 235, Toynbee, op. cit. p. 256. John Lydgate translated the *De Casibus* into English (from De Premierfait's French text) at Gloucester's request (Vickers, op. cit. p. 391).

Latin *Corbaccio*,[1] and a French *Decameron*.[2] Dante's *Commedia*[3] and the Latin text and commentary on it by Giovanni da Serravalle[3] were also to be found among the Duke's books, but it is doubtful whether he could read the *Commedia* in the original considering that he had the *Corbaccio* translated into Latin, and owned the *Decameron* in French. Other modern literary works in Humphrey's library were Del Monte's *De Vitiorum et Virtutum inter se Differentia*,[4] Lapo da Castiglionchio's *De Re Militari*,[4] Coluccio Salutati's *De Laboribus Herculis*,[5] Frulovisi's *De Republica*,[6] Bruni's *Isagogicon*,[7] and other writings,[7] and an unidentified work by Decembrio,[7] Poggio's *De Avaritia*[8] and perhaps the *De Varietate Fortunae*,[9] Andrea Fiocchi's *De Romanis Magistratibus*,[10] and, if these may be included amongst the humanistic works, several of Whethamstede's treatises, which had been given to him by the author.[11] The collection of manuscripts assembled by Gloucester was dispersed soon after its owner's death; this and the survival of only a few of his books constitutes a serious loss.

Throughout his career, Duke Humphrey kept up a close connexion with Oxford.[12] According to tradition the Duke had been in his youth a member of Balliol College:[13] whatever the truth may be, his attachment to this University strongly suggests that he was educated at one of its colleges, a thing not so unusual for a member of the royal family during the early fifteenth century.[14] In the later part of his life he appears as an unofficial protector of Oxford, and the numerous applications to him by the University

---

[1] Cf. *supra*, p. 46.

[2] Now MS. (B.N.) Fr. no. 12421.

[3] *Epistolae Academicae*, vol. I. p. 236. Cf. also Weiss, *Per la Conoscenza di Dante in Inghilterra nel Quattrocento*, p. 357.

[4] Cf. *supra*, pp. 25, n. 3, 51, n. 1.

[5] Now MS. (V.L.) Urb. no. 694. On this MS. cf. Ullman, *Manuscripts of Humphrey, Duke of Gloucester, passim*.

[6] *Epistolae Academicae*, vol. I, p. 236. He was probably also the owner of MS. College of Arms, London, Arundel, no. 12, containing Frulovisi's *Vita Henrici Quinti*.

[7] *Epistolae Academicae*, vol. I, pp. 235–6. Cf. also *supra*, pp. 49, n. 2, 59, n. 2, 64, n. 4.

[8] James, *A Catalogue of the Manuscripts . . . of King's College, Cambridge*, p. 81.

[9] Cf. *supra*, p. 20.

[10] *Epistolae Academicae*, vol. I, p. 235.

[11] Cf. *supra*, p. 34, n.1.

[12] On Gloucester's connexion with Oxford cf. Vickers, op. cit. pp. 397–409, *Epistolae Academicae*, vol. I, *passim*.

[13] Cf. *supra*, p. 39.

[14] Henry V is presumed to have been educated at the Queen's College, Oxford, (Ross, *Historia Regum Angliae*, p. 207). There is, however, no mention of him in the contemporary college records. Henry Beaufort, later Cardinal and Bishop of Winchester, resided in Peterhouse, Cambridge, in 1388–9 (*First Report of the Royal Commission on Historical Manuscripts*, London, 1870, p. 78).

F

authorities show how much his patronage was appreciated.[1]

The material welfare of the University was not, however, his sole interest. To him the advancement of learning was a matter for anxiety, and to this end he generously contributed both financially and with gifts of books. As early as 1433 he had manifested his intention of endowing some lectureships in Oxford,[2] and by 1435 he had presented books and a sum of money.[2] A letter written by the University to him in 1435 suggests that the lectureships were then established,[2] but scarcity of endowed lectureships was not the only difficulty facing the University at that time: lack of books and the means to acquire them were also felt very acutely, and accordingly, knowing the Duke's favourable disposition, the University begged him in 1437 to provide means of procuring books, and to found three new lectureships.[3] In this appeal the University was particularly fortunate. Hardly two years elapsed before Humphrey sent to Oxford a present of one hundred and twenty choice manuscripts, which included classical authors, both ancient and modern, besides translations from the Greek.[4] The translations of Greek works particularly delighted the Oxford authorities, who in a letter of acknowledgment to the Duke attempted to express their feelings of gratitude. At the same time statutes were passed by Convocation enacting rules for the library which was to harbour the Duke's donation, and forbidding anyone but their donor to borrow any books from it.[5]

Duke Humphrey's princely gift to Oxford was soon followed by other presents. Seven manuscripts were presented by him to the University in 1441,[6] and during the same year nine more were added by him.[6] As a sequence to such an unprecedented display of liberality Duke Humphrey's name was included in the University prayers in 1442.[6] But more tokens of his generosity

---

[1] Cf. the various letters addressed to him by the University in *Epistolae Academicae*, vol. I, *passim*.

[2] *Ibid.*, vol. I, pp. 107, 114–5, 139. It seems doubtful that Gloucester's intention was materialized before 1435, since during that same year the University complained to him of the lack of lectures, etc. (*Ibid.*, vol. I, pp. 128–30). Already in 1432 the University had sought Gloucester's help in inducing the Duke of Bedford to fulfil his promises of endowing some lectureships (*Ibid.*, vol. I, p. 83).

[3] *Ibid.*, vol. I, pp. 152–3. In this letter he was also asked to procure the promotion of graduates and obtain the books bequeathed by Henry V to the University.

[4] The University's letter of thanks is in *Ibid.*, vol. I, pp. 177–9. The indenture acknowledging the gift is dated 25 November, 1439, and is in *Ibid.*, vol. I, pp. 179–84.

[5] *Ibid.*, vol. I, pp. 188–91. These statutes were enacted on 25 November, 1439. On Gloucester borrowing a MS. from the University cf. *supra*, p. 62, n. 2.

[6] *Epistolae Academicae*, vol. I, pp. 197–8, 203–4, 217, 227–8.

were to reach the University: already in 1443 he intimated his intention to add to the books which he had presented so far,[1] and early in 1444 he fulfilled this promise by bestowing upon the University one hundred and twenty-nine manuscripts.[2] This collection, like the one presented five years earlier, also included an important number of classical and humanistic texts. In recognition of his munificence the Oxford authorities shortly afterwards sent a suggestion that the books presented by him should be housed in the new Divinity school then in construction, and that the new library should be named after him.[3] Finally he gave an oral promise that he would eventually present all his Latin books to the University,[3] a promise which he kept since at his death in 1447 his will was found to contain bequests of one hundred pounds to the Oxford school of Divinity, and all his Latin books to the University.[3] It is, however, extremely doubtful whether these legacies ever reached Oxford.[4]

The books presented by Gloucester served to stimulate the new and to revive much of the older learning. The translations of Greek authors were some justification for the statement on the part of the University that under his patronage Greek was coming to life.[5] Not the Greek language, be it understood, but a curiosity for things Greek which, together with an improved study of Divinity, more immediately promoted by Gloucester's donations, was destined in time to assist the University into an intellectual climate very different from that which Humphrey inhabited.

It is not easy to give an estimation of Humphrey's achievement in the humanistic field. His employment of Italians as secretaries, his relations with Bruni and Decembrio, his bibliophile activities, his efforts to advance learning in Oxford, show the direction of his intellectual leanings. The translations from the Greek which Bruni and Decembrio made at his request suggest some attraction to political philosophy, while the con-

---

[1] Cf. *supra*, p. 66, n. 6.

[2] The University's letter of thanks for this donation is in *Epistolae Academicae*, vol. I, pp. 240–2. The indenture acknowledging the gift is dated 25 February, 1444, and is in *Ibid.*, vol. I, pp. 232–7.

[3] *Ibid.*, vol. I, pp. 246, 286–7, 295–6. On Gloucester's will cf. Vickers, op. cit. pp. 442–3.

[4] The University was still trying to recover these books in 1453, (*Epistolae Academicae*, vol. I, p. 319). On previous attempts to secure them cf. *Ibid.*, vol. I, *passim*. At Gloucester's death his property was seized by the Crown and granted to King's College, Cambridge, (Vickers, op. cit. p. 303) where some of his books were already in 1452, cf. the 1452 library list of the college in James, *A Catalogue of the Manuscripts . . . of King's College, Cambridge*, pp. 72–83. For the view that part of Gloucester's library is included in this list cf. *Ibid.*, pp. 70–1.

[5] *Epistolae Academicae*, vol. I, p. 203. Cf. also *Ibid.*, vol. I, pp. 241, 245.

tents of his library hint to the catholicity of his reading. We know also that humanistic topics and news of the pursuits of Poggio, Guarino, and Bruni, were favourite subjects of conversation with him, and that he followed with interest the activities of the Italian world of learning. Neo-classical writings, and especially those by Petrarch and Boccaccio, aroused his appreciation, and the latinized Plutarchian biographies were equally welcome to him.

If we have enough material to establish Humphrey's attitude towards humanism, what we have concerning his actual learning is on the other hand rather disheartening. That he knew Greek is out of the question, and in spite of his having given a Greek name to one of his illegitimate children,[1] his acquaintance with Greek literature did not go far beyond the Latin translations of Plato, Aristotle, Plutarch, and St. Athanasius. As for his Latin scholarship, its standard seems doubtful. His Latin correspondence was certainly the work of secretaries,[2] and he doubtless had a marked predilection for Latin classics in French translations. Thus, he is known to have parted with the Latin original of a work, and to have retained a French version of it.[2] Besides this, perhaps an index to the shallowness of his Latin learning is provided by his notes of ownership on his books, which are invariably in French.[2]

As for his taste in classical and modern literature, he seems to have been above all interested in what might have proved of some practical value to him. Works of political philosophy, science, history, and rhetoric, appear to have been his favourites, possibly because of the use he could derive from their reading. Neither poetry nor plays were plentiful among his books, and possibly never exercised a strong appeal for him. That he was prepared to part with a considerable portion of his library during his lifetime also suggests that perhaps he was not as interested in its contents as one would think at first, and that possibly, like the bibliophile ridiculed in Sebastian Brant's poems, he preferred to look at rather than read his books.[3] On the other hand it is possible that he possessed duplicates of some of the volumes given away, as is suggested by extant manuscripts and by the '1452' catalogue of the library of King's College,

---

[1] His daughter Antigone who married Henry Grey, Earl of Tankerville, (Vickers, op. cit. p. 335).
[2] *Ibid.*, p. 414.
[3] S. Brant, *Narrenschiff*, Basle, 1499, sigg. a5ᵛ–a6ᵛ.

Cambridge,[1] while it is certain that even after the bestowal of his gifts to Oxford, he remained in possession of a substantial library.[2] He was no doubt the first Englishman to show a lively appreciation of humanism, and whatever the actual depth of his scholarship, he appears to have realized the difference between the works of humanists and schoolmen. He was also the first Englishman to aim at forming a fairly complete classical library and have recourse to expert advice in the formation of it. There is no doubt that his learned activities impressed his contemporaries, both in England and abroad, and there is enough evidence left to show how his importance in English culture was already appreciated during his lifetime.[3]

Altogether, Humphrey's achievement belongs rather to the sphere of patronage than to that of pure scholarship. As a scholar he did not go beyond reading his books, and discussing learned subjects: as a patron on the other hand he was instrumental in having several works translated for the first time into Latin, and bringing into England several classical and Renaissance texts hitherto unknown here. Through his patronage Italian humanists came to England, the book wealth of Oxford University was increased, and as a direct result of this, interest in polite letters in that University was to develop sufficiently to lay valuable foundations for what was going to be known later as the New Learning. Additional encouragement for scholarship was provided by his other benefactions to Oxford, thanks to which the University began to recover from the uncertain times it had known during the early years of the fifteenth century. Although an indifferent scholar himself, Humphrey was to prepare the ground for a favourable reception of humanism.

In all this his achievements were in many ways similar to those of such enlightened princes as Alfonso V of Sicily or Federico of Urbino, though with the difference that he was alone among his peers in England to encourage learning, while the majority of the courts of fifteenth century Italy protected and patronized scholars. The English humanism of Duke Humphrey's times had its origins in his household, and its development was mainly the outcome of his activities. From this point of view

---

[1] On which cf. *supra*, pp. 57, n. 4, 63, nn. 2, 11.

[2] That this was so is shown by his having possessed several Latin MSS. at the time of his death (*supra*, p. 67).

[3] Cf. for example the remarks of Aeneas Sylvius Piccolomini on the effects of his patronage, on which cf. *infra*, p. 83.

none of the subsequent patrons of letters in England during the fifteenth century can stand comparison with him, as none of them was able to exercise as much influence on the course of humanism in this country as Humphrey of Gloucester.

CHAPTER V

DUKE HUMPHREY's patronage had not been limited to Italians. He also encouraged and gave employment to learned Englishmen, some of whom were affected in a greater or lesser degree by humanism. Apart from the various English poets to enjoy Gloucester's protection,[1] a testimony of his fondness for letters scarcely germane with neo-classicism, it was in his household that Thomas Bekynton[2] shaped his career. Bekynton's rôle in the development of Renaissance learning in England must be sought chiefly within the province of administration, for it was reserved for him to raise the standards of official epistolography in this country by following classical models, and by a disregard of the formalities of medieval epistolary practice. Educated at Winchester College, where he resided from 1403 to 1408,[3] and New College, Oxford, of which he was a fellow from 1408 to 1420,[3] Bekynton had been brought up in the learning of the schools. It was perhaps his academic distinction that first attracted the attention of Duke Humphrey, who appointed him his chancellor about 1420,[3] an appointment soon followed by two lucrative ecclesiastical dignities.[4] Bekynton's office with the Duke lasted until about 1438. Now Frulovisi had been Gloucester's 'poet and orator' between 1436 and 1438,[5] and other humanists had also been in constant touch with the Duke. Hence it is natural to assume that Bekynton came under their influence. About 1438 Bekynton became Henry VI's secretary,[6] a post which prevented him from indulging in polite letters on the scale he would probably have liked, but which enabled him on the other hand to introduce new values into official epistolography. From 1438 until 1443, when he became Bishop of Bath and Wells and Keeper of the Privy Seal,[7] Bekynton participated in diplomatic missions

[1] On which cf. Vickers, op. cit. pp. 385–95.

[2] On Bekynton cf. especially *Official Correspondence of Thomas Beckington, The Register of Thomas Bekynton*, Perry, *Bishop Beckington and Henry VI*, Schirmer, op. cit. pp. 66–73. For his works cf. Tanner, *Bibliotheca Britannico-Hybernica*, p. 84.

[3] *Official Correspondence of Thomas Beckington*, vol. I, p. cxviii. He was certainly Gloucester's Chancellor in 1423, (*C.P.R.* vol. VII, p. 249).

[4] The Deanery of Arches, to which he was appointed on 11 February, 1422, (*Official Correspondence of Thomas Beckington*, vol. I, p. xx) and the Archdeaconship of Bucks which he was already occupying in 1424 (*The Register of Thomas Bekynton*, vol. I, p. viii).

[5] Cf. *supra*, pp. 42–3.

[6] Otway-Ruthven, op. cit. p. 154.

[7] *Official Correspondence of Thomas Beckington*, vol. I, p. xlv, *Handbook of British Chronology*, ed. F. M. Powicke, London, 1939, p. 75. He was Keeper until 11 February, 1444.

which included an embassy to the Count of Armagnac to arrange
a marriage between the Count's daughter and Henry VI.[1] Once
he had ceased to be Keeper he appears to have retired gradually
from politics and diplomacy, and to have dedicated himself
mainly to the care of his diocese until his death, as an old and
infirm man, in 1465.[2]

Besides contacts with Humphrey and his entourage, Bekynton
had also private links with Italian humanism, which were no
doubt equally instrumental in conditioning his outlook. From
about 1441 he can be found corresponding with Flavio Biondo,[3]
a distinguished humanist with whom he came in touch through
Angelo Gattola, a Papal official who had come to England in
1440 to bring the Red Hat to Cardinal Kemp, and who on his
return to the Curia had warmly recommended Bekynton to
the Italian scholar.[4] The reasons which gave rise to this correspondence were hardly of a scholarly order, the literary element
in it being incidental rather than the cause. What Bekynton
actually sought was a provision to the See of Bath and Wells
made vacant through Stafford's translation to Canterbury,[5]
and he rightly gauged the advantage he would derive if Biondo,
who enjoyed much influence at Rome, advocated his claims.
Nevertheless through this correspondence there arose a certain degree of friendship between the Englishman and the Italian
who had never met, and moreover Bekynton was enabled to
profit from the contacts with an Italian scholar who, like him,
alternated the pursuit of letters with official routine. Exchange of
letters and possibly reports from Gattola acquainted Biondo
with the tastes of his English friend; presents were exchanged by
both sides,[6] the gift sent by Biondo being a fine manuscript of
his *Decades*,[6] a work which according to its author was, like his
De Roma Triumphante, very well known in England.[7]

During his life Bekynton collected several ancient and modern

---

[1] An account of this mission is in *A Journal by One of the Suite of Tho. Beckington during an Embassy to Negociate a Marriage between Henry VI and a Daughter of the Count of Armagnac, A.D.* 1442, ed. H. N. Nicolas, London, 1828.

[2] Towards the end of his life he was licensed not to attend Parliament by both Henry VI and Edward IV because of his ill-health (Perry, op. cit. p. 271).

[3] On Biondo cf. Nogara, op. cit. His correspondence with Bekynton is in *Official Corres-pondence of Thomas Beckington*, vol. I, pp. 169–72, II, 241–2.

[4] *Ibid.*, vol. I, pp. 171–2.

[5] On 13 May, 1443 (Gams, op. cit. p. 183).

[6] *Official Correspondence of Thomas Beckington*, vol. I, pp. xxxi, 242. The *Decades* sent by Biondo is now MS. Corpus Christi Coll. Cambridge, no. 205.

[7] Nogara, op. cit. pp. 208, 212.

texts which are indicative of his tastes. Among these there were
the Latin poems of Francesco Pontano, presented by Vincent
Clement,[1] John Free's Latin Synesius,[2] very probably given by
John Tiptoft, Earl of Worcester, and the aforementioned works
of Biondo. But Bekynton's interest in the humanities was not
circumscribed within the sphere of bibliophily. Humanistic
influence is evident in his Latin correspondence,[3] which discloses
a real knowledge of the language as well as the right ideas on its
written use. His Latin prose has traces of the new Italian style,
and his fierce criticism of Abbot Whethamstede's Latinity[4]
betrays his feelings on the subject. His favourable attitude
towards polite learning is emphasized in his recommendations
to his young friend Richard Caunton, who was going to Rome to
pursue the study of oratory,[5] and in the enthusiasm with which he
welcomed humanistic manuscripts. Furthermore Bekynton's
admiration of the 'new Latin' is shown by his inclusion of one of
Petrarch's Latin Eclogues as an authority in his De Jure Regum
Anglorum ad Regnum Franciae.[6]

His official duties compelled Bekynton to remain within the
limits of book collecting, Latin letter writing, and private study.
Yet, despite his official preoccupations, he was able to promote
and foster humane studies in others. He protected, and perhaps
inspired, Thomas Chaundler and received the dedication of his
Latin works and a fine illuminated copy from the author.[7]
Moreover Bekynton knew many of the devotees of polite letters,
such as Adam de Moleyns,[8] Vincent Clement,[9] Andrew Holes,[10]
Piero del Monte,[11] and perhaps John Tiptoft.[12] Possibly some of
these were first attracted to classical learning by his enthusiasm.

[1] Official Correspondence of Thomas Beckington, vol. I, p. 178. Bekynton was also the owner of
a MS. collection of Medieval Latin poems, now MS. (B.L.) Add. A. 44, an article on which,
A. Wilmart, Le Florilège Mixte de Thomas Bekynton, will appear shortly in Medieval and Renaissance Studies.
[2] Mitchell, John Tiptoft, p. 166.
[3] Printed in Official Correspondence of Thomas Beckington. Letters by him are also in Letters
of Queen Margaret of Anjou and Bishop Beckington, and others Temp. Henry V and Henry VI, ed.
C. Munro, (C.S.) London, 1843.
[4] Official Correspondence of Thomas Beckington, vol. I, p. 116. For criticism of his friends'
Latin cf. also Ibid., vol. II, p. 172.
[5] Ibid., vol. I, p. 231.
[6] MS. (B.M.) Harl. no. 4763, ff. 55ᵛ–7ᵛ.
[7] Cf. infra, p. 134; Chaundler presented also other MSS. to Bekynton (Infra, p. 136, n. 2).
[8] Official Correspondence of Thomas Beckington, vol. I, p. 175.
[9] Cf. infra, p. 76.
[10] With whom he corresponded (Official Correspondence of Thomas Beckington, vol. I, pp.
225–6, 228–9, 233–4).
[11] Ibid., vol. I, p. 170.
[12] Cf. supra, n. 2.

But Bekynton's chief importance resides in his introduction of humane values in official epistolography. A schoolman by training, Bekynton conceived classical learning not only as an intellectual attainment but also as a thing of practical value. Thus he applied it to diplomatic prose, which he more than any other person in England disentangled from the medieval tradition of the *Cursus* and the involved phrasing so dear to Abbot Whethamstede and his admirers. What Frulovisi performed for the methods of English historiography, Bekynton did for the language of diplomacy, of which he was the chief ornament of his day.

Bekynton's introduction of Italian standards into the language of diplomacy owed part of its success to the receptive ground which it found. The Civil Service of the later Middle Ages had long traditions of literacy.[1] Its personnel was largely manned by clerks in holy orders who considered it a safe avenue to preferment. Vacant bishoprics were often bestowed upon civil servants and diplomatic missions entrusted to them. Although laymen belonged to it, the key positions were generally in the hands of ecclesiastics, who brought to them the benefits of University training as well as knowledge of Latin. The pursuit of *belles lettres* was not foreign to it. Chaucer, Hoccleve, and Richard de Bury, are outstanding examples of medieval bureaucrats dedicating their leisure to literature, but not the only ones of government officials alternating affairs with the pursuit of letters. Hence it is not surprising that the study of *Dictamen* and the Notarial Art had become fashionable in an atmosphere where skill in phrasing was sure of appreciation and could lead to advancement. It was the heyday of formularies which, as Richard de Bury's *Liber Epistolaris*[2] shows, interspersed specimens from the best dictaminal collections amongst the formulae of everyday use. *Artes Notariae*, handbooks on the *Cursus*, and collections of letters, like those by Peter de Vinea[3] and Thomas of Capua, were also among recognized helps, and formed part of the necessary equipment of the writer of state papers. Such a dependence from stylistic models in administrative practice should be particularly noted, as it discloses not only an appreciation of rhetorical values, but also a readiness to improve 'offi-

---

[1] Cf. T. F. Tout, 'Literature and Learning in the English Civil Service in the Fourteenth Century,' *Speculum*, IV (1929) pp. 365–89.

[2] On the *Liber Epistolaris* cf. Denholm-Young, *Richard de Bury*, pp. 140–4.

[3] On the diffusion of his letters in England cf. *supra*, p. 29, n. 2.

cial' diction from foreign models, and a reliance upon seeking inspiration from literary sources. This should especially be borne in mind in connexion with the stylistic changes introduced by Bekynton in official epistolography. When Bekynton became a member of the Royal Household through his appointment to the Royal Secretaryship, the methods and personnel of the administration presented on the whole the same characteristics as those of the preceding century. But Bekynton's former links with Humphrey's chancery had taught him to appreciate Italian scholarship, and thus his office gave him an opportunity to introduce more humane standards in official epistolography, and make it closer in style to the correspondence which reached him from the Curia and the chanceries of Italian princes. To write to Italy in a Latin not patently barbarous to Italian eyes was a matter of political prestige for a man with Bekynton's outlook. Thus during his term of office he endeavoured to introduce Italian values in the language of diplomacy. Such a change did not involve an abrupt departure from tradition. It merely implied a substitution of the letter book of the humanist for the dictaminal collections, and a knowledge of Latin inspired from classical instead of from medieval sources. Literary qualifications were to prove even more useful than ever. But their values were to be modified in accordance with modern Italian practice. In this Bekynton was successful. His letter books show the application of modern standards in diplomatic correspondence.[1] In an age when political value was attributed to rhetoric this met with approval. The usefulness of classical Latinity, especially in negotiations with the sophisticated courts of Italy, was accepted. Hence after him a good knowledge of humanistic Latin came to be considered a valuable asset for diplomatists. Probably Adam de Moleyns, Robert Flemmyng, Richard Bole, William Sellyng, John Shirwood, and John Doget, owed their careers to their literary qualifications as well as to political ability.

Of the lesser personalities around Bekynton, perhaps the most

---

[1] A fifteenth century counterpart of De Bury's *Liber Epistolaris* is MS. (B.M.) Cotton, Tib. B.VI, which includes official documents of the reign of Henry V and Henry VI and letters and orations by contemporary Italian humanists. It is almost certain that this formulary was prepared by or for Bekynton with whom it had already been connected (*The Correspondence of Thomas Beckington*, vol. I, p. XI). Another fifteenth century formulary also very probably once possessed by Bekynton and including state papers, letters by and documents connected with Bekynton, notes on *dictamen*, and part of the correspondence between Gloucester and Decembrio, is now MS. (B.L.) Ashmole, no. 789. Another collection of documents probably made by Bekynton is now MS. (B.M.) Cotton, Tib. B.XII.

striking, if scarcely the most respectable, was Vincent Clement,[1] a Spaniard who spent nearly all his life in England. This remarkable man, whom Gascoigne labelled with the title of *Doctor insolens*,[2] probably began his official career in England in 1438 when he obtained letters of denization.[3] Clement, whose aptitude for intrigue was undoubted, soon secured employment with the King and Gloucester, both of whom he represented in the Court of Rome as early as 1439.[4] Throughout his career in England, where he became Papal Collector in 1450,[4] he enjoyed the royal favour, and cumulated benefices to such an extent[5] as to arouse scandal in an age when pluralism was commonly accepted. While in England, Clement was on very friendly terms with Del Monte,[6] Bekynton,[6] and other prominent ecclesiastics, to whom he may have communicated his learned tastes. Though little more than a dilettante, his contribution to English humanism was not altogether negligible, for in presenting manuscripts to friends he was bringing neo-classical writings into the country. It was he who sent Bekynton the Latin poems of Francesco Pontano in 1442,[7] and who during Del Monte's visit to England presented him with manuscripts and arranged with him for the transcription of texts.[8] At a later stage Clement was apparently in touch with John Tiptoft, Earl of Worcester, who corresponded with him, possibly on matters connected with learning.[9] Del Monte's correspondence with Clement is evidence that the latter was not indifferent to the niceties of Latin style,[10] and though with him learning and all else was subordinate to the needs of career

[1] On Clement cf. Schirmer, op. cit. pp. 63–5, Mitchell, *John Tiptoft*, pp. 191–3, Calmette et Perinelle, *Louis XI et l'Angleterre*, pp. 12, 305–6.

[2] Gascoigne, op. cit. p. 28. Clement obtained a Divinity degree from Oxford, the University granting it, not without opposition, at the request of Henry VI (Schirmer, op. cit. pp. 64–5). Schirmer's view that opposition to Clement was really hostility towards humanism has no serious foundations.

[3] P.R. 1436–41, p. 312.

[4] *C.P.R.*, vols. VIII, pp. 224–5, X, p. 271.

[5] His benefices and offices included prebends at Lichfield, Wells, Hereford, and Lincoln, the Treasurership of Lichfield, and the Archdeaconships of Huntington, Wilts, and Winton (Le Neve, op. cit. vol. I, pp. 526, 582, 584, 630, II, pp. 213, 234, III, pp. 26, 51, 630).

[6] Del Monte's correspondence with Clement, whom he also recommended to Poggio, (Walser, op. cit. p. 452) is in MS. (V. L.) Vat. Lat. no. 2694, ff. 181^r–2^r, 185^r, 200^r–^{v}, 201^r–^{v}, 220^r–1^r, 221^v. Bekynton's correspondence with Clement is in *Official Correspondence of Thomas Beckington*, vol. I, pp. 160–1, 174–9. Clement was also acquainted with Adam de Moleyns, (*infra*, p. 81).

[7] Cf. *supra*, p. 73.

[8] MS. (V.L.) Vat. Lat. no. 2694, ff. 181^r–2^r.

[9] Mitchell, *John Tiptoft*, pp. 191–2.

[10] Schirmer, op. cit. p. 64, n. 28.

making, he must have possessed a remarkable classical culture. His notorious rapacity and lack of scruple rendered him unpopular in England, so that after endless complaints Pius II instructed his legate in England, Coppini, to remove him.[1] Yet even after this he occasionally appeared in the service of the English Crown during the Yorkist period although he had returned to his native country, where he alternated between the services of John II and Edward IV.[2]

Besides Bekynton and Clement, two English ecclesiastics resident for some years at the Court of Rome had each a part, though an unequal one, to play in introducing neo-classicism into England. Of these, Andrew Holes[3] has so far been deemed one of the early leaders of English humanism. But a closer acquaintance must deprive him of his laurels. Like Bekynton, Holes was educated at Winchester and New College, Oxford, of which he was a member from 1413.[4] After obtaining his Arts degree he proceeded to read for the Bachelorships of Civil and Canon Law,[5] on which subjects he is also known to have delivered lectures in Oxford.[5] While still there he had already begun to obtain ecclesiastical preferment,[6] and on 20 February, 1432, he was appointed Proctor of the Bishop of Bath and Wells at the Council of Basle.[7] Whether or not he actually went to Basle, it is known that he was already abroad in 1433, when he is found in Rome as a Papal Chamberlain.[8] Holes must soon have attracted favourable attention to himself in curial circles, as seven cardinals and many other important prelates attended his long Latin sermon in the Hospital of the Most Holy Trinity and St. Thomas of Canterbury on St. Thomas à Becket's day in 1433.[8] This

---

[1] On 9 August, 1460 (*C.P.R* vol. XI, p. 680). Clement was preparing to leave England in the following November (*Calendar of French Rolls*, p. 444).

[2] Calmette et Perinelle, op. cit. pp. 12, 305–6, J. Calmette, *Louis XI, Jean II et la Révolution Catalane* (1461–73), Toulouse, 1902, pp. 61, 542–3.

[3] On Holes cf. especially Schirmer, op. cit. pp. 105–6, Da Bisticci, op. cit. pp. 238–40.

[4] *Official Correspondence of Thomas Beckington*, vol. I, p. cxviii.

[5] *C.P.R.* vol. VIII, p. 459.

[6] He was already Rector of Davenham and Archdeacon of Anglesey in 1427, and Canon of York in 1431 (Le Neve, op. cit. vols. I, p. 114, III, p. 191, *C.P.R.* vol. VII, p. 499).

[7] *Register of John Stafford, Bishop of Bath and Wells*, 1425–43, ed. T. S. Holmes, (Somerset Record Society) London, 1915–6, vol. II, p. 183.

[8] Holes' sermon is in MS. National-Bibliothek, Vienna, no. 4139, ff. 61ʳ–9ʳ. Its title at fo. 61ʳ runs thus: (*S*)*ermo dictum per andream holes anglicum cubicularium s.d.n. anno a natiuitate domini Mccccxxxiij in hospitali anglicorum Rome, in festo sancti Thome martiris Cantuariensis quondam archiepiscopi in presencia VI reuerendissimorum dominorum Cardinalium et multorum honorabilium prelatorum in cuius sermonis exordio metrice plangit mortem magistri Guillermi Certeyn in artibus Floridique poete.* . . In 1450 Holes was appointed a procurator to recover money due in England to the English Hospice in Rome (Flynn, *Englishmen in Rome during the Renaissance*, p. 123).

sermon, the subject of which was St. Thomas à Becket, began with a lament for the death of William Certayn, an English ecclesiastic residing at the Curia:[1] fortunately it still survives to show what Holes really appreciated in classical scholarship. In this respect the omissions are of primary interest, for it contains no traces of neo-classical taste. Its conception, style, and similes, are those of a writer nurtured in the formal medieval education. Quotations or references are confined to Holy Scripture,[2] the Fathers,[2] Seneca,[2] and the *De Planctu Naturae* of Alain of Lille,[2] and the sermon reveals little beyond a capacity for writing Latin as it was understood during the Middle Ages, and a preference for scholastic rather than Ciceronian form. Holes spent several years at the Curia,[3] and therefore cannot have failed to encounter the humanists residing there. In 1437 he was appointed King's Proctor in the Court of Rome,[4] and followed the Papal Court in its move to Ferrara together with the Bishop of Bayeux and Robert Sutton.[5] It is unlikely that when at Ferrara Holes ever troubled to make the acquaintance of Guarino: instead he appears to have gone to study at the University of Padua, where he obtained a doctorate in Canon Law on 4 February, 1439,[6] after which he eventually rejoined the Curia in Florence.[7] The Florentine visit appears to have proved particularly congenial. Altogether he spent more than a year and a half in that town,[8] where he had chosen to remain even after the return of the Papal Court to Rome.[8]

Florence was then in every aspect the cultural capital of Italy, and here Holes kept open house and amidst routine affairs and pious reading entertained the leading scholars of the city.[9] According to his biographer, the Florentine bookseller Vespasiano da Bisticci, his learning impressed the men of letters with whom he conversed, while scholars of distinction like Carlo

---

[1] MS. National-Bibliothek, Vienna, no. 4139, ff. 61ʳ–2ʳ. This section is in elegiacs. The rest of the sermon is in prose.   [2] *Ibid.*, ff. 62ʳ, 64ʳ–ᵛ, 66ʳ, 67ᵛ.

[3] Holes remained in Italy until 1444. A safe conduct to him and ten companions returning to England was issued on 15 February, 1444 (*C.P.R.* vol. VIII, p. 296).

[4] Stevenson, *Letters and Papers Illustrative of the Wars of the English in France during the Reign of Henry the Sixth*, vol. I, p. 472.

[5] *Official Correspondence of Thomas Beckington*, vol. I, pp. 58–60.

[6] Zonta e Brotto, *Acta Graduum Academicorum ab anno Mccccvi ad annum Mccccl*, p. 283.

[7] On Holes in Florence cf. Da Bisticci, op. cit. p. 239. He must have been still there in 1443 since the Curia left Florence only during that year (Pastor, *History of the Popes from the Close of the Middle Ages*, vol. I, p. 332).

[8] Da Bisticci, op. cit. p. 240, *Vita Jannotii Manetti . . . auctore Naldo Naldio*, p. 546, *supra*, n. 7. According to Vespasiano, Holes remained in Florence in order to have books transcribed for him (Da Bisticci, op. cit. p. 239).

[9] *Ibid.*, p. 239, *Vita Jannotii Manetti*, p. 546.

Marsuppini, Matteo Palmieri, and Giannozzo Manetti, were glad
of an occasion to dispute with him on matters theological.[1]
The Florentine humanists perhaps appreciated Holes the more for
his lavish hospitality. Nevertheless fifteenth century humanism
still contained strong elements of scholasticism, so that Holes'
popularity is additional evidence that the dialectical skill of the
schools could yet obtain a measure of applause from the humanistic side. Judging from his only extant work, the sermon he
delivered in Rome, Holes can scarcely have comprehended the
finer and more distinctive traits in the mentality of his eminent
guests. But it is difficult to believe that he was not attracted,
even if unconsciously, by the neo-classical background, or at
least by the externals of this polite society: how else should he
have found the air of Florence so pleasant as to prolong his stay
far beyond necessity.

Besides disputation with the Florentine humanists, Holes
indulged in much book buying during his stay in Italy, and
purchased from the bookseller Vespasiano a large number of
manuscripts,[2] amongst them perhaps the fine Cicero now at New
College.[3] Doubtless the majority of the books which he collected
in Italy were Church Fathers and treatises on theology and
Canon Law,[4] but with them were probably works of classical
authors, and perhaps even some by those very humanists whom
he had befriended. So large was the collection that when he left
Italy in 1444 he was, according to Vespasiano, compelled to
return to England by sea in order to bring his books.[5] In
England Holes was acquainted with Bekynton[6] and Chaundler,[7]
and from Italy he had corresponded with Piero del Monte,
though solely on ecclesiastical business.[8] On his return home he
added yet more benefices to the ones he already held,[9] and from

[1] Da Bisticci, op. cit. p. 239.
[2] Ibid., p. 240. He had also scribes working for him while in Florence, (Ibid., pp. 239–40).
[3] MS. New Coll. Oxford, no. 249. This MS. was written in Italy during the fifteenth
century and belonged to Holes. (Ibid., fo. 1ᵛ).
[4] This is suggested by Vespasiano's account of him. MSS. (B.L.) Bodl. no. 247 and
Magdalen Coll. Oxford, no. 191, both of which were possessed by him, contain theology
and Canon Law.
[5] Da Bisticci, op. cit. p. 240.   [6] Cf. supra, p. 73.
[7] He must have been in contact with Chaundler not only at Winchester and Oxford, but
also at Wells where Holes was Archdeacon since 1450 (Le Neve, op. cit. vol. I, p. 160).
Chaundler mentions Holes in one of his Latin works (MS. New Coll. Oxford, no. 288, fo.
53ʳ); there is a representation of Holes in the New College MS. of Chaundler's works.
[8] MS. (V.L.) Vat. Lat. no. 2694, ff. 222ᵛ–3ʳ, 241ʳ–2ʳ.
[9] On Holes' benefices and dignities cf. C.P.R. vols. VIII, p. 526, IX, p. 82, Le Neve, op.
cit. vol. I, pp. 160, 509, 603. In 1442 Henry VI tried to secure the Norman bishopric of
Coutances for him (Official Correspondence of Thomas Beckington, vol. I, pp. 26–7).

the field of diplomacy he rose to a great office of state on his appointment to the Keepership of the Privy Seal in 1450.[1] Active politics did not long detain him, and after his tenure of office Holes appears to have spent his time until his death in 1467[2] in the enjoyment of his numerous benefices, the exercise of his ecclesiastical duties, and the pursuit of his favourite studies. Holes' correspondence with Bekynton and Del Monte gives no suggestion of his having been particularly interested in classical research, while his relations with the Florentine humanists indicate that Divinity was the common subject on which they met. His spare time in Florence was mainly employed in reading works of theology and Canon Law,[3] so that his services to humanism in England were probably limited to furnishing information about the Italians, and to the introduction of some manuscripts. As a whole Dr. Schirmer's judgment of him[3] must stand, for Holes was such an ingrained canonist that the atmosphere in which he spent a considerable time scarcely affected him, and his inclusion among the early English humanists is mainly due to Vespasiano's biography. But in spite of all his experiences in Italy must count for much, since he returned with an intimate knowledge of Florentine circles and what they stood for, so that even a bare description would stimulate emulation amongst English scholars.

If Holes' residence in Italy made little apparent impression upon his learning, a sojourn at the Court of Rome conditioned the intellectual outlook of Adam de Moleyns.[4] Nothing is known about his education, but his degrees in utroque[5] and his bequest of books to Oxford,[6] make it fairly certain that he was educated at that University. Already a Bachelor of Civil Law in 1430,[6] he probably became a member of the Papal household about this

[1] Stevenson, op. cit. vol. I, p. 514. He was still Keeper in February 1452 (P.R. 1446–52, p. 357) and was probably removed soon afterwards by Richard, Duke of York.

[2] According to Da Bisticci, op. cit. p. 240, Holes retired from secular activities after returning to England. Possibly such a retirement took place after he relinquished the Privy Seal, after which he disappears from politics. He was buried in Salisbury Cathedral (W. H. R. Jones, Fasti Ecclesiae Sarisberiensis, Salisbury, 1889, pp. 89, 338). Latin verses in his honour were placed after his death on the roof of Wells' Cathedral Hall (H. E. Reynolds, Wells Cathedral, Leeds, 1881, p. liii). His will is in Somerset Medieval Wills, 1383–1500, p. 213. The only MS. mentioned in his will is a Hymnary.

[3] Da Bisticci, op. cit. p. 239. Schirmer, op. cit. p. 106.

[4] On Moleyns cf. especially Leland, De Scriptoribus, p. 454, Schirmer, op. cit. pp. 103–5, and the article on him in the D.N.B.

[5] C.P.R. vol. VIII, pp. 178, 572.

[6] Register of the University of Oxford, vol. I, p. 287. On 10 February, 1450, Oxford University wrote to Moleyns' executors about his bequest of books (Epistolae Academicae, vol. I, pp. 281–2). He is already styled B.C.L. in 1430 (C.P.R., vol. VIII, p. 178).

time, and in all probability it was during the years that he spent at the Curia[1] that he became a friend of Poggio,[2] and came to cultivate letters and form that Latin style which was to gain the admiration of Aeneas Sylvius Piccolomini.[3] Moleyns had already become a Papal Chamberlain in 1434,[4] and in the following year he was sent to England by Pope Eugenius IV with a message for Cardinal Beaufort.[4]

Once back in England, Moleyns began a new career in the service of the Crown. In 1436 he was appointed Clerk of the Council,[5] and the experience gained by his residence abroad subsequently secured for him employment in diplomatic missions. These included embassies to Aix la Chapelle and Cologne in 1438,[6] and to Frankfurt in 1441.[6] Nor was Moleyns lacking in enlightened friends at home. Piero del Monte,[7] Richard Petworth,[8] Thomas Bekynton,[9] and Vincent Clement,[9] were closely acquainted with him. In 1442 Moleyns was once more at the Papal Court on a diplomatic mission[10] during which he saw much of Poggio, who in one of his letters to Petworth[11] warmly praises him. After this Moleyns' career was mostly occupied with the cares of State. Provided to the Bishopric of Chichester on

[1] He had already been at the Curia for some time at the beginning of 1434, when he was intending to return home (*C.P.R.* vol. VIII, p. 282). It is uncertain whether he left then, as he was at the Curia in September 1435, when a safeconduct was issued to him (*Ibid.*, vol. VIII, p. 285).

[2] Poggio refers to Moleyns as a mutual friend in a letter to Petworth written in 1442 (Walser, op. cit. p. 454), but probably they had met during Moleyns' early visit to the Roman Court. Poggio had signed the safeconduct issued to Moleyns in 1435 (*C.P.R.* vol. VIII, p. 285).

[3] Cf. *infra*, p. 83.

[4] *C.P.R.* vol. VIII, p. 282. His commission to go on a mission to Beaufort is dated 22 March, 1435 (*Ibid.*, vol. VIII, p. 218) but his departure must have been delayed since he was still at the Curia in September (*supra*, n. 1.). During this same month Henry VI wrote to the College of Cardinals proposing Moleyns for the vacant Archbishopric of Armagh (MS. Corpus Christi Coll. Cambridge, no. 170, p. 204).

[5] *Proceedings and Ordinances of the Privy Council*, vol. V, p. viii. In the spring of 1442 he had already resigned the clerkship and become a member of the Council (*Ibid.*, vol. V, p. 173).

[6] *Ibid.*, vol. V, pp. 89, 91. A 'protection' to Moleyns going to Frankfurt was issued on 3 December, 1441 (Rymer, op. cit. vol. XI, p. 53). On his other embassies cf. the article on him in the *D.N.B.*

[7] Del Monte mentions him in a letter to Pietro Barbo (MS. (V.L.) Vat. Lat. no. 2694, fo. 119ʳ) and when he left England he appointed Moleyns his locum-tenens and sub-collector (*C.P.R.* vol. VIII, p. 318). In 1444 Moleyns was commissioned with Bekynton and Stafford to enquire into Del Monte's past administration of the Collectorship (*C.P.R.* vol. VIII, p. 272).

[8] Cf. *supra*, p. 20.

[9] *Official Correspondence of Thomas Beckington*, vol. I, p. 175.

[10] His commission was issued on 12 March, 1442 (Rymer, op. cit. vol. XI, p. 3). He was also to ask for the canonization of King Alfred (*Official Correspondence of Thomas Beckington*, vol. I, p. 119).

[11] Walser, op. cit. p. 454.

G

23 September, 1445,[1] and Keeper of the Privy Seal from 1444 to 1449,[2] he held at Suffolk's side a key position in English politics until his tragic death at Portsmouth on 9 January, 1450.[3]

In spite of his many occupations Moleyns found some time for humanistic pursuits. Besides assembling a collection of manuscripts about which we could wish to know more,[4] he successfully cultivated an elegant Latin style free from the conventions of Latin prose as taught during the Middle Ages. His correspondence with Aeneas Sylvius Piccolomini,[5] at that time a secretary in the Imperial Chancery, was concerned with an amicable exchange of news and recommendations. Indeed their almost conscious reluctance to discuss the technical aspects of scholarship imports a refined enlightenment to their communications, which if hardly surprising on the part of the daring author of *Euryalus and Lucrece* was decidedly unconventional for a Keeper of the Privy Seal. The familiar but sophisticated manner, so attractive in a Petrarch, and too often obscured by the pedantry of the later Renaissance, imparted grace and charm to the correspondence of the two civil servants, severed by distance, and yet alike in their devotion to literature amidst the cares of state.

In the one surviving letter of Moleyns,[6] he begins by placing his own and his correspondent's name at the opening and so proceeds to salute the Piccolomini. The choice of words, the construction and phraseology, are obviously inspired by classical models, and show the writer's close association with humanistic culture. In style and Latinity, Moleyns appears from this letter to have been on the same level as most Italian humanists of his time, and by far superior to any of his English contemporaries, Bekynton included. It is consequently no wonder that Aeneas Sylvius, who had visited England and was acquainted with the state of learning here, should have been pleasantly surprised. In

---

[1] *C.P.R.* vol. IX, p. 514.

[2] Moleyns became Keeper of the Privy Seal on 11 February, 1444, and resigned the office on 9 December, 1449, (Rymer, op. cit. vol. XI, pp. 53, 255).

[3] Ramsay, *Lancaster and York*, vol. II, p. 104.

[4] All that is known about Moleyns' books is that he bequeathed some to Oxford (*supra*, p. 80).

[5] In 1443 Piccolomini wrote to Moleyns asking for Henry VI's support of the Imperial efforts to secure Church unity (*Der Briefwechsel des Eneas Silvius Piccolomini*, vol. I, pp. 156–7), thus starting a correspondence with him printed in *Ibid.*, vol. I, pp. 156–7, 324–6, 561–2. In one of these letters Piccolomini thanks for a present from Moleyns' niece, (*Ibid.*, vol. I, pp. 324–6).

[6] *Ibid.*, vol. I, p. 172. This letter was probably written in 1443.

one of his letters to Moleyns, he declared that his Latin was the best written in England since Peter of Blois, and attributed the high degree of Moleyns' classical learning to the wise patronage of Humphrey, Duke of Gloucester.[1]

Moleyns' achievement is particularly important in showing the standards to which an Englishman could attain at a time when neo-classicism was just being slowly introduced into England. That the scope of his genius was so far limited, must be sought for in the nature of his occupations, which were such as to preclude him from taking an active part in the extension of humanism. His position was too eminent to allow of his teaching, and his offices perhaps too exacting to furnish him with the necessary leisure for the composition of literary works. Thus his generous instincts were limited to letter writing and book collecting. Alone among the Englishmen of his time, Moleyns found genuine praise abroad for his Latin learning. But like Bekynton, and after him Grey and many others, he was handicapped by his station in life: had this been less exalted and his career less successful, his learning would perhaps have proved more fruitful.

---

[1] *Der Briefwechsel Des Eneas Silvius Piccolomini*, vol. I, p. 325. He also mentions Gloucester's patronage in a letter to Sigismund of Austria (*Ibid.*, vol. I, p. 227). Aeneas Sylvius came to England in 1435–6, but it is most unlikely that he exerted any influence here. On his journey from Scotland into England cf. J. Wilson, 'The passage of the Border by Aeneas Sylvius in the winter of 1435–6,' *Transactions of the Cumberland and Westmoreland Antiquarian and Archaeological Society*, new series, XXIII (1923) pp. 17–28. While in London he was shown an ancient Latin version of Thucydides in St. Paul's Cathedral (*Aeneae Silvii Opera*, Basileae, 1571, p. 652).

CHAPTER VI

DURING the fifteenth century several English students attended Italian Universities to continue their studies after taking their degrees at Oxford or Cambridge. Englishmen were driven to taking post-graduate courses in Italy during this century mainly as a result of the Hundred Years War, which had made difficult their attendance at the University of Paris, to which they had formerly resorted. Amongst the Italian Universities, those of Padua and Bologna[1] appear to have been patronized especially by Englishmen, the majority of whom were in holy orders and read in the faculties of theology or decrees.

Naturally several humanists were to be found teaching at these Universities, but it would be a very serious mistake to assume that every English student who went to study in Italy came under the spell of humanism during his residence there. Just as a large proportion of the English prelates who resided at the Curia remained impervious, so did the majority of English students in Italy return with their scholastic outlook untouched by the Renaissance. Some, however, like William Grey and Robert Flemmyng, proved better disposed or more receptive and were won for the New Learning while studying at the University of Padua, while others, like John Free and John Gunthorpe, went expressly to Italy to attend humanistic lectures.

During the first half of the fifteenth century two schools directed by humanists enjoyed a great reputation throughout Italy. The first of these was that kept at Mantua by the celebrated Vittorino da Feltre,[2] which was attended by pupils of every rank, and in the organization of which may perhaps be detected the foundations of the modern English Public School system of education. The other, which was in reality rather a department of the local University than a school, was that kept by Guarino da Verona in Ferrara from 1429 until his death in 1460,[3] and which included pupils drawn from several European countries.[4]

---

[1] On English students at Padua and Bologna during the fifteenth century cf. especially Mitchell, *English Students at Padua*, 1460–75, and Mitchell, *English Law Students at Bologna in the Fifteenth Century.*

[2] For Vittorino da Feltre and his school cf. W. H. Woodward, *Vittorino da Feltre and other Humanist Educators*, Cambridge, 1897.

[3] On which cf. Sabbadini, *La Scuola e gli Studi di Guarino da Verona.* On Guarino at Ferrara cf. Bertoni, *Guarino da Verona tra Letterati e Cortigiani a Ferrara.*

[4] Guarino's foreign pupils are mentioned in his funeral oration by Ludovico Carbone in Bertoni, op. cit. pp. 160–75. On Englishmen in Ferrara during the fifteenth century cf. R. J. Mitchell, 'English Students at Ferrara in the Fifteenth Century', *Italian Studies*, I (1937) pp. 75–82.

Amongst fifteenth century humanists Guarino held a position of great eminence. A pupil of Emanuel Chrysoloras,[1] he had spent some time during his youth in Constantinople,[1] where he had perfected his knowledge of Greek, and gathered together an important collection of manuscripts of ancient Greek authors.[2] On his return from Greece, Guarino had embarked upon a teaching career, and before settling at Ferrara in 1429, he had taught the humanities in Venice,[3] Florence,[3] and his native Verona.[3] Besides his teaching and lecturing activities, Guarino composed treatises, made translations from the Greek, emended classical texts, and kept up a voluminous correspondence[4] with the principal Italian scholars of his time, thus keeping himself acquainted with the latest trends of the humanistic world, and the most recent discoveries of ancient texts.

Guarino's method of teaching the classics consisted in dividing his courses into three parts, elementary, grammatical, and rhetorical, more or less according to the divisions advised by Quintilian. The grammatical course, which followed the elementary one, was divided into methodical and historical sections, and mainly dealt with the acquisition of historical and mythological knowledge. The last and most advanced course, the rhetorical, was mainly dedicated to an explanation of Quintilian and the *Rhetorica ad Herennium*. Besides this, Guarino used to request his pupils to write Latin exercises under the form of letters to him, which he then corrected and discussed with them, and he also lectured on the texts of various important authors, both Latin and Greek.[5]

By the end of the first half of the fifteenth century Guarino and his school had acquired an international reputation. In England Humphrey of Gloucester was acquainted with his achievement, and took much interest in Guarino's writings and studies.[6] Some of Guarino's letters were sufficiently appreciated to be included in a formulary prepared almost certainly at Christ Church, Canterbury, about 1450,[6] and in this monastery the monk Henry Cranebroke is known to have copied some of

---

[1] Sabbadini, *Guarino da Verona e il suo Epistolario edito e inedito*, pp. 56–7.

[2] On which cf. H. Omont, 'Les MSS. Grecs de Guarino', *Revue des Bibliothèques*, V (1892) pp. 78–81.

[3] Sabbadini, *Guarino da Verona e il suo Epistolario edito e inedito*, pp. 58–70.

[4] Published by R. Sabbadini in *Epistolario di Guarino Veronese*.

[5] Sabbadini, *Il Metodo degli Umanisti*, pp. 40–4, Sabbadini, *La Scuola e gli Studi di Guarino da Verona*, pp. 35–7.

[6] Walser, op. cit. p. 172, n. 2; *supra*, pp. 50, n. 4, 64, n. 7; *infra*, pp. 129, 131.

Guarino's works into his own notebook.[1] Moreover, some of
Guarino's writings were to be found in England during the first
half of the fifteenth century,[1] and the evidence would suggest
that the popularity of his school in this country was perhaps due
more to the dissemination of his writings and to the 'propaganda' of former pupils like Piero del Monte,[2] than to the Englishmen who happened to attend the Council of Ferrara in 1438.[3]
It is true that some of Guarino's English pupils, like Grey,
Flemmyng, and Tiptoft, had studied at the University of Padua
before coming to his school. Yet it seems probable that although
they doubtless heard more of his great reputation while in
Padua,[4] they were already familiar with his name and perhaps
with some of his works before leaving England, and had already
decided to attend his courses when they left their own country.

As far as we know, the first Englishman to attend the lectures
of Guarino was William Grey, later Bishop of Ely.[5] Before going
to Ferrara Grey had studied at Oxford, where he lived in Balliol
College. After obtaining his arts degree, Grey continued to keep
his rooms in Balliol, which were famed in academic circles for
the books collected there,[6] and thanks to his influential position,
he was a son of Sir Thomas Grey of Heton[7] and had been Archdeacon of Northampton from 1434,[8] he was elected Chancellor
of Oxford University in 1440 or 1441, an office he kept until
1442, when he was probably succeeded by Thomas Gascoigne.[9]
Although little is known about Grey's life in Oxford save that
he held the Chancellorship, studied Divinity, and collected books,
it seems possible that his subsequent well-known interest in
classical scholarship had its beginnings during his Oxford
residence. Duke Humphrey's first large donation of manuscripts
reached Oxford in 1439;[10] hence knowing Grey's bibliophile
leanings, and considering his position in the University, it is

---

[1] Cf. *supra*, p. 85, n. 6.
[2] Cf. *supra*, p. 24.
[3] Like Andrew Holes, cf. *supra*, p.78.
[4] Cf. *infra*, p. 88.
[5] On Grey cf. especially Schirmer, op. cit. pp. 116–21, Da Bisticci, op. cit. pp. 213–5, Leland, *De Scriptoribus*, pp. 461–2, and the article on him in the *D.N.B.*
[6] *et est utrumque opus Lire Cantabrigie, et eciam magister Willelmus Grey habet idem opus Oxonie in camera sua in aula Ballioli*, Gascoigne, op. cit. p. 185. Grey's MSS. of Lyra are now MSS. Balliol Coll., Oxford, nn. 166b, 171.
[7] A. R. Wagner, 'William Grey Bishop of Ely,' *T.L.S.*, 9 June, 1932, p. 427.
[8] Le Neve, op. cit. vol. II, p. 58. On his numerous benefices and dignities cf. *Ibid.*, vols. I, p. 613, II, pp. 221, 404, III, pp. 140, 171, 183, 453.
[9] *Registrum Cancellarii*, vol. I, pp. xxxvi–vii.
[10] *Supra*, p. 66.

practically certain that he must have had access to these books before leaving Oxford.[1] These and other texts, which possibly came into his hands, may have originated in him that curiosity for the antique which was to increase considerably during his visit to Italy. That such interest had already been aroused in him before reaching Italy would appear from some manuscripts, which were written for him during his visit to Cologne, and which contain classical and neo-classical texts,[2] which would hardly have been commissioned save by a person interested in humanism.

Grey's main interest was, however, not the study of ancient and humanistic literature but theology,[3] and it was with a view to furthering his knowledge of this subject that he went abroad once his term as Chancellor of Oxford had expired. He left England during the autumn of 1442[4] with a numerous retinue, which included two fellows of Balliol College, Richard Bole, afterwards Archdeacon of Ely, and Nicholas Saxtoun, in order to go to Cologne to read at that University. Once there he proceeded to be incorporated with Bole and Saxtoun into the faculty of Divinity as Masters of Arts of Oxford, the incorporation taking place on December 1st, 1442.[5] During his visit to that city Grey also appears to have alternated the study of theology with book collecting, his additions to his library including classical and humanistic texts as well as treatises on Divinity and Canon Law.[6] Grey left Cologne for Italy in somewhat dramatic circumstances. His open display of wealth had been noticed by some local robbers, who planned to watch for his departure in order to capture him and hold him up to ransom once he was outside the city walls. But Grey became aware of the danger.

[1] This is very probable considering the immediate popularity of Gloucester's gifts in University circles, cf. *Epistolae Academicae*, vol. I, pp. 245–6.

[2] Now MSS. (C.U.) Dd. XIII. 2 (Cicero) copied by T. Werken for Grey in 1444, Balliol Coll. Oxford, no. 295, (Works of Sicco Polenton) copied by the same scribe in 1445, almost certainly for Grey. Vespasiano states that Grey was already aware of Italian prominence in the classics before leaving England, and that he thought he could become acquainted with neo-classicism only in Italy, (Da Bisticci, op. cit. p. 213).

[3] His studies and the remains of his library witness to such an interest.

[4] *Calendar of French Rolls*, p. 355.

[5] Keussen, *Die Matrikel der Universität Köln*, vol. I, p. 457. On Bole cf. *infra*, pp. 96–7. Saxtoun presented MSS. Balliol Coll. Oxford, nn. 25, 74, 101, 146b (Petrarch, Cicero *Pro Archia*), 153, 265, to the College.

[6] Cf. *supra*, n. 2; Besides Werken, scribes patronized by Grey in Cologne included a *Thialmann filius Reyneri* who copied MS. Balliol Coll. Oxford, no. 28 in 1442, (he also transcribed MSS. Corpus Christi Coll. Cambridge, no. 68, Gonville and Caius Coll. Cambridge, no. 114) and perhaps Heinrich Horn of Dusseldorf who copied MS. Balliol Coll. Oxford, no. 130. On Bole transcribing MSS. for Grey while in Cologne cf. *infra*, p. 96. On Grey's acquiring MSS. in Cologne cf. also Da Bisticci, op. cit. p. 214.

Hence he departed in secret with only one companion, both disguised as Irish pilgrims, while his physician kept calling at his former residence so as to hide his departure from ill wishers. The ruse proved successful and Grey reached Italy safely.[1] If the testimony of Vespasiano da Bisticci is to be relied upon, he first went to Florence, where he bought several books from his future biographer Vespasiano,[2] and then to Padua, where he continued his theological studies, and obtained a degree in Divinity on 14 September, 1445.[3] Vespasiano tells us also that it was while in Padua that Grey heard of Guarino's reputation, and made up his mind to move to Ferrara to attend that famous school after completing his studies in the University.[4] This may be quite possible, especially as we know that Grey was in contact with humanists in Padua: the famous physician and humanist Giovanni Marcanova was one of Grey's *testes* for his degree,[5] and may have persuaded him to follow Guarino's lectures. Nevertheless it is equally possible that Ferrara and the school of Guarino had been included in his original plans before leaving England.

The date of Grey's departure from Padua is not known, but it is probable that he left shortly after obtaining his degree, arriving in Ferrara during the autumn of 1445 in time for the beginning of the academic year.[6] In Ferrara Grey attended Guarino's lectures, almost certainly the rhetorical course,[7] and besides studying the

[1] Da Bisticci, op. cit. p. 214. Probably Grey did not leave Cologne before 1444 since one of his MSS. (now MS. Balliol Coll. Oxford, no. 69), was completed there on 8 February, 1444. MS. Balliol Coll. Oxford, no. 124b (written in 1444) may also have been acquired by him there.

[2] Da Bisticci, op. cit. p. 214. As MSS. were copied for Grey in Florence in 1448–9 (*infra*, p. 92, n. 1) it seems probable that he visited Florence in 1447 or 1448. Grey owned also a MS. copied in 1446 by the same scribe who prepared two of the MSS. made in 1448–9, (*infra*, p. 92, n. 1) which was probably copied expressly for him, and which, if so, suggests an earlier visit.

[3] Da Bisticci, op. cit. p. 214. Grey's *assignatio punctorum* took place on 3 September, 1445, his *licentia privati examinis* following three days later (Verrua, *Umanisti ed altri studiosi viri italiani e stranieri*, p. 78). His disputations took place on September 11, his *disputantes* being Gerolamo d'Assisi and Niccolò da Treviso (Zonta e Brotto, op. cit. p. 389). His degree was conferred upon him on the same day (Verrua, op. cit. p. 78).

[4] Da Bisticci, op. cit. p. 214. He is mentioned among Guarino's pupils in the funeral oration of the latter, (Bertoni, op. cit. p. 167).

[5] Verrua, op. cit. p. 58.

[6] It is almost certain that Grey left Padua for Ferrara shortly after taking his degree, since he remained in Ferrara for some time and it is known that he left that town in 1446 when he took up his duties as Proctor in Rome (*infra*, p. 89). He was in Ferrara in 1446 since a MS. was copied in his house there during that year (*infra*, p. 89, n. 5). Grey probably arrived in Ferrara in time for the beginning of the academic year which then began about the middle of October (*Epistolario di Guarino Veronese*, vol. III, p. 500).

[7] This is obvious: his University education would have provided him with enough knowledge to dispense with the more elementary courses.

classics appears to have taken a keen interest in philosophy.[1] Instead of living in lodgings like the average student, he kept up his own impressive household, as he had done in Cologne,[2] indulging at the same time in patronage and book collecting.[3] It was while he was at the school of Guarino that Grey came across the humanist Niccolò Perotti, then a young and needy scholar.[4] The unusual gifts of the young man made a considerable impression upon Grey, who perceiving his ability, and being acquainted with his circumstances, invited him to settle in his household and study at his expense.[4] In 1446 Perotti was already established in Grey's house,[5] and thanks to his patron's liberality he found himself provided with the necessary means to purchase the books he needed, and pay for his studies. In return he perhaps copied some manuscripts for his patron, but evidence on this point is not conclusive.[5]

Grey's visit to Ferrara was not a long one. On 18 November, 1445, Grey, who since leaving England had succeeded Bekynton in a prebendary stall at Lichfield,[6] was appointed Henry VI's Proctor in the Court of Rome,[6] so that during 1446, after scarcely one year in Ferrara, he was compelled to leave the school of Guarino to take up his new duties in Rome.[7] With him went his protegé Perotti, but shortly after they had settled there the young Italian left his patron, to enter with the latter's permission the household of Cardinal Bessarion in order to improve his knowledge of Greek.[8] After the death of Pope Eugenius in 1447, Grey soon gained the favour of Pope Nicholas V who shared his love of books, and had once been a noted professional humanist.[9] As a result of this at the end of 1448 Grey was already a Papal

---

[1] Bertoni, op. cit. p. 167. The philosophical works formerly in his library confirm this.

[2] Da Bisticci, op. cit. pp. 213–4.

[3] *Ibid.*, p. 214. Cf. also *infra*, n. 5.

[4] On Perotti cf. Mercati, *Per la Cronologia della Vita e degli Scritti di Niccolò Perotti*. Among Grey's reasons for asking Perotti to join his household there was also that Grey wanted a resident scholar in his house, (Da Bisticci, op. cit. p. 214).

[5] Cf. MS. (V.L.) Vat. Urb. no. 1180 (containing grammatical treatises including the *Rhetorica* of Chirius Consultus Fortunatianus) fo. 118ʳ: *Apuleii fragmentum de diphthongis quod in uetustissimo codice repertum est finit feliciter per Nicolaum Peroctum cum Ferariae apud magnificum et generosissimum uirum d. Guilielmum Grai esset duodeuicesimumque aetatis suae annum ageret*. As Perotti was born in 1429 (Mercati, op. cit. p. 17) this MS. was written in 1446. It is unlikely that this MS. was made for Grey for it bears Perotti's arms. It is, however, highly, probable that Grey availed himself of Perotti's ability as a scribe.

[6] Le Neve, op. cit. vol. I, p. 613, P.R. 1441–6, p. 390.

[7] Da Bisticci, op. cit. p. 214. As Perotti was already in Bessarion's house in 1446 (Mercati, op. cit. p. 31) Grey must have left Ferrara in 1446, possibly during the autumn.

[8] Da Bisticci, op. cit. pp. 147, 210, 214–5.

[9] On the early career of Nicholas V cf. G. Sforza, *La patria, la famiglia e la giovinezza di papa Niccolò V*, Lucca, 1884.

Protonotary,[1] and when the See of Lincoln fell vacant in 1450, he was unsuccessfully provided to it.[1] Failure with Lincoln does not appear to have discouraged Nicholas V from his intention of bestowing an English bishopric upon Grey: hence when four years later the Bishopric of Ely fell vacant, he was, this time successfully, provided to it by the Pope.[2]

During his sojourn at the Curia Grey's position placed him in close contact with many of the humanists residing there, who must have encouraged him to join in their pursuits. Cardinal Bessarion, with whom he was on good terms, was among them:[3] another was Poggio, who, after Grey had returned to England, wrote to him from Florence tendering his congratulations on his elevation to the Bishopric of Ely, offering advice, and asking him to write from England.[4] Nor did the patronage which had distinguished Grey in Ferrara end once Perotti had left him: the poet Capgrave, when ill in Rome in 1450, was visited and kindly treated by him,[5] and the scribe Werken, whom he had first met in Cologne, is found working for him in Rome.[6] In addition to the books which Werken was preparing for him, Grey acquired several other manuscripts in Rome, with the result that when he finally settled again in England in 1454,[7] his collection of classical

---

[1] C.P.R. vol. X, pp. 388–9, 508. The bishopric was given instead to John Chedworth after Grey had surrendered his provision, (Ibid., vol. X, p. 600).

[2] On 21 June, 1454, (Ibid., vol. X, p. 698).

[3] His acquaintance with Bessarion is disclosed by Perotti's becoming a member of that Cardinal's household thanks to Grey's influence with him (Da Bisticci, op. cit. pp. 214–5). Edward IV's copy of the 1471 edition of Bessarion's orations is in the Vatican Library (J. Philippe, Origine de l'Imprimerie à Paris d'aprés des documents inedits, Paris, 1885, p. 95).

[4] Mai, op. cit. vol. X, pp. 296–7. Grey was very popular at the Curia, (Da Bisticci, op. cit. p. 215).

[5] J. Capgrave, Liber De Illustribus Henricis, ed. F. C. Hingeston, (R.S.) London, 1858, p. 221. Capgrave dedicated his commentaries on the Creed and the Acts to Grey. Grey's copies of these are now MSS. Balliol Coll. Oxford, nn. 189–90. Capgrave may have derived his knowledge of Domenico di Bandino's Encyclopedias (Ye Solace of Pilgrims by John Capgrave, ed. A. C. Mills, Oxford, 1911, pp. 13, 43, 45, 49) from the MSS. of that work owned by Grey, on which cf. infra, p. 94. Grey took also an interest in the English Hospice in Rome (Flynn, op. cit. p. 130).

[6] Cf. the colophon of MS. Balliol Coll. Oxford, no. 238, pt. 2: Iste liber inceptus erat Colonie anno Domini 1447 20 die mensis Decembris et finitus est Rome anno Domini 1448 et 10 die mensis Februarii. T. Werken. Some of the volumes of this MS. were written by Laurence Dyamant. His colophon shows that the MS. was transcribed for Grey: Laurencius Dyamantis scripsit ad institucionem eggregii ac perfulgentis uiri domini Guillermi Grai. . . As Werken was in Cologne in 1447 he must have joined Grey in Rome and not have gone to Italy with him.

[7] Grey was already in England in September 1454, when he was consecrated Bishop at Mortlake (Le Neve, op. cit. vol. I, p. 339). But he may have settled here again in 1452, when he was sent home to bring the pallium to Cardinal Kemp (C.P.R. vol. X, p. 603). On the other hand Vespasiano states that he was in Rome when he was provided to the See of Ely (Da Bisticci, op. cit. p. 215). He must have been in England from the second part of 1451 to the beginning of 1452 since letters of protection for his journey to Rome were issued on 15 October, 1451, and 12 March, 1452 (Calendar of French Rolls, pp. 387, 391).

and neo-classical writings had assumed respectable proportions.

During his tenure of the Bishopric of Ely, Grey found himself burdened with state business as well as ecclesiastical duties: during the course of the Civil War he served on a commission for arbitration between the Dukes of York and Somerset.[1] But politically his sympathies were decidedly Yorkist, and in June 1460 it was he and George Neville, Bishop of Exeter, who took an armed force to join the Earls of Warwick and Salisbury.[2] From 25 October, 1469, until the following July Grey occupied the office of Treasurer,[2] and after Edward IV's restoration he found more employment from the Crown in diplomatic and political capacities.[2] Always, whether in his diocese or in his Manor of Holborn, he appears to have lived in great state and followed his favourite studies until his death on 4 August, 1478.[3]

According to Vespasiano, Grey purchased books in Cologne, Florence, Padua, and Ferrara,[2] and the remains of his collection confirm the statement of his biographer. He had begun to collect already during his residence in Oxford, where his private library seems to have enjoyed a certain reputation in academic circles.[5] Several of his books were actually acquired by him in Oxford: others probably came to him from relatives, as was the case with his copy of Higden's *Polichronicon*,[6] some he obtained possibly from religious institutions.[7] But the main bulk, and by far the most important part of his collection, was acquired by him during his travels abroad. In Cologne he not only purchased several manuscripts, but he also encouraged members of his own household, like Richard Bole, and local scribes, like Theodorick Werken, who later joined him at Rome in 1448, to copy manuscripts for him.[8] When he reached Florence he immediately

---

[1] Rymer, op. cit. vol. XI, p. 362.

[2] Worcester, *Annales Rerum Anglicarum*, p. 772; P.R. 1466–77, pp. 176, 211. In 1471 he was one of the ambassadors treating with the Scots (Rymer, op. cit. vol. XI, pp. 717, 748, 776).

[3] Le Neve, op. cit. vol. I, p. 339; Wharton, *Anglia Sacra*, vol. I, p. 672.

[4] Da Bisticci, op. cit. p. 214.

[5] Cf. *supra*, p. 86; MSS. Balliol Coll. Oxford, nn. 23, 40, 42, 229, were almost certainly purchased by Grey in Oxford.

[6] Now MS. Balliol Coll. Oxford, no. 236.

[7] Like MS. Balliol Coll. Oxford, no. 178, which he probably obtained from St. Mary's, Woburn.

[8] MSS. Balliol Coll. Oxford, nn. 13, 124b, were probably acquired by Grey in Cologne; on other MSS. acquired there by him cf. *supra*, p. 87, n. 6. For Bole as Grey's scribe cf. *infra*, p. 96. The following MSS. were transcribed by Werken for Grey: MSS. Balliol Coll. Oxford, nn. 66, 67a, 328, pts. 1(?), 2, and the MSS. mentioned *supra*, p. 87, n. 2. On Werken in Rome cf. *supra*, p. 90. Grey may have brought Werken to England with him, this being suggested by MS. Balliol Coll. Oxford, no. 34, which was finished by this scribe in London

went to see the famous bookseller Vespasiano da Bisticci,[1] and he befriended while there the scribe Antonio Mario,[1] who with another Florentine scribe, Gherardo del Ciriagio,[1] prepared several manuscripts for him. More books were obtained by him in Padua, Ferrara, and in Rome, where besides purchasing many he employed scribes.[2] Foreign and especially German scribes appear to have found favour with Grey, who even after his return to England availed himself of the services of Reynbold, a German scribe working in Oxford, who transcribed several theological treatises for him during the period 1461–65.[3]

Unlike such continental bibliophiles of his time as Federico da Montefeltro, he does not appear to have disapproved of printing, since there is now preserved in Balliol College a printed Josephus,[4] formerly in his library. Grey's library[5] shows clearly that theology of a Scotist complexion was his main interest. Of the extant manuscripts once possessed by him the majority contain theological treatises. An important minority, however, is constituted by classical and modern writings, amongst which are to be found several Latin translations from the Greek. The Renaissance versions of Greek authors suggest Grey's special interest in philosophy: amongst them were Aristotle's *Politics*[6] and *Ethics*,[6] the pseudo Platonic *Axiochus*,[7] and Plato's *Eutiphron*,[7] *Timaeus*,[7] and *Apologia Socratis*.[8] He also owned Rinuccio Aretino's Latin text of the Brutus correspondence,[9] Fran-

in 1462. Werken was still alive in 1478, when he finished a two volume St. Jerome now MSS. Trinity Coll. Cambridge, nn. 990–1.

[1] Da Bisticci, op. cit. p. 214. MSS. Balliol Coll. Oxford, nn. 78b, 154, 248e, all of which belonged to Grey, were copied by Antonio Mario in 1446, 1448, and 1449. Nn. 78b and 154 were made expressly for Grey, this being shown by scribal notes, cf. for instance no. 154, fo. 2ʳ: *Lege feliciter mi suauissime Ghuighlelme*. Mario worked for Vespasiano (Mazzatinti, *La Biblioteca dei Re d'Aragona*, pp. X–XI). MS. Balliol Coll. Oxford, no. 248b was copied by Gherardo del Ciriagio in 1448. Grey obtained it in all probability from Vespasiano, since it is known that Ciriagio worked for Grey's biographer (MSS. (V.L.) Vat. Urb. nn. 1314, 1323).

[2] Cf. *supra*, p. 90.

[3] Now MSS. Balliol Coll. Oxford, nn. 202–6, 209, 216, 291. Reynbold was working in Oxford as early as 1453, (MS. (B.L.) Ballard, no. 40, fo. 70ʳ).

[4] Weiss, *The Earliest Catalogues of the Library of Lincoln College*, p. 354, n. 20.

[5] Besides his MSS. now in the Library of Balliol College, Oxford, a list of which is in H. O. Coxe, *Catalogus Codicum MSS. qui in Collegiis Aulisque Oxoniensibus hodie adservantur*, part I, *passim*, Grey owned the following MSS.: MSS. (B.M.) Royal, 7.F.XII, (B.L.) Bodl. nn. 252, 312, 753, Laud. Misc. no. 209, (C.U.) Dd. XIII. 2, Ff.IV.11, Kk.IV.2, Musée Plantin, Antwerp, nn. 52, 77, Bibliothèque de la Ville, Douai, no. 750. Leland's account of Balliol library includes several classical and humanistic MSS. now there no longer, the majority of which came doubtless from Grey. Cf. Leland, *Collectanea*, vol. IV, pp. 60–7.

[6] MS. Balliol Coll. Oxford, no. 242.

[7] Now part of MS. Balliol Coll. Oxford, no. 131.

[8] Now part of MS. Balliol Coll. Oxford, no. 315.

[9] Now part of MS. Balliol Coll. Oxford, no. 131.

cesco Filelfo's version of two orations of Lysias and one of
Dio Crysostomos,[1] Valla's Thucydides,[2] Plutarch's *De Virtute et
Vitio*[3] latinized by Cencio Romano, Lucian's *De Amicitia*,[3] and
the Latin Aesop by Rinuccio Aretino.[4] Strangely enough Grey
does not appear to have possessed the modern translations of
Plutarch's *Lives* which were so popular during the fifteenth century, but of course it is possible that he had a copy of them now
lost. Several other humanist translations from the Greek are
registered by Leland in his account of Balliol College Library.[5]
But this is not in itself proof that Grey was once their owner,
although it is quite probable that most of them came from him.
Some medieval translations of Greek ecclesiastical authors were
also to be found in Grey's library alongside with that of St. John
Crysostomus by Ambrogio Traversari.[6] Instead no original
Greek texts appear to have been owned by him, while the only
evidence of any interest in the Greek language is provided by a
Graeco-Latin dictionary,[6] a medieval compilation of little value,
possibly similar to the *Verba greca et interpretaciones lingue latine*
given to Oxford by Duke Humphrey.[7]

Passing to the Latin classics, besides several works well-known
throughout the Middle Ages, Grey possessed the *Panegyrici
Veteres*[8] and Pliny's *Panegyric to Trajan*,[8] both of which had only
been discovered by Giovanni Aurispa in 1433 in Mainz,[9] the
Natural History of the Elder Pliny[10] and the pseudo-Plinian *De
Viris Illustribus*,[10] the compilations of Nonius Marcellus[10] and
Festus Pompeius,[10] the latter a very rare text even in Italy until
the end of the fifteenth century,[11] Quintilian,[12] Cicero's Letters[13]
and various of the recently discovered orations and rhetorical
works.[14] Besides these, the *Ars Rhetorica* of Chirius Consultus
Fortunatianus, and the treatise on diphthongs by the Pseudo-

---

[1] Cf. *supra*, p. 92, n. 9.
[2] MS. (C.U.) Kk. IV.2.
[3] Now part of MS. Balliol Coll. Oxford, no. 315.
[4] Now part of MS. Balliol Coll. Oxford, no. 131.
[5] Leland, *Collectanea*, vol. IV, pp. 60–7.
[6] MSS. Balliol Coll. Oxford, nn. 154–5.
[7] Cf. *supra*, p. 63.
[8] Now part of MS. Balliol Coll. Oxford, no. 315.
[9] *Carteggio di Giovanni Aurispa*, ed. R. Sabbadini, Roma, 1931, p. 82.
[10] Now part of MSS. Balliol Coll. Oxford, nn. 249, 262, 237.
[11] Sabbadini, *Scoperte*, vol. II, p. 222.
[12] Now MS. Balliol Coll. Oxford, no. 138.
[13] Now MS. Balliol Coll. Oxford, no. 248c. This MS. includes fourteen books of letters
Ad Atticum, and the sixteen books of letters *Ad Familiares*.
[14] Now MSS. Balliol Coll. Oxford, nn. 248a, b, d, e, (C.U.) Dd. XIII. 2. Grey owned also
a précis of the *Pro Ligario*, now part of MS. Balliol Coll. Oxford, no. 128.

Apuleius were probably also in his hands, since Perotti made a copy of both in Grey's house in Ferrara.[1] Neither historians nor poets occupy a prominent place in the collection. On the other hand treatises on grammar and rhetoric are common. Among the Latin authors Cicero occupies the main place with several sumptuously prepared volumes, a clear indication that their owner shared the humanists' devotion for this author.

Of much interest also is the contemporary side of the library. Besides the writings of early humanists and poligraphers like Domenico di Bandino,[2] Benvenuto da Imola,[3] and Petrarch, of whom he possessed the letters,[4] Grey owned works by Valla,[5] Flavio Biondo,[6] Tortellio,[6] Aurispa,[7] Poggio,[7] Bruni,[8] Gasparino Barzizza,[9] Guarino,[9] Francesco Barbaro,[9] Bartolomeo Fazio,[9] and perhaps Giovanni da Ravenna[10] and Sicco Polenton.[10] Nor should it be omitted to mention that he owned a copy of Richard de Bury's *Philobiblon*,[11] a book which doubtless appealed to his bibliophile instincts.

William Grey left his collection to the library of Balliol College, where part of it is still kept.[12] According to Leland,[13] he

[1] Cf. *supra*, p. 89, n. 5.

[2] His copy of the *Fons Rerum Memorabilium* is now MS. Balliol Coll. Oxford, no. 238.

[3] Grey's copy of Benvenuto's commentary on Lucan is now MS. Balliol Coll. Oxford, no. 144. He also owned Dionigi da Borgo San Sepolcro's commentary on Valerius Maximus, his copy being now MS. Balliol Coll. Oxford, no. 122.

[4] Now MS. Balliol Coll. Oxford, no. 126.

[5] Besides Valla's Thucydides, (*supra*, p. 93) he probably owned the copy of the *Elegantiae* and the *in Raudensem* and *in Facium* now MS. Balliol Coll. Oxford, no. 233.

[6] Grey owned Biondo's *Italia Illustrata* and Tortellio's *De Orthographia*, his copies being now MSS. Balliol Coll. Oxford, nn. 286, 290.

[7] He possessed Aurispa's *De contentione praesidentiae Alexandri Hannibalis, etc.*, and an oration of Poggio. Cf. MSS. Balliol Coll. Oxford, nn. 125, 315.

[8] Besides several of his versions from the Greek, Grey possessed Bruni's preface to the *Phaedo*, now part of MS. Balliol Coll. Oxford, no. 125, the *Isagogicon*, *Commentaria Rerum Graecarum*, and a Latin version of three speeches from the ninth book of the *Iliad*. Grey's copy of these is now part of MS. Balliol Coll. Oxford, no. 315.

[9] Grey's copy of Barzizza's letters is now MS. Balliol Coll. Oxford, no. 132. His MS. of Guarino's orations and letters is now MS. Balliol Coll. Oxford, no. 135. He also owned MS. Balliol Coll. Oxford, no. 125, which includes orations by Guarino, Barzizza, and Barbaro. His copy of Fazio's *In Laurentium Vallam Grammaticum* is in MS. Balliol Coll. Oxford, no. 131.

[10] Grey was probably the owner of MSS. Balliol Coll. Oxford, nn. 288, 295, which contain works by Giovanni da Ravenna and Sicco Polenton.

[11] Now MS. Balliol Coll. Oxford, no. 166a.

[12] Although we possess no contemporary evidence on it, it seems certain that Grey's books reached Balliol after his death. That they were acquired by the college after 1475 is quite certain since they include a printed Josephus (*supra*, p. 92) issued about 1475. Grey contributed to the building of Balliol Library. His coat of arms is still to be found on two of the library windows.

[13] Leland, *Collectanea*, vol. IV, p. 23. No trace of these MSS. is to be found either in the library of Peterhouse, nor in its catalogue compiled in 1418–81, printed in James, *A ... Catalogue of the Manuscripts ... of Peterhouse, Cambridge*, pp. 3–26. Possibly Grey never pre-

also presented several books to Peterhouse, Cambridge, of which
he was Visitor as Bishop of Ely, and the Master of which, John
Warkworth, was one of his chaplains. As a collection it was no
doubt one of the most important of its kind formed by an Englishman during the fifteenth century, and it is doubtful whether
even the library assembled by John Tiptoft, Earl of Worcester,[1]
exceeded it in numbers and variety of contents. It is chiefly of
importance because it contained works hitherto unknown in
England which became available to at any rate some Oxford
scholars after 1478.

The position of Grey in the history of English humanism
should, like that of Humphrey, Duke of Gloucester, be viewed
from the angle of patronage rather than that of actual scholarly
achievement. His main intellectual interest seems to have been
Divinity, and although he was genuinely interested in things
classical, it is very doubtful that he ever went beyond reading his
books. That he knew Greek is unlikely, although opportunities
for learning it were amply available to him in Ferrara. The absence of Greek texts in his library, as well as the omission of Greek
quotations in Free's letters[2] to him, corroborates the already
strong suspicion that he knew no Greek, for it seems probable
that Free would have flaunted his knowledge of it in his letters
if it would have been understood by his patron.

If Grey's scholarship was indifferent,[3] his patronage was
undoubtedly discriminating and far reaching. Thanks to him
Perotti could pursue his studies,[4] Free was able to go to Italy,[4]
and Balliol College acquired a very large collection of classical
and humanistic manuscripts. There is no doubt that we owe
much of Free's brilliant achievement to Grey, since it seems very
unlikely that he could have distinguished himself as a classical
scholar had he remained in England. This places Grey on a level
with Duke Humphrey, and if the latter exceeded him in his
patronage of Italian scholars, Grey was on the other hand re-

sented MSS. to this college but gave some to his chaplain John Warkworth who was Master
of Peterhouse from 1473 to 1498. Warkworth was a benefactor of his college library, and
consequently it is possible that Leland may have seen Grey's name on some MSS. presented
by Warkworth, and inferred from that that Grey had given them.

[1] On which cf. *infra*, p. 117.

[2] Free's letters to others contain occasional quotations in Greek, (Schirmer, op. cit. p.
131.

[3] A letter of Grey to the Convent of Ely written in 1465 is in MS. Lambeth Palace, no.
448, fo. 99ʳ; but it is probably the work of a secretary and suggests no classical influences.

[4] Cf. *supra*, p. 89, *infra*, p. 107.

sponsible for the beginnings of one of the greatest fifteenth century English humanists.

The bibliophile and classical interests of Grey were shared by his secretary, Richard Bole.[1] The connexion between them had in all likelihood originated at Balliol College, where Bole held a fellowship[1] at the time of Grey's residence there. When Grey went to Germany in 1442, Bole accompanied him and matriculated with him at Cologne University;[2] it is not known, however, whether he also followed him to Ferrara and Rome.[2] From 1452–6 Bole held a prebend in St. Paul's, London,[3] and he was 'King's Clerk' in 1458,[4] when he was appointed with John Tiptoft, Earl of Worcester, and others to bring Henry VI's obedience to the newly-elected Pius II.[4] In 1467 at the latest he rejoined his friend Grey who appointed him Archdeacon of Ely during that year.[5] Like Grey, Bole was one of the early benefactors of Balliol College Library, the books he presented to it bearing witness to his literary inclinations. The twelve manuscripts given by him to his college include Petrarch's *Secretum*,[6] Poggio's *De Vera Nobilitate* and *De Avaritia*,[6] Gasparino Barzizza's *De Elocutione*,[7] a *Lexicon* of Servius' commentary on Vergil by Guarino,[8] and the Letters of Leonardo Bruni.[9] Amongst these Guarino's *Lexicon* is particularly interesting, and it is possible that it came from Grey, from whom may also have come the other manuscripts in Bole's collection executed by the scribe Werken.[10] Besides being a discriminating bibliophile, Bole was also an accomplished scribe. During his visit to Cologne he is known to have transcribed texts for Grey,[11] but his skill was also

---

[1] On Bole cf. Mitchell, *John Tiptoft*, pp. 74–5. On his being a fellow of Balliol cf. MS. Balliol Coll. Oxford, no. 258, fo. 1ᵛ.

[2] Cf. *supra*, p. 87. His appointment as a *procurator* to recover money in England due to the English Hospice in Rome in 1450 (Flynn, op. cit. p. 123) suggests a visit to Rome. His name may on the other hand have been suggested by Grey who was also connected with the Hospice (*supra*, p. 90, n. 5).

[3] Le Neve, op. cit. vol. II, p. 430. He appears as Prebendary of St. Mary Southwell, in 1450 (Flynn, op. cit. p. 123).

[4] P.R. 1452–61, p. 487.

[5] Le Neve, op. cit. vol. I, p. 351. Bole died in 1477 (*Ibid.*, vol. I, p. 351).

[6] Now MS. Balliol Coll. Oxford, no. 127 (copied by T. Werken in 1450).

[7] Now part of MS. Balliol Coll. Oxford, no. 123. This MS. contains also a commentary on Sallust and a treatise by Giles of Rome.

[8] In MS. Balliol Coll. Oxford, no. 287 (copied by T. Werken in 1450). On this *Lexicon* cf. Sabbadini, *Il Metodo degli Umanisti*, pp. 31–2. The *Lexicon* in this MS. is the shorter of the two recensions distinguished by Sabbadini.

[9] Now MS. Balliol Coll. Oxford, no. 310, (copied by T. Werken in 1449).

[10] Now MSS. Balliol Coll. Oxford, nn. 34, 127, 287, 310.

[11] MS. Balliol Coll. Oxford, no. 78a (St. Augustine), was written by Bole in Cologne for Grey in 1442. The Sallust transcribed by Bole is now MS. Balliol Coll. Oxford, no. 258.

applied to increase his own collection as is testified by a Sallust which he finished in 1461.[1]

So far all the exponents of modern learning in England belonged to the patron and bibliophile type. Altogether they shared but few of the activities of the Italians, while perhaps their main characteristic was potentiality rather than actual achievement. Mere capability is, however, not enough to launch an intellectual movement, and had English humanism not acquired a fresh impetus, its development would probably have come to a standstill. A new kind of scholar, who was a compromise between the type exemplified by Bekynton, Moleyns, and Grey, and the average Italian humanist, began, however, to be found in England after the middle of the fifteenth century, and is the product of the school of Guarino.

The first Englishman presenting such features was Robert Flemmyng, the second English pupil of Guarino, who became Dean of Lincoln in 1452. A nephew of Richard Flemmyng, Bishop of Lincoln and founder of Lincoln College, Oxford, he was born about 1415.[2] Through family influence he soon found his way open to ecclesiastical preferment, and shortly after matriculating at Oxford University he obtained his first benefice, a prebend in Lincoln Cathedral.[3] At Oxford he lived in University College where he occupied rooms from January 1430,[4] and after obtaining his arts degree he continued to reside there,[4] probably in order to read Divinity. In 1438 Flemmyng, then a Master of Arts,[4] was elected one of the University Proctors.[5] This and his continued residence in rooms in college until the summer of 1443,[6] suggests that he had planned to take up an academic career, perhaps as a fitting introduction to advancement in the church. During 1443 Flemmyng left Oxford in order to pursue his theological studies abroad, and during the summer of 1444 he matriculated in the University of Cologne.[7] It is

[1] Cf. *supra*, p. 96, n. 11.

[2] On Flemmyng cf. especially Schirmer, op. cit. pp. 141–9, Leland, *De Scriptoribus*, pp. 460–1, Tanner, op. cit. p. 287. The *D.N.B.* gives a short account of him in the article on Richard Flemmyng. The year of Flemmyng's birth is unknown, but his going to Oxford in 1430 suggests that he was born about 1415.

[3] Le Neve, op. cit. vol. II, p. 187. He was installed into it by proxy on 3 August, 1430.

[4] The rolls of the *Computus* of the *Procurator* of University College, Oxford, still preserved in the college treasury, show that Flemmyng took a room there as a *commensalis* together with John Flemmyng in January 1430, and kept it until 1432 when he started to occupy a room alone. He is styled *Magister* for the first time in the *Computus* from Pentecost 15 Henry VI to Pentecost 16 Henry VI.   [5] *Register of the University of Oxford*, vol. I, p. 23.

[6] *Computus*, Easter 22 Henry VI–Pentecost 23 Henry VI.

[7] Keussen, op. cit. vol. I, p. 477.

H

uncertain whether Grey was still in Cologne when Flemmyng arrived: whatever the case as they had probably met at Oxford, it seems likely that Flemmyng's travels were inspired by Grey's previous peregrinations.[1]

The length of Flemmyng's visit to Cologne is uncertain, but it is certain that he did not take a degree there since in 1446 he was still reading theology, this time at Padua, where he obtained his Bachelorship of Divinity on September 4th of the following year.[2] Already while in Padua Flemmyng had begun to take an interest in things classical. This is shown by his transcribing there Cicero's *De Officiis*.[3] Moreover, the script of this copy displays very marked humanistic characteristics, no doubt derived from the study of contemporary Italian manuscripts, and proves that Flemmyng was already by that time under the influence of humanism. It was doubtless this interest in polite letters that induced him after accomplishing his theological studies to follow the lectures of Guarino da Verona, as William Grey had done before him.[3] It is not known exactly when Flemmyng went to Ferrara: however, it seems quite certain that he went there after obtaining his degree at Padua, and that he did not remain there after 1451.[4] During his attendance at Guarino's school, Flemmyng gained some knowledge of Greek, while his Latin acquired a neo-classical flavour which, in spite of its short-comings, shows the thoroughness of his attempts to capture the spirit of humanism. Flemmyng's return to England was followed by advancement in the church. In 1452 he was admitted Dean of Lincoln Cathedral:[5] in 1453 he was already a chaplain to Henry VI:[5] two years later he was declared qualified for the Chancellor-ship of Oxford University though not a doctor.[6] Attainment of

[1] On which cf. *supra*, pp. 87–90.

[2] Verrua, op. cit. p. 77. His presence in Padua is also recorded on 29 January, 1446, when he was one of the witnesses to Thomas Balscott's degree (*Ibid.*, loc. cit.).

[3] Cf. *infra*, p. 103 n. 6. On Grey at Ferrara, cf. *supra*, pp. 88–9.

[4] Flemmyng cannot have gone to Ferrara to read under Guarino before the autumn of 1447 since he was in Padua until then. He must have left Ferrara not later than 1451 since he was already in England in January 1452, when he was installed Dean of Lincoln Cathedral. The possibility of his reading under Guarino at a later date is excluded as he must have already known Greek in 1453, when he borrowed a Greek MS. (*infra*, p. 99,). Moreover, when he visited Italy as King's Proctor he would have been unable to live in Ferrara, as is shown by the case of Grey who had to leave that town after being appointed to that office (*supra*, p. 89). The only contemporary source for Flemmyng's attendance of Guarino's school is Carbone's panegyric of Guarino (Bertoni, op. cit. p. 167). Leland, *De Scriptoribus*, p. 460, states that Flemmyng was a pupil of Battista Guarino, but Leland was clearly con-founding Battista with his father.

[5] On 21 January, 1452, (Le Neve, op. cit. vol. II, p. 33). *C.P.R.* vol. X, p. 130.

[6] Boase, op. cit. vol. I, p. 23. This is the only known instance of such a dispensation, which shows the University's anxiety to place him under an obligation.

an important ecclesiastical position had not, however, caused him to set aside his literary interests. His borrowing of a Greek manuscript from Derley Priory in 1453[1] suggests that he had not relinquished his Greek studies, and that perhaps he was anxious to obtain as many Greek books as he could lay hands on. Luckily for Flemmyng's intellectual pursuits he was soon to return to Italy. Ludovico Carbone in his funeral panegyric of Guarino states that it was Flemmyng's proficiency in the humanities that caused his appointment as King's Proctor in Rome in 1455.[2] That this was the only reason that led to such an appointment may perhaps be open to doubt, but it almost certainly was one of the main causes for it, other reasons being obviously his knowledge of Italy and his personal ability. For motives unknown to us Flemmyng did not leave for Rome then: however, his commission was renewed two years later,[3] and both in 1457[4] and 1458[4] he was appointed also King's Orator to Pope Callixtus III. Actually his departure from England must have taken place before the autumn of 1458 when he was to be found at the Court of Rome, and was appointed an Apostolic Protonotary by Pope Pius II.[5] The Roman Curia with its establishment of distinguished scholars could but prove a congenial residence for Flemmyng, who doubtless while there collected most of the classical and modern texts which he presented to Lincoln College in 1465.[6] His appointment as King's Orator with John Tiptoft in 1459[7] on an embassy which never materialized was made during this visit, but political events in England were soon to terminate his 'Roman career.' As a supporter of Henry VI Flemmyng could hardly expect employment from the Yorkists: it is therefore

[1] Now MS. (B.L.) Laud. Gr. no. 28 (St. Basil's *Liturgy*). The following note on fo. 1ʳ shows how it reached Flemmyng: *Iste liber est de abbathia de Derley accomodatus uenerabili uiro magistro Roberto Flemmyng decano Lyncolnie in uigilia epiphanie anno Domini mcccclij.*

[2] Bertoni, op. cit. p. 167. He was appointed Proctor in Rome on 18 March, 1455, (P.R. 1452–61, p. 277).

[3] On 4 February, 1457 (*Ibid.*, p. 336).

[4] *Ibid.*, pp. 362, 424. Flemmyng was still in England in 1457 (MS. Lincoln Coll. Oxford, no. 63, fo. 5ʳ).

[5] Flemmyng's presence at the Roman Curia in 1458 is proved by his appointment as Protonotary which enjoined him to take his oath of office before the Cardinal of San Lorenzo in Damaso (*C.P.R.* vol. XI, p. 681). Had he been in England at the time he would have been required to take the oath before an English Bishop, as was for instance the case of Thomas Chaundler when he was made a Protonotary in 1480 (*Ibid.*, vol. XIII, p. 80). Flemmyng must have already taken his oath on 23 November, 1458, when he was styled 'Protonotary' in a Papal letter (*Ibid.*, vol. XI, p. 517).

[6] On this collection cf. Weiss, *The Earliest Catalogues of the Library of Lincoln College, passim.*

[7] P.R. 1452–61, p. 487. The commission describes Flemmyng as 'King's Clerk.'

not surprising to find that his proctorship came to an end with
the accession of Edward IV to the English throne in 1461. It is
true that already in the spring of 1460 he was planning a return
to England:[1] none the less this was not due to the termination of
his office then, since his successor, Francesco Coppini, the notorious Bishop of Terni, whom Pius II had sent to England as legate
in 1458 and who had only too readily identified himself with
the Yorkist cause, was only appointed King's Proctor in Rome
in 1461.[2] Back in England Flemmyng went once more to live in
University College, Oxford, where he occupied rooms during the
period 1462–72.[3] His activities during this time are unknown,
though one can easily conjecture that he must have continued
with his favourite studies. But a donation of classical and
modern texts made by him to Lincoln College, Oxford, in 1465,[4]
attracts attention during these otherwise obscure years for his
biography. Lincoln was, like University College, an Oxford
foundation dedicated exclusively to the pursuit of Divinity. By
1465 Flemmyng had already the experience of two long visits to
Italy and was well imbued with the spirit of neo-classicism.
Hence it appears practically certain that behind this donation
rested a desire to improve the theological studies pursued in
Lincoln College through the introduction of Italian values.
Had it not been so why should he have showered upon those
medievally minded theologians a valuable collection of texts of
purely classical interest?

The Court of Rome doubtless made a strong appeal to
Flemmyng. Not only did he return to Rome, but he also
followed the Papal Court to Tivoli during the summer of 1473.[5]
The nature of his curial duties at this time is uncertain: on the
other hand, we know that this visit lasted at least until the end of
1477,[6] and that Flemmyng found sufficient leisure to dedicate
himself to the pursuit of letters. Some of his Latin poems were

---

[1] A safeconduct to him and his retinue to the number of twelve returning to England was
issued in Siena on 26 April, 1460 (*C.P.R.* vol. XI, p. 574).

[2] *P.R.* 1461–7, p. 55.

[3] *Computus*, 2 Edward IV–12 Edward IV.

[4] Weiss, *The Earliest Catalogues of the Library of Lincoln College*, p. 356, n. 61. Until Flemmyng's gift neither classical nor humanistic texts were to be found in Lincoln College. Cf.
the '1474' list of the college library in *Ibid.* which discloses that the only literary MSS.
there were Flemmyng's.

[5] Where he first conceived the *Lucubratiunculae Tiburtinae*. That his stay with the Papal
Court in Tivoli must have taken place in 1473 is clear, as this was the first year before 1477
(when the *Lucubratiunculae* was finished, cf. *infra*, p. 102) in which Sixtus IV spent the
summer at Tivoli (Pastor op. cit. vol. IV, p. 249).

[6] When he finished the *Lucubratiunculae* in Rome (*infra* p. 102, n. 4).

composed during this second 'Roman period' which also witnessed the rise of his friendship with the famous humanist and Papal Librarian, Bartolomeo Platina, whom one may well imagine watching over Flemmyng's studies in the Vatican Library.[1] The year 1478 saw Flemmyng's return to England and installation in the Prebend of Leighton Buzzard in Lincoln Cathedral.[2] As far as we know he never left his native country again, and he died in 1483.[3]

How Flemmyng's interest in humanism arose must remain a matter for conjecture. Yet when we realize that he only left Oxford in the summer of 1443, it seems reasonable to suggest that he saw some of the books given by Gloucester to the University in 1439, and that these were instrumental in attracting him towards classicism. To this may be added the likelihood that he had already heard in Oxford of Guarino's reputation as a humanist and teacher,[4] and that this stimulated a desire in him to go to Italy to learn the humanities at his school.

Flemmyng occupies a prominent position in the history of early English humanism because of his Latin writings, his bibliophily, and his knowledge of Greek. This knowledge, so far denied to fifteenth century Englishmen, he doubtless acquired from Guarino,[5] and soon the study of things Greek became one of his favourite intellectual pursuits. The compilation of a Graeco-Latin dictionary now lost but which was seen by Leland,[6] a task probably suggested to him by his teacher Guarino,[6] testifies to his painstaking study of that language. His industry in this respect is also emphasized by the numerous Greek notes which he scribbled on the margins of his books.[7] No doubt his proficiency in Greek was not such as to rival Free's mastery of that language. Nevertheless it is evident that Flemmyng was sufficiently well acquainted with it to understand classical texts and

---

[1] On his knowledge of the library and friendship with Platina cf. *Lucubraciuncularum Libri Duo*, ff. 13ᵛ–14ʳ.

[2] On December 3rd (Le Neve, op. cit. vol. II, p. 172).

[3] On August 12th. He was buried in Lincoln Cathedral; his will was proved on 23 August, 1483 (*Ibid.*, vol. II, p. 33).

[4] On Guarino's reputation in England cf. *infra*, p. 107, n. 6.

[5] This seems certain since he knew Greek in 1453 (*supra*, p. 99), and he could not have learnt it at Oxford or Cologne. It is also most unlikely that he could have learnt it in Padua, since Greek was not taught at that University during Flemmyng's visit to that town.

[6] Leland, *De Scriptoribus*, p. 461. Guarino encouraged his pupils to compile lists of Greek words (Sabbadini, *Il Metodo degli Umanisti*, p. 33).

[7] Cf. MSS. Lincoln Coll. Oxford, nn. 41, 43, 46, 84, and especially the notes in no. 43, ff. 18ʳ, 35ʳ, 107ʳ, etc. The note on fo. 107ʳ is especially interesting as it is a quotation from Euripides, an author also mentioned in the *Lucubratiunculae*.

write in Greek characters without difficulty.[1] Passing to his
Latin scholarship, we know that Flemmyng wrote several poems
and epistles.[2] Unfortunately these are now lost, but there luckily
remains a volume of Latin verse by him printed in Rome during
the last quarter of the fifteenth century,[3] which is valuable for
our knowledge of his Latin learning. This work, which he
entitled *Lucubratiunculae Tiburtinae*, was first conceived, as its
title shows, during his stay with the Papal Court at Tivoli in
1473, and was finished in Rome in 1477.[4] The *Lucubratiunculae*
opens with praises of Sixtus IV and his birthplace Savona,
followed by the history of the Pope's youth. Sixtus IV's anxiety
to embellish Rome, the jubilee of 1475, and the restoration of the
Lateran and the Sixtine Bridge, occupy several lines of the poem.
The Sixtine chapel is described, the Vatican library is compared
with that of Alexandria, and the learning of its librarian, Platina,
is extolled, all to the greater glory of Sixtus IV. The second
book of the *Lucubratiunculae* begins with a description of the
plague that ravaged Rome in 1475–76 obviously modelled in
part upon Lucretius' account of the plague in Athens.[5] Short
panegyrics of each of the Pope's relatives follow, and it ends
with a final laudation of the poem's hero, Pope Sixtus IV.

The value of the *Lucubratiunculae Tiburtinae* is more historical
than literary. Its hexameters contain a large number of false
quantities, and possess neither the fluency nor the elegance of
those of contemporary Italian humanists. Nevertheless it is
quite evident that Flemmyng strove to give a classical atmosphere to his work. His diction, his metaphors, attempt to be
those of a humanist. It is true that his prosody is often faulty and
his Latinity unsatisfactory when judged by Italian standards;
yet when we bear in mind that the *Lucubratiunculae* was the work

---

[1] Cf. *supra*, p. 101, n. 7.

[2] Pits, *Relationum Historicarum de Rebus Anglicis*, p. 659, assigns the following works to
Flemmyng: '*Lucubrationum Tiburtinarum Libri Duo, Epistolarum ad diversos librum unum,
Carmina diversi generis librum unum, Dictionarium Graeco-Latinum, et alia non pauca.*'

[3] Hain, no. 3612. The only known MS. of the *Lucubratiunculae* is MS. National-Bibliothek,
Vienna, no. 2403. This is a copy executed in Italy during the last quarter of the fifteenth
century, and, judging from its appearance, a presentation copy. Textual differences make it
obvious that it is not a transcript of the printed text. A MS. including the *Lucubratiunculae*
as well as poems by Free and Widow was seen by Leland (Leland, *De Scriptoribus*, p. 486).
On the *Lucubratiunculae* cf. Mann, op. cit. pp. 3–7.

[4] Cf. MS. National-Bibliothek, Vienna, no. 2403, ff. 30ʳ⁻ᵛ: *Lucubraciuncularum tiburtinarum cuiusdam protonotarii de sanctissimo ac beatissimo in christo Patre et domino nostro Sixto
quarto diuina prouidentia summo maximoque Pontifice liber secundus qui apologeticus est explicit,
exactus quidem completusque Romae ipsis nonis decembribus Anno grattae Mcccclxxvii. Ponti-
ficatus uero ipsius sanctissimi domini nostri anno septimo.*

[5] *Lucubraciuncularum Tiburtinarum Libri Duo*, ff. 17ᵛ–21ʳ.

of an Englishman with a schoolman's education, whose first direct contacts with Italian scholars began after he reached an age when it is no longer easy to assimilate a new culture, it can but seem remarkable because of its freedom from scholastic convention, and its classical form and execution. As a historical document, besides giving us an insight into its author's capacities and being the earliest appreciation of an aspect of the Renaissance written by an Englishman, the *Lucubratiunculae* is particularly important for giving us details of Sixtus IV's youth not to be found elsewhere,[1] and for furnishing the only contemporary mention of Sixtus IV's writings.[1]

The collection of Robert Flemmyng is doubtless, after Grey's, the most important one assembled by an Englishman during the fifteenth century, of which we still possess a fairly large part. As in Grey's library, theology is dominant; yet a substantial place is occupied by classical and humanistic works. Part of Flemmyng's books were purchased by him in Italy:[2] others were obtained by him in Oxford,[3] from monasteries,[4] and probably a few in Cologne during his visit there:[5] one at least, Cicero's *De Officiis*, he copied himself.[6] What makes this library particularly important is the presence of Greek manuscripts in it. Of these, two containing St. Basil's *Liturgy*,[7] the *Acts of the Apostles*,[8] and St. Paul's *Epistles*,[8] are still extant: the Graeco-Latin Dictionary mentioned by Leland[9] is now lost. Besides original Greek texts, Flemmyng owned also modern translations of classical and ecclesiastical Greek authors, which included Leonardo Bruni's translation of the *Ethics*,[10] the latinized Plutarch's *Lives*,[11] the

[1] Pastor, op. cit. vol. IV, pp. 205, 209.

[2] The literary MSS. presented by Flemmyng to Lincoln College are of Italian origin and were doubtless purchased there by him. Leland, *De Scriptoribus*, p. 461, states that he bought MSS. in Italy.

[3] Like for instance MS. Lincoln Coll. Oxford, no. 105.

[4] Like for instance MS. Lincoln Coll. Oxford, no. 63.

[5] Some of Flemmyng's books are of German origin and were probably acquired by him in Cologne. MS. Lincoln Coll. Oxford, no. 34 is probably one of these.

[6] Now MS. Lincoln Coll. Oxford, no. 43. That Flemmyng was its scribe is shown by the following note on the last flyleaf: *Constat Magistro Roberto fflemmyng quem scripsit manu propria*. On the same flyleaf we find the date 10 October, 1446, this being very probably the date when the transcription of the text was finished. The Italian character of part of its handwriting, the Italian style of its decorations, and its having been completed by October 1446, make it certain that this MS. was copied by Flemmyng in Padua. On fo. 129ʳ Flemmyng copied the passage on Cicero in Silius Italicus, *Punica*, VIII, 408–11, which appears sometimes in MSS. of the *De Officiis* (Sabbadini, *Storia e Critica di Testi Latini*, Catania, 1914, p. 166).

[7] Cf. *supra*, p. 99, n. 1.   [8] Now MS. Lincoln Coll. Oxford, Gr. no. 82.

[9] Cf. *supra*, p. 101.   [10] Now MS. Lincoln Coll. Oxford, no. 21.

[11] Weiss, *The Earliest Catalogues of the Library of Lincoln College*, p. 350. Flemmyng's copy is probably MS. Lincoln Coll. Oxford, no. 111.

Comparationes Parvae of that author translated by Guarino da Verona,[1] Diogenes Laertius in Traversari's Latin text,[1] and a translation from St. John Crysostomus by George of Trebizond.[1]

The Latin side of the collection is equally characteristic of its owner's tastes. Neither Humphrey nor Grey appear to have been particularly interested in poetry. But Flemmyng delighted in the composition of Latin verse: it is therefore natural to find Latin poets and their commentators among his books. He possessed the whole of Horace,[2] the commentaries on this poet by Porphyrion[2] and the Pseudo Acron,[2] both uncommon texts during the fifteenth century: besides these, he owned Lactantius Placidus on Statius,[2] Aelius Donatus on the Comedies of Terence,[3] the *Interpretationes Vergilianae* of Tiberius Claudius Donatus,[3] and Servius' commentary on Vergil:[3] and most important of all, he was probably the first fifteenth century Englishman to possess the *Comoediae* of Plautus.[4] Other rare Latin texts in his possession were the Letters of the Younger Pliny[5] and the pseudo-Plinian *De Viris Illustribus*,[5] Cicero's Letters[6] and several volumes of his works,[7] a complete Aulus Gellius,[8] a Livy in three volumes,[9] the *Vitae* of Cornelius Nepos,[9] and Caesar's *Gallic War*.[9] Modern works in his library included Valla's *Elegantiae*,[10] Boccaccio's *De Casibus*[10] and *De Claris Mulieribus*,[10] Bruni's *Isagogicon*,[11] and the *Adnotatio de duobus Pliniis* by Johannes Mansionarius.[12]

Through his familiarity with neo-classical manuscripts Flemmyng acquired a neat italic handwriting often to be found on the margins of his books, a clear indication also of his study of them.[13] The eventual fate of his collection is well-known. As we saw, he had already presented part of his library to Lincoln College in 1465: the rest of it he also bequeathed to that same foundation,[14] where most of it is still to be found.[15]

[1] Now MSS. Lincoln Coll. Oxford, nn. 60, 46, 35.
[2] Weiss, *The Earliest Catalogues of the Library of Lincoln College*, p. 350.
[3] Now MSS. Lincoln Coll. Oxford, nn. 45, 44, 91.
[4] Weiss, *The Earliest Catalogues of the Library of Lincoln College*, p. 350.
[5] Now part of MS. Lincoln Coll. Oxford, no. 77.
[6] Now MS. Lincoln Coll. Oxford, no. 42.
[7] Weiss, *The Earliest Catalogues of the Library of Lincoln College*, p. 349.
[8] Now MS. Lincoln Coll. Oxford, no. 59.
[9] Weiss, *The Earliest Catalogues of the Library of Lincoln College*, p. 349.
[10] Now part of MSS. Lincoln Coll. Oxford, nn. 32, 60.
[11] Weiss, *The Earliest Catalogues of the Library of Lincoln College*, p. 350.
[12] Now part of MS. Lincoln Coll. Oxford, no. 77.
[13] Cf. the notes in MSS. Lincoln Coll. Oxford, nn. 39, 43, 46, 59, 84, 91, and especially his note in no. 93, fo. 1ʳ.
[14] Leland, *De Scriptoribus*, p. 461.
[15] Cf. Coxe, op. cit. part I, section on the MSS. of Lincoln College, *passim*.

The rôle of Robert Flemmyng is of much importance in the history of humanism in England. As the first fifteenth century Englishman to learn Greek and extend his activities beyond book collecting and patronage, his career inaugurated a more advanced type of learned pursuits. As a 'Maecenas' he contributed to the introduction of humane standards into Oxford, and to the bringing of theology into contact with neo-classicism. Though his plans could only mature slowly, they are none the less suggestive of his enthusiasm. His giving away of cherished texts is indicative not only of the quality of his patronage, but also of his firm intention to advance learning. Although his Latin poetry is poor in quality and metrically unsound, it shows determined efforts to conform with humanistic models, and a painstaking study of the Latin poets. In spite of the nature of his early education, some of his intellectual pursuits were very close to those of the Italians. His learning Greek, his writings, his copying classical texts, his patronage, his close study of his books, all testify to a genuine enthusiasm for classical culture.

CHAPTER VII

IF Flemmyng's literary career constituted a decisive step towards higher standards in English humanism, with John Free these standards were elevated so far as to arouse admiration even in Italy. Until Free neo-classicism in England had been practically the close preserve of princes like Humphrey, Duke of Gloucester, or prominent prelates like Bekynton and Grey. As a result of this humanism had never formed a full time pursuit, but rather an occasional diversion from theological studies or political preoccupations. With Free we find humane studies first taken up by an Englishman as a career, and with results which were not reached again until the time of Grocin, Linacre, and Colet.

The year of John Free's birth is not known[1], and even his birthplace seemed until now doubtful. However, it now appears fairly certain that he was born in London and that he spent the early years of his life in Bristol.[1] From school Free went to Oxford, where he matriculated in 1445,[2] and where he obtained a fellowship at Balliol College open only to London-born persons.[2] Three years after matriculation, in December 1448, he supplicated for the degree of Bachelor of Arts,[3] which was eventually granted to him in June 1449.[3] After obtaining his first degree in Arts, Free continued his studies in Oxford, and in 1454 he incepted Master of Arts.[3] After this he still continued to reside

[1] On Free cf. especially Schirmer, op. cit. pp. 121–34, Leland, *De Scriptoribus*, pp. 466–8, Spingarn, *Unpublished letters of an English Humanist*. As Free matriculated in Oxford in 1445, (*infra*, n. 2) he was probably born about 1430. When in Italy Free latinized his name into Frea, (Weiss, *A letter Preface of John Free to John Tiptoft, Earl of Worcester*, p. 102, MS. (B.L.) Bodl. no. 80, fo. 3ʳ). William of Worcester calls him *ffreas* (*MS*. Balliol Coll. Oxford, no. 124, fo. 153ʳ), and states that he was born in Bristol (*Ibid.*, ff. 1ʳ, 153ʳ, MS. (B.L.) Auct. F.3.25, fo. 1ᵛ). On the other hand a note by a fifteenth century Vicar of St. Michael's Church, Bristol, states: *Magister Iohannes ffree . . . natus erat in ciuitate Londoniarum et pro Londoniensi electus est et admissus socius in collegio Ballioli*, (MS. Balliol Coll. Oxford, no. 124, fo. 153ʳ). The vicar's statement should be accepted as reliable since he was in charge of the church of which Free had been rector, and was acquainted with some of Free's Bristol relations. Cf. *Ibid.*, loc. cit.: *Iste magister Iohannes free beneficiatus erat bristollie quoniam rector sancti michaelis ibi in monte et plures ibi habuit manentes de affinitate, quos ibi noui postquam ego sum effectus uicarius ibi S. Michaelis et prior Kalendarum*. It seems consequently established that Free was London-born and probably spent his earlier life in Bristol. Leland states that he was London born (Leland, *De Scriptoribus*, p. 466).

[2] As he supplicated at the end of 1448 that three years in the Faculty of Arts should be sufficient for his B.A. (University Archives, Oxford, *Register Aa5*, fo. 21ʳ) his matriculation must have taken place in the autumn of 1445. On his Balliol fellowship cf. *supra*, n.1.

[3] *Register of Oxford University*, vol. I, p. 1.

there,[1] preparing himself at the same time to take holy orders, which he received not later than 1456 in the Diocese of Bath and Wells.[1] It was about 1456 or during this very year that Free attracted the attention of William Grey, Bishop of Ely. Grey, who had returned from Italy a few years before, wanted to send a nephew of his to Ferrara to read under Guarino, and was then looking for a suitable companion for the youth. Somehow Free, who had already begun to take a serious interest in classical studies, was brought to his notice and accordingly appointed to the post.[2] Actually Grey's nephew died before the time came for him to leave for Italy, yet Free was sent to Ferrara at the Bishop's expense.[2] Apparently Free's friends were against his going abroad, but Grey, evidently attracted by the idea of becoming the patron of a potentially distinguished scholar, persuaded him to go none the less.[2]

Free left England during the second half of 1456 reaching Ferrara during the autumn.[3] He started immediately to attend the lectures of Guarino da Verona, so that the time he spent there proved particularly profitable to him. During his visit he was able to acquire a thorough knowledge of Greek, improve his Latin style, and enter into friendly relations with other humanists residing in Ferrara, such as Janus Pannonius, Gerolamo Castiglione, and Ludovico Carbone, with all of whom he was to correspond later,[4] and probably with his compatriot John Gunthorpe, who was also reading under Guarino.[5] As a student he followed Guarino's usual advice to his pupils to practice the writing of Latin epistles as a form of exercise: one of these, written in November or December 1456, is still extant. This letter is addressed to Guarino, and in it Free tells how the previous lesson of Guarino on Cicero encouraged him to write, and of the fame of Guarino in England.[6] Besides this, his activi-

---

[1] Free was one of the trustees transferring a tenement and garden to the Master and Fellows of Balliol College on 7 September, 1456, (*Oxford Balliol Deeds*, ed. H. E. Salter, (O.H.S.) Oxford, 1913, p. 216). Free is described as clerk of the Diocese of Bath and Wells in 1459 (*C.P.R.* vol. XI, pp. 536, 571).

[2] Spingarn, op. cit. pp. 59, 63. Leland states erroneously that Free had been urged to go to Italy by some Italian merchants he had met in Bristol, (Leland, *De Scriptoribus*, p. 467).

[3] He was already in Ferrara on 22 October, 1456 (*Epistolario di Guarino Veronese*, vol. III, p. 500).

[4] Free's letter to Carbone and a fragment of a letter to Castiglione are in Schirmer, op. cit. pp. 130, n. 154, 131, n. 155. His letter to Pannonius is dated 22 October (1456) and is in Spingarn, op. cit. pp. 60–1. For the date of this letter and the identification of its addressee with Janus Pannonius cf. *Epistolario di Guarino Veronese*, vol. III, p. 500. Carbone mentions Free in his panegyric of Guarino (Bertoni, op. cit. p. 167).

[5] *Infra*, p. 123.

[6] The letter is in *Epistolario di Guarino Veronese*, vol. II, pp. 652–3. Free was not flattering

ties included the taking of copious lecture notes,[1] the composition of at least one Latin oration,[2] as well as the increasing of
his small stock of books by copying ancient and modern texts.[3]

The residence of Free in Ferrara was, however, rendered less
enjoyable to him by lack of means. Apparently after his arrival
there he received no money from his patron for some time, thus
being forced to pawn books and clothes with the local Jewish
moneylenders in order to subsist.[4] However, after repeated
appeals for assistance Grey again resumed his allowance to him,
so that in a letter written in 1458 Free could be bold enough to
ask for an increase in order to purchase Greek manuscripts.[5]
Free's letters from Ferrara show the rapidity with which he
assimilated the teaching of Guarino. They are the letters of a
writer who can express himself in Latin with elegance and liveli-
ness, and has a vast store of classical knowledge at his disposal
which he knows how to display. The influence of Cicero on this
correspondence is obvious, and the precepts of Guarino to his
pupils on the subject of epistolography are obviously followed.[6]
Hence events, such as the death of Lorenzo Valla, or the festivities that took place in Ferrara to celebrate the election of Pope
Pius II, are incorporated amidst private news and conventional
flattery.[7]

Ferrara did not hold Free for very long for sometime after the
summer of 1458 he left for Padua,[8] which then shared with
Montpellier a deserved prominence in the teaching of medicine.

Guarino. That the latter's reputation stood high in England already during the first half
of the fifteenth century is undoubted. Gloucester was anxious to possess versions from the
Greek by him and was an admirer of his scholarship (*supra* p. 50, n. 4, Walser, op. cit. p.
172, n. 2). Guarino's works were appreciated at Christ Church, Canterbury, where some of
his writings were transcribed (*infra*, pp. 129, 131). Guarino's reputation in England must
have been fostered by Del Monte and Frulovisi, both of whom had been his pupils, and by
Grey and Flemmyng after their return home.

[1] The notes on classical poets in MS. (B.L.) Bodl. no. 587, ff. 137ʳ-55ʳ, 179ʳ-190ʳ were
taken by Free at Guarino's lectures. That they are in Free's hand is obvious on comparison
with other items in Free's handwriting. That they derive from Guarino's lectures is suggested by their similarity with other notes taken at the courses of that humanist. The notes
in MS. (B.M.) Cotton, Julius F.VII, fo. 219ʳ (owned by William of Worcester) are also
probably by Free.

[2] Printed in Schirmer, op. cit. p. 129, n. 148. This is not a letter as Schirmer thinks but, as
its phraseology shows, an oration probably composed as an exercise.

[3] MS. Balliol Coll. Oxford, no. 124, and part of MS. (B.L.) Bodl. no. 587 were copied by
Free, the latter almost certainly at Ferrara.

[4] Spingarn, op. cit. p. 64. On Free's lack of funds at Ferrara cf. also *Ibid.*, pp. 59, 62–5.

[5] *Ibid.*, p. 54.

[6] On these precepts cf. Sabbadini, *Il Metodo degli Umanisti*, pp. 44–5.

[7] Spingarn, op. cit. pp. 52–4, 57.

[8] Free was still in Ferrara in August 1458, since he describes in a letter to Grey the
festivities held there on the arrival of the news of the election of Pius II (*Ibid.*, pp. 52–4).

Free, who was by then the possessor of two valuable benefices,[1] very likely obtained through Grey, probably went there in order to study that science,[2] which already counted several distinguished humanists amongst its students, without renouncing his literary pursuits. The actual length of Free's visit to Padua is uncertain. But it is known that he was still there on 21 March, 1461,[3] and that besides learning medicine and perhaps some Hebrew,[4] he lectured on the classics in that University. In Padua he was not forgetful of his Ferrara friends:[5] moreover, he made new friendships there including the humanist Ognibene da Lonigo, whom he brought to Tiptoft's notice,[6] and Andronicus Callistus,[7] a Greek of distinction then a tutor in the household of the Florentine refugee Palla Strozzi. If Leland is to be relied upon, it was at this time that Free was requested to compose a Latin epitaph for Petrarch's tomb at Arquà,[8] which, if true, can only be indicative of the high estimation in which Free's learning was held by the Italians. It was also in Padua that he came across John Tiptoft,[9] to whom he dedicated some Latin poems now lost[10] and a translation of Synesius' *Laus Calvitii*.[10]

In his Synesius Free chose to translate the text freely, and yet to avoid the licences taken in the field of translating even by great

[1] A church in the Diocese of Ely and one in that of Lincoln (*C.P.R.* vol. XI, pp. 536, 573). As he is already mentioned as in possession of them in Papal letters issued in May 1459, it seems certain that he already possessed these benefices in 1458.

[2] MS. Balliol Coll. Oxford, no. 124, flyleaf and fo. 1ʳ, Leland, *De Scriptoribus*, pp. 467–8. Leland adds that Free took up medicine as a profession.

[3] Mitchell, *John Tiptoft*, p. 65. Verrua suggests that Free may have been the *Doctor Anglensis* whose *cassationem et subrogationem fratris magistri Gerardi loco suo* in the University of Padua took place in 1462 (Verrua, op. cit. p. 77).

[4] This is suggested by a note by Free in MS. Balliol Coll. Oxford, no. 124, fo. 25ᵛ.

[5] Like Carbone and Castiglione to whom he addressed letters from there (*supra*, p. 107).

[6] *Infra*, p. 115, n. 7.

[7] Schirmer, op. cit. p. 131, n. 154. Callistus was in Padua in 1461 (Legrand, *Bibliographie Hellenique*, vol. I, p. 21).

[8] Leland, *De Scriptoribus*, p. 468. The epitaph is in Leland, *Collectanea*, vol. III, p. 6.

[9] This seems certain since Free was in Padua during at any rate most of the time that Tiptoft spent there.

[10] The poems '*in quibus Bacchus expostulat cum capro vitem arrodente*' (Leland, *De Scriptoribus*, p. 467), a MS. of which was seen by Leland among John Redman's books (*Ibid.*, p. 486); another copy was among the MSS. presented to Jesus Coll. Cambridge, by Gunthorpe (Leland, *Collectanea*, vol. IV, p. 16). These poems must have been inspired by the classical fable of the goat and the vine, on which cf. W. R. Halliday, 'The Fable of the Goat and the Vine,' *Annals of Archaeology and Anthropology*, XI (1918), pp. 95–102. The only known MS. of the Synesius (the presentation copy to Tiptoft), is MS. (B.L.) Bodl. no. 80; another copy was seen among Gunthorpe's books at Jesus College, Cambridge, by Leland (Leland, *Collectanea*, vol. IV, p. 16). Rhenanus' edition of Free's version is in Erasmus, *Morias Encomium*, Basileae, 1515. Free's introduction to Tiptoft is in Weiss, *A Letter-Preface of John Free to John Tiptoft, Earl of Worcester*, pp. 102–3. The version was already finished in the summer of 1461 (*Ibid.*, p. 102).

humanists like Bruni and Valla.[1] His attempt at reproducing the
character of the original proved fairly successful, while his
rendering of Greek particles shows that his understanding of
them was approaching that of the most distinguished Italian
scholars of his time. His rendering of the epithets occurring in
the frequent Homeric passages quoted by Synesius is sound, and
witnesses his acquaintance with the peculiarities of the Homeric
dialect. As we saw, Free had not chosen to translate literally:
thus he occasionally omits words or even entire sentences. But
on the whole he is fairly faithful to his original, and altogether
he succeeds in giving an attractive rendering. The version of
Synesius was conceived by him more as a work of art than as
a mere latinizing of the original text. Praised, edited, and
glossed, by Beatus Rhenanus during the sixteenth century, the
translation retained its popularity in the face of the more fastidious during the High Renaissance.

Besides dedicating works to Tiptoft, Free probably served
him as a secretary as well as a bibliographical adviser. It is very
likely that he wrote letters on his behalf[2] and procured books for
his library, the latter a practice he probably continued even after
Tiptoft's return to England.[3] After 1462 we lose sight of Free
altogether. According to Leland he went to Florence and then
to Rome,[4] where he apparently gained the favour of Pope Paul II,
who is supposed to have provided him to the vacant Bishopric of
Bath and Wells, and where he died in 1465, rumours of poisoning
being associated with his untimely death.[4]

Free was never a wealthy man, and consequently some of his
manuscripts were written by himself. Of these, we still possess
the *Ars Rhetorica* of Chirius Consultus Fortunatianus[5] and other
short rhetorical treatises,[5] and some excerpts from Pliny's
Natural History[5] and Poggio's translation of Diodorus,[5] all of

[1] On humanist methods of translation from the Greek cf. Sabbadini, *Il Metodo degli
Umanisti*, pp. 23–7.
[2] Comparison with Free's extant letters makes possible an attribution to him of the letter
sent by Tiptoft to the University of Oxford from Padua in Tait, *Letters of John Tiptoft,
Earl of Worcester, and Archbishop Neville to the University of Oxford*, pp. 571–2.
[3] Weiss, *The Library of John Tiptoft, Earl of Worcester*, p. 160.
[4] Leland, *De Scriptoribus*, p. 467. The only contemporary mention of Free's provision to
the See of Bath and Wells is in a note by William of Worcester (MS. Balliol Coll. Oxford,
no. 124, fo. 1ʳ). There is no mention of such a provision in extant Papal records, and
Worcester himself states that Bekynton was succeeded to the See of Bath and Wells by
Robert Stillington (Worcester, *Annales Rerum Anglicarum*, p. 783). Stillington was provided
to Bath and Wells on 30 October, 1465 (*C.P.R.* vol. XII, p. 468), consequently if Free's
provision did actually take place, he must have already been dead by then. About the
rumours that Free was poisoned cf. Leland, *De Scriptoribus*, p. 468.
[5] Now part of MSS. (B.L.) Bodl. no. 587, Balliol Coll. Oxford, no. 124.

which show how his handwriting had assumed the indubitable characteristics of that of the Italian humanists. From Free's correspondence with Grey we know that he was also anxious to purchase Greek books.[1] One of these, a fourteenth century manuscript containing some plays by Sophocles and Euripides, a few of Pindar's *Olympic Odes*, and Theocritus' *Idylls*, is still extant,[2] and with this we are forced to conclude our meagre list of the volumes once possessed by Free which have reached us. After his death part of his library came into the possession of John Gunthorpe, who was in Italy when Free died:[3] another part of it came into the hands of William of Worcester,[4] who may have acquired it from some relative of its late owner.

An examination of the career and achievement of John Free places him beyond all doubt above every fifteenth century English humanist before the time of Grocin and Linacre. His Latin style manifests his ability to escape from the medieval tradition which had dominated his early education, and to write in an elegant language modelled upon the ancients and similar to that used and perfected by the Italians since the days of Poggio. In the field of Latin poetry he showed himself, if Petrarch's Latin epitaph quoted by Leland[5] is to be reckoned as his work, competent enough to write hexameters not only metrically faultless, but also permeated with a grace perhaps reminiscent of the exquisite productions of Basinio or Politian. His Synesius shows besides his command of Greek that he was able to translate like a humanist: his library and his quotations in his letters testify to his widespread study of Greek literature, just as his lecture notes indicate his interest in Latin letters.[6]

Altogether, Free was from every point of view the equal of his humanist friends, Carbone, Castiglione, and Janus Pannonius: but amongst these he was closest of all to Pannonius, whose accomplishments, like Free's, were not helped by native literary tradition. His financial conditions doubtless contributed to the

---

[1] *Supra*, p. 108.   [2] Now MS. (B.L.) Auct. F.3.25.   [3] *Infra*, p. 123.
[4] William of Worcester owned MSS. Balliol Coll.Oxford, no. 124, and (B.L.) Auct. F.3.25.
[5] *Supra*, p. 109.
[6] The *D.N.B.* gives the following as Free's works: (1) *Cosmographia Mundi cum naturis arborum*, (2) Letters, (3) Version of Synesius, (4) Petrarch's epitaph, (5) Letters to Tiptoft, (6) *Contra Diodorum Siculum poetice fabulantem*, (7) Latin poems and epigrams, (8) *Expostulatio Bacchi ad Tiptoft*, (9) Version of some minor works of Xenophon. Of these nn. 5, 7, 8, 9 are lost, 1 is to be identified with the excerpts from Pliny in MS. Balliol Coll. Oxford, no. 124, while 6 is Free's transcript of Poggio's Latin Diodorus in *Ibid.*, and not a treatise against Diodorus as stated in *Ibid.*, fo. 153ʳ. On this version being by Poggio and not by Free cf. Zeno, op. cit. vol. I, pp. 41–3. As for 9 there is no conclusive evidence that Free translated any works of Xenophon.

successful development of his classical learning: had it not been for his poverty his efforts would perhaps not have exceeded those of Robert Flemmyng. Unfortunately his individuality did not stand out so sharply against the general background of Italian civilization, and his early death prevented his return to England. His influence on English humanism is confined to his relations with Tiptoft, and perhaps with John Gunthorpe. Still as the first Englishman to become a professional humanist and reach the standards of the Italians, he forms a definite new step in the early history of English humanism.

Just as Free was the only Englishman who was able to assume the entire personality of the typical Italian scholar of his time, his patron, John Tiptoft, Earl of Worcester, was the English nobleman of his age who came closest to the Italian prince of the Renaissance. There are many elements in Tiptoft's career which are reminiscent of Italian rulers of the fifteenth century. He resembles them especially in his political and intellectual outlook, in his attitude towards humanism, and in his generous patronage of scholars which endeared him to the Italians. Brought up in England, Tiptoft appears to have been so receptive of the cultural and political theories of the Renaissance, that one can say of him what the Milanese ambassador Alberico Malletta said of Louis XI: 'one would say that he has always lived in Italy.'[1]

John Tiptoft[2] was the son of John, Lord Tiptoft, a former Speaker of the Commons during the reign of Henry IV, and was probably born in 1427.[3] In 1440 he made his first appearance in Oxford as a *commensalis*, that is to say a lodger who was not a fellow, of University College, where he occupied rooms until 1443,[3] for the greater part of the time with a John Hurlegh, probably his tutor, who later became his chaplain.[3] Robert Flemmyng was also living in University College during Tiptoft's stay there;[4] hence considering the limited number of residents in that college in those years, it seems practically a certainty that they made each other's acquaintance there. Tiptoft possibly also met at that time William Grey, who was in Oxford until 1442,[5] and he is known to have started a friendship

[1] Quoted by C. Petit-Dutaillis in his chapter on Louis XI in *The Cambridge Medieval History*, vol. VIII, p. 305.

[2] On Tiptoft cf. especially Mitchell, *John Tiptoft*, and Schirmer, op. cit. pp. 107–16. To the bibliography in Mitchell's work one may add, H. S. Pancoast, 'Notes on John Tiptoft, Earl of Worcester,' *P.M.L.A.* XI (1896) pp. 7–9.

[3] Mitchell, *John Tiptoft*, pp. 11, 14.   [4] *Supra*, p. 97.   [5] Cf. *supra*, p. 86.

there with John Ross, who later advised him to visit the Holy Land.[1] It is likely that while at Oxford Tiptoft had an opportunity of perusing Duke Humphrey's books, access to which had perhaps the effect of awakening in him some interest in polite learning. In 1443 Tiptoft succeeded to his father's title,[2] and soon afterwards he began to take an active part in politics. As a politician he possibly started by siding with Cardinal Beaufort, who remembered him in his will,[3] later supporting Richard, Duke of York, to whose influence he probably owed the Earldom of Worcester which was bestowed upon him in 1449.[4] Besides taking part in politics he appears to have indulged, though perhaps rather mildly, in literature, this being suggested by some correspondence exchanged in 1452 with Henry Cranebroke, a monk from Christ Church, Canterbury.[5] Although the style of Tiptoft's extant Latin letter to Cranebroke shows an attempt to balance the sentences with care, the structure of the periods is not happy. Its numerous barbarisms manifest the deficiencies of its writer's classical education; his reference to the euphuisms of Cranebroke's letter as written *stylo tulliano* hints only too openly at his limited understanding of Cicero. Still Tiptoft's epistle, whatever the standard of its Latinity, and in spite of its obvious shortcomings, does also suggest a certain stylistic preoccupation and a lively interest in Latin elegances.

Meanwhile Tiptoft's political career was advancing rapidly. In April 1452, he succeeded Lord Beaumont in the post of Treasurer,[6] a position he kept until 7 October, 1454,[6] and in 1454 he also became one of the 'Keepers of the Sea.'[6] By this time political conditions in England were rapidly reaching a crisis on the Lancastrian–Yorkist issue. Its final outcome seemed, however, uncertain. Hence in order to avoid committal with either party he decided to go abroad until the political horizon appeared less unsettled. It was perhaps in response to his own desire that he was appointed in 1457, with Robert Flemmyng and others, to go to Rome to express the King's obedience to Pope Callixtus III.[7] This embassy did not materialize; none the

---

[1] Ross, op. cit., p. 5.   [2] Mitchell, *John Tiptoft*, p. 14.
[3] Radford, op. cit. p. 295.   [4] Mitchell, *John Tiptoft*, p. 19.
[5] Part of this correspondence is in Schirmer, op. cit. pp. 110, 115. A letter from Cranebroke to Tiptoft is in MS. (B.M.) Royal, 10. B.IX, fo. 122ʳ.
[6] Mitchell, *John Tiptoft*, pp. 23–4.
[7] *Ibid.*, p. 27. Two years later Tiptoft was appointed one of Henry VI's ambassadors to Pius II, but also this embassy did not take place (*Ibid.*, p. 61).

I

less shortly after January 1458, Tiptoft was able to leave England for a pilgrimage to the Holy Land in accordance with the former advice of the friendly Ross.[1] Alongside with reasons dictated by expediency,[2] Tiptoft's departure may have also been occasioned partly by a desire to perfect his studies in Italy. By the time he went abroad both Grey and Flemmyng had returned from their continental tours, and the possibility that he may have been advised by one of them to go to Padua and Ferrara should not be overlooked.

During May 1458 Tiptoft reached Venice, where on the seventeenth of that month he left on a Venetian galley for the Holy Land,[3] his fellow passengers including the famous condottiere Roberto da Sanseverino, with whom he made friends, and who was later to write a spirited account of the journey.[4] After an uneventful pilgrimage Tiptoft landed again in Venice on 6 September, 1458,[5] from where he moved to Padua to begin his studies at the University.[5] The charge of having introduced the 'law of Padua' into England, which was brought against him,[6] is not in itself conclusive evidence that he read in the faculty of Civil Law: still it is possible that he may have done so considering that he had already followed the arts courses at Oxford, that he was not in holy orders, and that medicine was an unlikely pursuit for a person of his standing. In Padua Tiptoft maintained a household of his own, and soon established friendly relations with men of letters, like Ognibene da Lonigo[7] and Galeotto Marzio,[7] and with Englishmen studying there, like Peter Courtenay, whom he presented with a choice Sallust purchased from Vespasiano,[8] and John Free, who probably served him as secretary during his visit.[8] Tiptoft's stay in Padua

---

[1] Cf. *supra*, p. 113. Letters of attorney on his going abroad were issued on 28 January, 1458, (*Calendar of French Rolls*, p. 425).

[2] Da Bisticci, op. cit. p. 403, Weiss, *A Letter-Preface of John Free to John Tiptoft, Earl of Worcester*, p. 103.

[3] Weiss, *The Library of John Tiptoft, Earl of Worcester*, p. 161, n.3.

[4] R. di Sanseverino, *Viaggio in Terra Santa*, ed. G. Maruffi, Bologna, 1898.

[5] Weiss, *The Library of John Tiptoft, Earl of Worcester*, p. 161, n. 3. He went to Padua shortly after landing in Venice on his return from the Holy Land, and had already been there for some time in January 1459, (*Ibid.*, p. 161, n. 5).

[6] Warkworth, *Chronicle*, p. 5, Da Bisticci, op. cit. p. 404. According to Vespasiano Tiptoft went to Padua in order to study Latin letters, (*Ibid.*, p. 403).

[7] Cf. *Infra*, p. 115. As Marzio was in Padua in 1460 (Bertoni, op. cit. p. 166) it seems certain that Tiptoft met him there. Marzio corresponded with Tiptoft (Weiss, *The Library of John Tiptoft, Earl of Worcester*, p. 163, n. 25). A letter of Janus Pannonius to Marzio written in 1464 suggests that Marzio had an engagement with Tiptoft should the latter return to Italy (*Galeottus Martius Narnensis, Epistolae*, ed. L. Jushaz, Roma, 1930, p. 6).

[8] Weiss, *Another Tiptoft Manuscript*, p. 234; *supra*, p.110.

began about January 1459,[1] and he was still there at the beginning of 1461.[1] Nevertheless during this period he spent several
months away visiting other Italian towns, and attending the
school of Guarino da Verona at Ferrara.[2] There he doubtless
came into touch with members of the ruling family of Este, and
had the opportunity of exercising his patronage on Ludovico
Carbone, to whom he suggested in vain a visit to England in his
employment.[2] He also became friendly with his teacher Guarino,[2]
and may have met John Gunthorpe, then a student reading
under that humanist.[3] Florence and Rome were amongst the
towns visited during this tour of Italy,[4] and in the former city he
called at the bookshop of his future biographer, Vespasiano da
Bisticci, from whom he commissioned various books for his
library,[4] and he attended at least one of John Argyropoulos'
lectures in the *Studio*.[4] At the Papal Court he was formally
received by Pope Pius II, before whom he delivered a Latin
oration which, according to John Free, moved the Holy Father
to tears.[5] Pius II appears to have been aware of Tiptoft's interests, and from his opinion of him[5] it is obvious that he appreciated the Earl's intellectual powers.

Tiptoft's Italian journeys enabled him to collect a considerable
library, which impressed his Italian contemporaries to the point
of charging him with spoliating their country of its book wealth.[6]
Besides collecting manuscripts on a large scale, he also patronized those scholars with whom he came into contact, chiefly by
encouraging them to prepare and dedicate to him Latin translations of Greek authors. Thus, Ognibene da Lonigo dedicated to
him a latinized Xenophon,[7] and Francesco Griffolini prepared

[1] Weiss, *The Library of John Tiptoft, Earl of Worcester*, p. 161, n. 5.
[2] Tiptoft's visit to Ferrara must have taken place in 1459 or 1460. He had already left
when Guarino died at the end of 1460 (Bertoni, op. cit. pp. 167–8). On his invitation to
Carbone cf. *Ibid.*, loc. cit. A letter of Guarino to Tiptoft was in Tiptoft's lost letter-book
(Weiss, *The Library of John Tiptoft, Earl of Worcester*, p. 163, n. 25).
[3] *Infra*, p. 123.
[4] Da Bisticci, op. cit. p. 403. In Florence Tiptoft must have met Giovanni di Cosimo de
Medici, to whom he sent a collection of songs set to music on 17 December, 1460, offering
at the same time to supply more in the future (C. S. Gutkind, *Cosimo de Medici*, Oxford,
1938, p. 213, n. 2), and with whom he corresponded, (Mitchell, *John Tiptoft*, p. 65).
[5] Weiss, *A Letter-Preface of John Free to John Tiptoft, Earl of Worcester*, pp. 102–3. His
visit to the Pope is also mentioned by Caxton, (*The Prologues and Epilogues of William
Caxton*, p. 47). His oration was probably delivered during the summer of 1460, this being
suggested by a Papal safeconduct issued to him on 16 October, 1460 (*C.P.R.* vol. XI, p.
580). For Pius II's opinion of Tiptoft cf. Weiss, *A Letter-Preface of John Free to John Tiptoft,
Earl of Worcester*, pp. 102–3.
[6] Weiss, *The Library of John Tiptoft, Earl of Worcester*, p. 157.
[7] Printed at Reggio Emilia about 1494, Hain, no. 16225. Ognibene was recommended to
Tiptoft by Free (MS. (B.L.) Bodl. no. 80, ff. 3ʳ–4ᵛ). Tiptoft owned Ognibene's commentary
on Juvenal (*infra*, p. 117 n. 6).

at his request a Latin text of Lucian's *Calumnia*.[1] Contacts with Italian humanism had enabled Tiptoft to realize the inferior quality of his fellow Englishmen's Latin scholarship, and inspired in him a desire to introduce more humane standards into England. His love of letters, and perhaps an ambition to become another Humphrey, aroused him to act. Hence while in Padua he conceived a scheme for the improvement of English letters. This was to be effected through a donation to the University of Oxford of choice Latin writings upon which students would be able to model their style. With such an end in view he addressed from Padua a letter to the University of Oxford in which he made his offer, accompanied by a list of the works he intended to include in his gift.[2] As was only natural such a proposal met with immediate acceptance. In their reply to him the University authorities expressed their gratitude, and, in order to ensure the fulfilment of his intention, added with timely flattery that they had decided to establish him as successor to the late Duke of Gloucester in their affections.[2] But it seems unlikely that the 'second Humphrey' fulfilled his promises this time. Further steps in connexion with this scheme appear to have been left to his last will,[3] when it was obviously too late for him to supervise its working. When Tiptoft left Italy in the summer of 1461 to return to England,[4] he brought with him not only a very valuable collection of books, but also the interested admiration of those humanists whom he had captivated by the generosity of his patronage and the candour of his manners. Once back in England Tiptoft was caught up in the whirlpool of politics, which eventually led to his execution in October 1470[4] during the Lancastrian restoration. But even during this period of acute political activity he is known to have pursued his studies. More books came from Italy[5] and Germany[5] to swell his library, and when he went to Ireland as Deputy in 1467 he brought with him a substantial part of it, which was still there at the time of his death.[6]

---

[1] On this version cf. Weiss, *The Library of John Tiptoft, Earl of Worcester*, p. 162, n. 15. Griffolini, who incidentally mentions Tiptoft in a letter to Francesco Pellato (*Phalaris Epistulae*, Tarvisii, 1471, fo. 61ᵛ) possibly met Tiptoft in Florence (Mitchell, *John Tiptoft*, pp. 73–4).

[2] For Tiptoft's letter cf. *supra*, p. 110, n.2. The University's reply is in *Epistolae Academicae*, vol. II, p. 355.

[3] Cf. *infra*, p. 118.

[4] He landed in England on 1 September, 1461, (Weiss, *The Library of John Tiptoft, Earl of Worcester*, p. 162, n. 20). For the date of his execution cf. *Ibid.*, p. 163, n. 28.

[5] *Ibid.*, p. 160, *infra*, p. 117.

Weiss, *The Library of John Tiptoft, Earl of Worcester*, p. 163, n. 33.

Tiptoft's library[1] doubtless constituted one of the most important collections of his time assembled by an Englishman, so that even its few remains are enough to give us a clear idea of its wealth. Already before going to Italy he had in all probability started to collect books.[2] But the most important section of his library was formed during his stay in that country. His Italian purchases were not limited to the *scriptorium* of Vespasiano, from whom he obtained the Sallust now at Copenhagen,[3] but, as both Vespasiano[4] and Carbone[4] tell us, he bought books wherever he went during his Italian peregrinations. An important part of his collection was very probably acquired in Padua,[5] whence more volumes were sent to him once he had returned to England, probably through the agency of John Free.[5] Manuscripts acquired by him in Italy included, besides the Sallust already mentioned, works by Ognibene da Lonigo,[6] Francesco Griffolini,[6] Basinio da Parma,[6] Bartolomeo Fazio,[7] Petrarch,[7] Porcellio[7], John Free,[7] and probably also writings by other scholars with whom he had established contacts during his visit to Italy. Of particular importance were his copies of recently discovered Latin classical authors, amongst which there were Lucretius' poem,[8] Tacitus' *Dialogus de Oratoribus*,[9] and Suetonius' *De Grammaticis et Rhetoribus*,[9] all these being probably the first manuscripts of them to reach England after their discovery by Poggio[10] and Enoch of Ascoli.[10] Unlike his biographer Vespasiano, Tiptoft does not appear to have been prejudiced against printing: two printed bibles were imported by him from Cologne in 1468.[11] Thus from

[1] On Tiptoft's Library cf. Weiss, *The Library of John Tiptoft, Earl of Worcester*, Mitchell, 'A Renaissance Library: The Collection of John Tiptoft, Earl of Worcester', *The Library*, XVIII (1937) pp. 67–83.
[2] MS. (B.M.) Royal 18.D.IV, (Lydgate's *Fall of Princes*) probably came into his possession before his departure for Italy.
[3] On which cf. Weiss, *Another Tiptoft Manuscript, passim*.
[4] Da Bisticci, op. cit. p. 403, Bertoni, op. cit. pp. 167–8. Carbone also stated that Tiptoft had spoliated the libraries of Italy (*Ibid.*, loc. cit.).
[5] Weiss, *The Library of John Tiptoft, Earl of Worcester*, p. 160.
[6] Tiptoft's MS. of Ognibene's commentary on Juvenal is now MS. (B.L.) Arch. Selden, B.50. Doubtless he owned copies of the versions which Ognibene and Griffolini had dedicated to him. His copy of Basinio's *Astronomicon* is now MS. (B.L.) Bodl. no. 646.
[7] A MS. containing several works by Fazio, Petrarch, and Porcellio, and formerly in Tiptoft's library is now MS. St. John's Coll. Cambridge, no. 226. Tiptoft's copy of Free's Synesius is now MS. (B.L.) Bodl. no. 80. Besides this he doubtless owned MSS. of those other works which Free had dedicated to him.
[8] Now MS. (B.L.) Auct. F.1. 13.
[9] Now MS. (B.M.) Harl. no. 2639.
[10] On which cf. Sabbadini, *Scoperte*, vol. I, pp. 108–9, 140–1, II, pp. 25–6, 192.
[11] Weiss, *The Earliest Catalogues of the Library of Lincoln College*, p. 354, n. 19.

what we know, it is possible to conjecture that his library must have contained a very important range of both ancient and modern authors, besides probably a large number of medieval writings: as such, from the point of view of classical as well as neo-classical studies, its almost total loss is much to be regretted. The fate of this library is not devoid of interest. Already while in Padua Tiptoft had, as we saw, planned to present some books to Oxford:[1] that this intended donation took place is doubtful. On the other hand, we know that his will contained bequests of manuscripts to both Oxford and Cambridge Universities,[2] doubtless with a view to introducing humane standards into England. Apparently some difficulty in obtaining these books was experienced by the legatees, with the result that shortly after Tiptoft's death they appealed to George Neville, Archbishop of York and Chancellor of England, for help in obtaining their legacies.[3] What eventually happened is not known, but it is probable that only a part of the books, if indeed that, did finally reach the two Universities, for it is doubtful whether Neville was able to secure the volumes left in Ireland.[3]

Many factors must be considered in estimating the extent of Tiptoft's learning. His library shows beyond doubt his humanistic leanings, which are confirmed by his activities in Italy, and his relations with Italian scholars and with Free.[4] Besides this, his writings and his political outlook should not be overlooked. The works assigned to him[5] consist of English translations of Cicero's *De Senectute*[6] and *De Amicitia*,[6] of Buonaccorso da Montemagno's *De Nobilitate*,[6] and of select passages from Caesar referring to Great Britain,[7] several ordinances issued by him as High Constable of England,[8] two orations, one to the citizens of Padua[9] and one to Pope Pius II,[9] a volume of Latin letters,[10] and a chronicle.[11] Of these, neither the chronicle nor the trans-

---

[1] Cf. *supra*, p. 116.
[2] Weiss, *The Library of John Tiptoft, Earl of Worcester*, pp. 158–9.
[3] *Ibid.*, p. 159.
[4] On Free and Tiptoft cf. *supra*, pp. 109–10.
[5] A list of writings attributed to Tiptoft is in *The Chronicles of the White Rose of York*, pp. 192–3. On Tiptoft's works cf. Mitchell, *John Tiptoft*, pp. 172–94, Lathrop, *The Translations of John Tiptoft*.
[6] Printed by Caxton at Westminster in 1481, (Gordon Duff, no. 103).
[7] Printed by William Rastell, London, 1530.
[8] On these ordinances, which were issued on 29 May, 1466, cf. Mitchell, *John Tiptoft*, pp. 101–3.
[9] *The Chronicles of the White Rose of York*, p. 193, Weiss, *A Letter-Preface of John Free to John Tiptoft, Earl of Worcester*, p. 102.
[10] Now lost but formerly in the Library of Lincoln Cathedral (Tanner, op. cit. pp. 716–7).
[11] Now MS. Thirlestane House, Cheltenham, Phillips, no. 11301. Rather than a chronicle

lations of Caesar and of the *De Senectute* are his works:[1] the letters
and the orations are now lost. Tiptoft's two versions do not
rank high as specimens of the art of translating. The *De Amicitia*
shows that he possessed neither complete mastery of the
language of the original nor the faculty of lucid expression: it is
in many ways reminiscent of a schoolboy's Latin 'unseen' and
contains several mistakes. All that it suggests is that Tiptoft
was unable to understand with ease such a comparatively simple
text as Cicero's *De Amicitia*. Perhaps Tiptoft made this version
prior to his visit to Italy, for it displays such a mediocre knowledge of Latin as to make its execution after he had studied at
Ferrara and Padua unlikely. A slight improvement marks his
handling of Buonaccorso da Montemagno's work. Here mis-
translations are fewer than in the *De Amicitia*, the prose is more
fluent and mature. This may be due partly to a better understanding of humanistic than of classical Latin, which suggests
possibly that it was made after Tiptoft's return from Italy.

The evidence of Tiptoft's Latin scholarship, as provided by
his two translations and his correspondence with Cranebroke,
hints that the Latin oration which so much moved that accomplished humanist, Pope Pius II, and the Latin letter addressed
from Padua to the Oxford authorities, were probably the work of
scholars in his pay rather than his own composition. The style
of the latter is especially much too classical to have been written
by the translator of the *De Amicitia*, and it may have come from
the pen of John Free.[2] If available information reveals Tiptoft
to have been but an indifferent Latin scholar, his patronage
shows that, like Humphrey, Duke of Gloucester, he liked latinized Greek works and was anxious to have Italian humanists in
his pay. His advances to Carbone and his links with Marzio
make this clear, while the unqualified praise of him by the
scholars whom he encountered is suggestive of generosity in
his patronage. Tiptoft's fondness for Latin texts of Greek
authors also points clearly to an ignorance of Greek: but this is
not to be wondered at. After all, when he went to Italy he had
already reached an age when a language is no longer to be learnt

it is a collection of extracts from St. Augustine, Geoffrey of Monmouth, the metrical life of
William of Wykeham, and the 1399–1437 version of the Latin *Brut*. Its attribution to Tiptoft,
to whom it may have belonged, is due to the following fifteenth century note on fo. 1[r]:
*Cronica Regum Anglie in diuersis historiographis per Dominum Wigornii sparsim collecta. Sheld-
uuych.*

[1] Lathrop, op. cit. pp. 497–9.
[2] Cf. *supra*, p. 110, n. 2.

with ease, and thus his failure to apply himself to a task requiring much industry and patience may perhaps be excused.

Italian fifteenth century politics were conditioned by expediency rather than morality.[1] When power was based upon prestige, and a ruler's self preservation was dependent on political success, it was imperative for princes to strengthen the weaknesses of their rule by devices often ethically objectionable. Italian opinion did not condemn such methods. The Italians had accepted brutality and deceit as instruments of government, and political theorists from Frulovisi to Guicciardini had portrayed rather than moralized upon political practice. In a way the Italians stood for subtlety rather than force and realism rather than theory. To conquer by mere show of strength was considered almost clumsy and lacking in polish. But to circumvent successfully an opponent was considered a proof of finesse deserving of the applause of connoisseurs. Politics had practically become one of the liberal arts, and the use of letters, sculpture, painting, and architecture, for political ends was universally accepted. The Italian *Principe nuovo* was a 'Maecenas' whose patronage ranged from the fine arts to political murder. He was a dilettante in scholarship but no theorist. In government he did not follow rules but treated each situation by its own merits. Francesco Sforza or Lorenzo de Medici did not seek guidance from handbooks. They appreciated realities and acted in what they judged to be the most advantageous way. Their real and sole deity was success, and to its attainment everything else was to be sacrificed.

The obvious implications in the policy of Italian petty princes had not been missed by foreign rulers interested in statecraft. Louis XI and Ferdinand the Catholic, both keen students of Italian politics, assumed a modified Italian outlook suitable to local conditions. In this lay the success of their policies, since both Louis and Ferdinand realizing the difference between their countries and Italy, had been able to practise the spirit of Italian politics within the letter of customary government. As a politician and diplomatist Tiptoft could but be influenced by Italian theories. The political outlook of the average fifteenth century Italian prince may have inspired his Irish policy. He appears to have shared with his contemporary, Charles of Burgundy, the

[1] On Italian politics during the early Renaissance cf. for instance C. Benoist, *Le Machiavellisme*, vol. I, Paris, 1907.

Italian view that 'dead men make no war',[1] and his actions conformed to some extent with the totalitarian theories set forth in Frulovisi's *De Republica*,[2] which he may have read in Ferrara. The charge that Tiptoft introduced the 'law of Padua'[3] into this country is not to be interpreted as the result of an attempt to replace the Common Law with the Civil Law of Rome, but rather of his frequent summary administration of justice, which appeared both foreign and objectionable to his fellow citizens. A realist and an authoritarian, he had learned from his Italian experience the importance of state supremacy as means of consolidating the monarchy, and avoid its subordination to the feudal nobility; and like his contemporary, Sir John Fortescue, he was aware of the danger of the 'over mighty subject'.[4] Thus Tiptoft's political practice and the theory upon which it rested had as its ends a monarchy as conceived by Louis XI and later by Henry VII.[5] The main difficulty in adapting English opinion to such views was that they were modelled upon foreign conceptions, and were utterly alien to English political tradition. As a result they were at first much resented although they were accepted later at the hands of the Tudors, who rendered them more adaptable to an English setting.

Tiptoft is doubtless one of the most interesting, if not the most attractive product of Italian influence upon Englishmen. The strong humanistic interests perhaps already latent in him before his visit to Italy, went beyond book collecting and patronage, and in his case the Renaissance was able to exert a vigorous influence not only on his literary tastes but also on his political and moral outlook. His general attitude towards humane learning suggests his acceptance of the Italian notion of humanism as the only begetter of glory. That such a view, as well as an appreciation of the political potentialities of polite letters, may have conditioned his intellectual outlook and prompted his patronage of Italian scholars, is quite possible. Why should he otherwise have invited Carbone to come to England, and encouraged the men of letters in his Italian entourage to compose epistles and

---

[1] Da Bisticci, op. cit. p. 205.   [2] On the *De Republica* cf. *supra*, p. 44 .
[3] Cf. *supra*, p. 114.
[4] Sir J. Fortescue, *The Governance of England*, ed. C. Plummer, Oxford, 1885, p. 130.
[5] Tiptoft's political outlook is illustrated not only by his policy as High Constable of England and Deputy and Lieutenant of Ireland, on which cf. Mitchell, *John Tiptoft*, pp. 81–99, 112–35, but also by his last remarks to the friar accompanying him to the scaffold (Vespasiano, op. cit. pp. 404–5), and by his judgment of Sir Ralph Grey (Warkworth, op. cit. pp. 38–9).

orations on his behalf? Possibly Gloucester's example was in his mind, and he was intending to continue his activities. If so Oxford had struck the right note in hailing him as a second Humphrey. Like Humphrey's his Latin learning remained mediocre. Nevertheless, the eagerness with which he pursued his studies, the range of his intellectual activities, and the influence he exercised, are sufficient to make him the most striking figure in the history of English humanism since the days of Humphrey of Gloucester. His employment of well-known literary men like Marzio and Free indicates his discrimination, since there doubtless were less accomplished humanists eager to serve him. The remains of his library show his anxiety to collect the latest discoveries in Latin literature as well as the latest neo-classical writings, while his bequests of books and his promises to Oxford University make it manifest that he had the advancement of learning at heart. To estimate Tiptoft as a man one needs to judge him according to fifteenth century moral standards: to estimate his accomplishments as a scholar it is necessary to bear in mind the limitations of his early education. That his learning impressed his Italian as well as his English contemporaries,[1] indicates how the importance of his learned activities was perceived already during his age.

Tiptoft's studies in Italy coincided with those of another Englishman, John Gunthorpe,[2] a pupil at Guarino's school in Ferrara, where he was very likely a fellow student of John Free. What brought Gunthorpe to Italy must remain matter for conjecture, since our knowledge concerning his early life is limited to a few fragments of information. These are, however, sufficient to disclose to us that he received his University education at Cambridge, where he was probably a Master of Arts already in 1452.[3] In 1454–5 he appears as one of the University Proctors,[4] an office clearly indicative of an active part in academic affairs. Perhaps it was in Cambridge that a desire to go and read under

---

[1] On contemporary opinion of Tiptoft's scholarship cf. *The Prologues and Epilogues of William Caxton*, p. 47, Da Bisticci, op. cit. p. 403, Bertoni, op. cit., pp. 167–8, Weiss, *A Letter-Preface of John Free to John Tiptoft, Earl of Worcester*, pp. 102–3, Ross, op. cit. p. 5, and his Canterbury obituary in Mitchell, *John Tiptoft*, p. 136. Some obituary verse probably about Tiptoft are in M. R. James, *A Descriptive Catalogue of the Manuscripts in the Library of St. John's College, Cambridge*, Cambridge, 1913, p. 130.
[2] On Gunthorpe cf. especially, Schirmer, op. cit. pp. 134–9, M. Schutt, 'Bishop (*sic*) Gunthorpe,' *Modern Language Review*, XXIII (1928) pp. 42–3, Leland, *De Scriptoribus*, pp. 462–3, and the article on him in the *D.N.B.*
[3] MS. (C.U.) Ff. VI.20, fo. 450ʳ.
[4] *Grace Book A*, p. 1.

Guarino first arose in him, a desire possibly stimulated by current accounts of Guarino's teaching ability and contacts with someone who, like Grey and Flemmyng, had been in contact with the Italian scholar. In the summer of 1460 Gunthorpe had already been in Ferrara[1] for some time, and was then attending Guarino's courses on rhetoric.[2] He had by then also succeeded in learning some Greek,[3] and had established cordial relations with Ludovico Carbone,[4] and doubtless with other resident men of letters. Like Free, he proved a very diligent student, took copious notes at Guarino's lectures,[5] and employed part of his leisure in transcribing classical texts to enrich his store of books; a Seneca copied by him in Ferrara in 1460[6] shows not only that Italian calligraphic fashions were influencing his handwriting, but also that he was acquiring skill as a scribe. At the end of 1460 Guarino died at the advanced age of ninety, and shortly after this at the latest Gunthorpe left Ferrara. He may have subsequently visited Padua and Rome; in fact his coming into possession of part of Free's books[7] suggests his presence in Rome when the latter died there in 1465.

It appears to have been the practice of both Lancastrians and Yorkists to choose for diplomatic missions persons with an experience of foreign countries and a good knowledge of Latin. Gunthorpe was fully qualified in these respects. Hence he had not long to wait after his return home[8] before obtaining employment from Edward IV. He had only been in England a short time, when in 1466 his recent appointment as chaplain to the

---

[1] Since he finished then the transcription of a MS. in Ferrara (*infra*, n. 6).

[2] *Infra*, n. 6.

[3] Notes in Greek in Gunthorpe's hand appear in MSS. (B.M.) Harl. no. 2485, ff. 56ʳ, 197ʳ, etc., (B.L.) Bodl. no. 587, fo. 83ᵛ. It seems certain that Gunthorpe learnt Greek at the school of Guarino.

[4] Bertoni, op. cit. p. 167.

[5] Gunthorpe's marginal notes on his transcript of Seneca's *Tragedies*, now MS. (B.M.) Harl. no. 2485, were taken at Guarino's lectures on this text. This is proved by Gunthorpe's reference to Guarino's lectures on that text, (*infra*, n. 6), and by the following note at fo. 68ᵛ of his transcript: *primo modo leget guarinus*. The *Tragedies* of Seneca were one of the subjects of Guarino's 'grammar courses' (Sabbadini, *La Scuola e gli Studi di Guarino da Verona*, p. 36).

[6] Now MS. (B.M.) Harl. no. 2485. That Gunthorpe was its scribe is disclosed by the colophon at fo. 197ʳ: *Finis tragediarum Lucii Auli Anei Senece Cordubensis script. manu propria mei Iohannis Gunthorp de Anglia tunc studentis poeticę in inclita ciuitate Ferarię legente tunc eas Guarino Veronensi oratore prestantissimo. completus est iste liber. Tercio Nonas Augusti anno domini* 1460 *Pio secundo senensi pontificante.*

[7] Leland, *De Scriptoribus*, p. 463. One of Free's MSS. subsequently owned by Gunthorpe is now part of MS. (B.L.) Bodl. no. 587.

[8] He was already back in England in 1465 when he purchased a Macrobius, now MS. Trinity Coll. Cambridge, no. 824, in London.

King[1] was followed by membership of an embassy to Henry
IV of Castile,[1] during which he delivered some Latin orations.[2]
Despite his diplomatic work, the world of learning still exercised
attractions for Gunthorpe, who on his return from Castile went
to Cambridge to conclude his studies in Divinity.[3] He had by
then also become the Queen's secretary[4] and Warden of King's
Hall, Cambridge,[4] yet the holding of such posts did not prevent
him from participating in more embassies abroad. Thus when in
1468 the Anglo-Burgundian friendship was being cemented by
the marriage of Charles of Burgundy to Margaret of York, he
was sent to Bruges to take part in the marriage festivities, a
mission which involved the delivery of several Latin speeches
before the Duke and his court.[5] Gunthorpe's work as a diplomatist and his favour with the Crown contributed to his receiving valuable dignities in the Church, such as the Archdeaconry
of Essex[5] and the Deanery of Wells, which he obtained in 1472.[6]
As time went on his links with the Court became closer; in 1475
he accompanied Edward IV on his expedition to France in the
capacity of almoner,[7] and in 1481 he became Dean of the Chapel
Royal.[7] During the short reign of Richard III he was appointed
Keeper of the Privy[7] Seal; but after the accession of Henry VII
in 1485 he was still entitled to consideration despite his former
political attachments, and already in 1486 he was engaged on
royal business.[7] He continued to be occupied with public and
ecclesiastical duties until his death which occurred in 1498.[8]

[1] Rymer, op. cit. vol. XI, p. 572.
[2] On these orations cf. *infra*, p. 125.
[3] *Grace Book A*, p. 67. The study of letters at a University was one of the exceptions
enabling Gunthorpe to enjoy his benefices though non resident (*C.P.R.* vol. XIII, p. 445).
[4] He was styled King's clerk and Queen's secretary in his appointment as Warden of
King's Hall on 30 September, 1467 (*P.R.* 1466–77, p. 32). Gunthorpe resigned the Wardenship in January 1473 (*Ibid.*, p. 367).
[5] *Infra*, p. 125, n. 3. According to the Flemish chronicler A. de Roveere, Gunthorpe
and the Bishop of Tournay spoke for more than an hour at Sluys on 29 June, 1468. Gunthorpe spoke in Latin and the Bishop in French and both were, according to Roveere,
quite unintelligible (MS. Bibliothèque Royale, Bruxelles, Van Hulthem, no. 787, ff.
19ᵛ–20ʳ). Gunthorpe was Archdeacon of Essex from 1472–8 (Le Neve, op. cit. vol. II.
p. 335).
[6] *Ibid.*, vol. I, p. 152. He had also been Chief Almoner to the King since 9 December,
1469 (Rymer, op. cit. vol. XI, p. 637).
[7] *Edward IV's French Expedition*, ed. F. P. Barnard, Oxford, 1925, p. 127, *P.R.* 1476–85,
p. 250. He was appointed Keeper of the Privy Seal on 6 July, 1483 (Rymer, op. cit. vol. XII,
p. 194). The *Liber Rubeus* of Wells shows that he was already engaged on business with the
King in 1486 (H.M.C., *Calendar of the Manuscripts of the Dean and Chapter of Wells*, London,
1914, pp. 101, 109, etc.). On 15 December, 1486, he was made an ambassador to treat with
the Archduke Maximilian, and in March 1488 he was appointed to an embassy to Isabella
of Castile, (Rymer, op. cit., vol. XII, pp. 319, 336).
[8] Gunthorpe's will was made on 25 June, 1498, and proved on 26 August, 1498, and is in

As a diplomatist and politician, Gunthorpe was no doubt endowed with remarkable abilities, his employment by Henry VII after having served Edward IV, Edward V, and Richard III, being clearly indicative of this. As a scholar he closely resembled Flemmyng with whom he was probably acquainted. Like him, he knew Greek,[1] composed Latin verse, and gathered together an important collection of classical and modern manuscripts. Gunthorpe's Latin poems are not extant, but Leland, who relied on hearsay, states that they were by no means indifferent.[2] His Latin letters[2] are also lost, so that his Latin speeches are his only literary remains. These orations[3] are naturally of much importance for any estimate of Gunthorpe's achievement. With their style modelled upon Cicero, and their general effect reminiscent of formal eloquence as practised by the Italians, these orations manifest not only Guarino's influence on their author, but also a desire to conform with humanist standards. This is furthermore emphasized by the wealth of words but paucity of facts, by the evident love of similes and examples drawn from Roman history, and by the sacrifice of matter to form. It is obvious from these orations that Gunthorpe had studied the art of writing in the new style, and that his training at Ferrara had freed him from any influence of Latinity as taught in academic England during the fifteenth century. Further insight into Gunthorpe's intellectual outlook is given by the remains of his library, and by some information about it furnished by Leland.

Gunthorpe collected most of his library during his visits abroad. Besides purchasing books, he added to its bulk by transcribing texts himself and by becoming the possessor of part of Free's library at that scholar's death in Italy.[4] During the sixteenth century a substantial part of Gunthorpe's books were housed in Jesus College, Cambridge, where they were seen by

Somerset Medieval Wills, 1383–1500, pp. 361–2. No MSS. are mentioned in it. Gunthorpe died on June 26, since this is given as the anniversary day of his death in the obituary of the Grande Chartreuse (C. Le Couteaulx, *Annales Ordinis Cartusiensis*, Monstrolii, 1887–8, vol. II, pp. 459–60).

[1] *Supra*, p. 123.   [2] Leland, *De Scriptoribus*, p. 463.

[3] The autographs of Gunthorpe's orations to Henry IV of Castile and the Duke of Burgundy are in MS. (B.L.) Bodl. no. 587, ff. 73ʳ–93ʳ. The following is a list of them: (1) ff. 73ʳ–6ᵛ. To the King of Castile, delivered on 23 October, 1466. (2) ff. 77ʳ–ᵛ. To the same? (3) ff. 78ʳ–9ʳ. To the Duke of Burgundy. (4) ff. 79ʳ–80ᵛ. To the same? (5) ff. 81ʳ–2ᵛ. To Henry IV of Castile. (6) ff. 84ʳ–7ᵛ. To the Duke of Burgundy and his bride Margaret of York, delivered at Bruges on 8 July, 1468. (7) ff. 88ᵛ–9ʳ. To the Duke of Burgundy. (8) ff. 90ʳ–2ʳ. To the same on his marriage to Margaret of York. (9) ff. 92ᵛ–3ʳ. To the same and his bride. Passages from some of these speeches are printed in Schirmer, op. cit. p. 139, n. 184.

[4] *Supra*, p. 123, n. 7.

Leland, according to whom they included the *De Ingenuis Moribus* by Vergerio, Petrarch's *De Vita Solitaria*, the *De Re Uxoria* by Francesco Barbaro, and writings by Free.[1] Besides these, Gunthorpe owned the Latin text of the *Odyssey* by Francesco Griffolini, which he purchased in London in 1475,[2] as well as other Greek authors latinized by Bruni, Perotti, and Guarino,[2] and possibly the works of Frulovisi.[3] Among Latin manuscripts in his collection, there were the pseudo-Ciceronian *Synonima*[4] and Seneca's *Tragedies*,[5] both copied by himself, the rare *Ars Rhetorica* by Chirius Consultus Fortunatianus transcribed by John Free,[6] some of Free's lecture notes and letters,[6] and several well-known works such as the *Satires* of Persius.[7] Printed copies of Pliny's *Natural History*,[8] and Dionigi da Borgo San Sepolcro on Valerius Maximus,[8] once possessed by him, suggest that perhaps he owned other printed books.

As a scholar Gunthorpe is above all important as personifying with Flemmyng the typical English humanist of his time, to whom literary pursuits were mainly a recreation from political and ecclesiastical affairs. His public career indicates how already during the third quarter of the fifteenth century humanistic culture was becoming a valuable asset for public employment, as it had been in Italy since the end of the fourteenth century. But his success naturally prevented him from teaching, and thus, like the other four English pupils of Guarino, he failed to establish in this country any direct continuity with the teaching of that great humanist. In so far as the development of English humanism during the fifteenth century is concerned, the rôle played in it by the English pupils of Guarino da Verona was not

[1] Leland, *Collectanea*, vol. IV, p. 16. Gunthorpe's MSS. must have reached Jesus College after 1484 since MS. Jesus Coll. Cambridge, no. 49 was purchased by Gunthorpe on 20 December, 1484. This is the only MS. given by Gunthorpe still to be found in Jesus College. According to Leland, Gunthorpe's books ended partly at Oxford and partly at Cambridge. (Leland, *De Scriptoribus*, p. 463).

[2] Now MSS. (C.U.) Mm. III. 4, St. John's Coll. Cambridge, no. 61.

[3] In MS. St. John's Coll. Cambridge, no. 60.

[4] Now part of MS. (B.L.) Bodl. no. 587. On this MS. cf. *supra*, pp. 108, n. 1, 110.

[5] *Supra*, p. 123.

[6] Now part of MS. (B.L.) Bodl. no. 587.

[7] Gunthorpe's Persius is now MS. Henry Huntingdon Library, San Marino, E.L.34.B.6. Besides those mentioned already Gunthorpe owned the following MSS.: MSS. (C.U.)Dd. VII. 1–2, Dd. X.29, Ff.VI.20, Corpus Christi Coll. Cambridge, no. 164, Emmanuel Coll. Cambridge, no. 3, Sidney Sussex Coll. Cambridge, no. 46, (B.M.) Cotton, Tib.A.IX, Harl. no. 654, Royal, 9.E.I, 15.C.XIV, Sion Coll. London, Anc. I.40.2.–L.23.

[8] Now Dean and Chapter Library, Wells, B.1.20, and (B.L.) Auct. N.4.4. The Pliny is the Venetian edition of 1472 (Hain, no. 13089), and the Dionigi is the Strassburg edition by the 'R' printer (Hain, no. 4103). The latter was purchased by Gunthorpe on 7 February, 1475.

one of direct personal influence. Their stations in life and activities in other fields prevented them from handing on directly the culture they had acquired in Italy, so that apart from influencing casually a few friends, and introducing here some texts hitherto unknown, they played no part in the general development of English humanism. Learning was for them, with the exception of Free, only a leisured pursuit, almost a relaxation from heavier duties, and because of this Grey, Flemmyng, Tiptoft, and Gunthorpe, stand isolated as scholars. It is possible that their examples inspired others to follow in their footsteps, and it is certain that they were able to spread Italian knowledge through their donations of books and their patronage. But it would be impossible to trace to them the beginning of new traditions in fifteenth century English culture. Perhaps the chief interest of their achievements is that they prove how already by this time Englishmen could understand modern values and assimilate the new culture found in Italy. Guarino's English pupils made some impression in Ferrara: the memory of them lingered there after they had left, so much so that each of them was individually praised in Carbone's funeral panegyric of Guarino,[1] while their examples gave occasion to the same Carbone to assure Borso d'Este some years later that good orators were to be found in England.[2] Battista Guarino also, in singing the praises of his late father, did not forget to mention that pupils had come to hear him even from England 'which was out of the world.'[3]

[1] Bertoni, op. cit. pp. 167–8.
[2] B. Botfield, *Praefationes et Epistolae Editionibus Principibus Auctorum Veterum Praepositae* Cambridge, 1861, p. 132.
[3] *Epistolario di Guarino Veronese*, vol. III, p. 500.

CHAPTER VIII

By the beginning of the second half of the fifteenth century humanism had begun to establish itself in England, as is disclosed by the active interest taken in it in the monastery of Christ Church, Canterbury, and in the University of Oxford. The awakening curiosity in these places appears to have coincided with the activities of the English pupils of Guarino da Verona, and although less important judged by individual achievement, it none the less contributed largely to the background of English culture at the eve of the Reformation.

Amongst English monasteries Christ Church, Canterbury, occupied an exalted position. With the Cathedral inside its boundaries and with its chapter's right to elect the Archbishop, its prominence was assured. Other monasteries, like Westminster, Glastonbury, or St. Albans, could also claim antiquity and wealth, but Canterbury eclipsed them all in prestige. The cult of St. Thomas à Becket had proved valuable. It attracted crowds of pilgrims from all England to worship at his shrine, as well as precious gifts from English and foreign royalty. Besides forming the centre of the spiritual capital of England, Christ Church had stood out as a citadel of learning since the earliest days of English Christianity. Archbishops and priors had supported scholarship and a sumptuous library,[1] including Greek manuscripts[2] and Latin classics little known even in Italy before Petrarch,[2] bore witness to the outlook of generations of priors and monks. Nor did Christ Church rely solely upon its own resources for the erudition of its members. With the rise of the universities the value of academic training was recognized there. Monks were sent to Oxford, Cambridge, and abroad, and from the second half of the fourteenth century promising young monks were sent as a matter of routine to Canterbury College, Oxford,[3] to read for degrees. An institution of the prominence of Christ Church was bound to be in close contact with Rome.

---

[1] On which cf. James, *The Ancient Libraries of Canterbury and Dover*, *passim*.

[2] These included a Greek *Octateuch* now MS. (B.L.) Can. gr. 35. On Greek MSS. at Canterbury cf. James, *The Ancient Libraries of Canterbury and Dover*, pp. lxxxv–vii. The medieval Christ Church catalogues in *Ibid.*, pp. 1–172, include some rare classical texts such as Vitruvius, a complete Quintilian, and Pompeius on Donatus, (*Ibid.*, pp. 47, 78, 85).

[3] A history of Canterbury College, Oxford, is being prepared by Mr. W. A. Pantin of Oriel College, Oxford.

Monks were often sent there to supplicate for fresh privileges, and at home cordial relations with Papal Collectors and the episcopate were normal features. The powers of the chapter, especially during *sede vacante*, entailed intercourse with the Council, while the priors of Christ Church, whose privileges included political as well as spiritual powers, were often employed on state missions. Both its importance and its geographical position made foreign intercourse frequent. Foreign prelates and Papal officials and foreigners visiting England came to Canterbury: Manuel Palaeologos went there in 1400,[1] and the Emperor Sigismund worshipped at St. Thomas's shrine in 1416.[2] Such a concourse of visitors made an international centre of Canterbury,[2] and ensured valuable contacts to anyone interested in classical letters there.

It was probably through contacts with Papal officials and with Englishmen already under the spell of their learning, like Richard Petworth,[3] that some interest in polite letters began to be developed by some of the Christ Church monks about the middle of the fifteenth century. Already about 1440–50 the monk William Chart[4] appears to have attempted occasionally to write Latin letters on the Italian model,[4] and although his attempts were a failure, yet they are indicative of some interest in humanism at Canterbury at that time. Humanistic writings like the *Exhordia* of Gasparino Barzizza and letters of Poggio, Guarino da Verona, and Francesco Barbaro, were to be found there, and there they were collected and transcribed. The insertion of part of Petworth's Latin correspondence in a manuscript collection made at Christ Church about this period, and including the works mentioned above,[5] suggests Petworth as the source of these texts, especially as we know from other documents of his relations with the monastery.[6]

---

[1] Schirmer, op. cit. p. 14.
[2] *Chronicles of London*, ed. C. L. K. Kingsford, Oxford, 1905, p. 124. On visitors at Christ Church cf. Stone, *Chronicle, passim.*
[3] On Petworth's relations with the Canterbury monks cf. *supra*, p. 20.
[4] William Chart (II) became a monk at Christ Church in 1437 and died in Ireland in 1458 (Stone, op. cit. p. 75). He should be distinguished from William Chart (I) who died at Canterbury in 1417 after having been Treasurer, Penitentiary, and Warden of Canterbury College (*Ibid.*, p. 9). Two Latin letters by William Chart (II) and one addressed to him are in MS. Imperial University Library, Tokyo, A. 100.1300, (Weiss, *Some Unpublished Correspondence of Guarino da Verona*, p. 111). The letter to Chart mentions his literary studies.
[5] Now MS. Imperial University Library, Tokyo, A.100.1300. For a description of this MS. and its contents cf. Lobel, *A fifteenth cent. MS. in private hands*, and Weiss, *Some Unpublished Correspondence of Guarino da Verona*, pp. 110–3.
[6] *Supra*, n. 3.

K

Besides Chart, the monastic community possessed in Henry Cranebroke another member with a bent towards classicism. Cranebroke had entered the Benedictine order in 1435,[1] and had been made an acolyte on 5 March, 1436.[1] He must have shown some promise of scholarship soon after entering the monastery, for he had not been there many years when he was sent to Canterbury College, Oxford, where he held a fellowship in 1443-4.[2] It is very likely that it was in Oxford that he met John Tiptoft, with whom he is known to have been on friendly terms,[3] and it is possible that while there he was able to examine some of Duke Humphrey's books, which may have aroused his curiosity for things classical. In 1444 Cranebroke was ordained priest,[4] and as his name then ceases to appear in the Canterbury College accounts, he probably left Oxford during that year to return to Canterbury, where he died in 1466.[5] Cranebroke's interest in classicism is displayed by his correspondence with Tiptoft,[6] and by one of his notebooks which is still extant.[7] But although Tiptoft referred to one of Cranebroke's letters as 'Ciceronian',[8] his correspondence shows hardly any modern influence. With its euphuisms reminiscent of Abbot Whethamstede, its barbarisms, and its weak attempts at reproducing a classical style, this correspondence indicates merely how its author's handicaps were too great to enable him to imitate Cicero with any success. His and William Chart's attempts at writing in elegant Latin are, however, valuable historically as signs that there were already at that time people at Canterbury who were no longer satisfied with the traditional medieval style, and were attempting to shape their Latin more in conformity with classical models.

[1] MS. Corpus Christi Coll. Oxford, no. 256, fo. 117ʳ. Lambeth Palace, *Register of Archbishop Chichele*, vol. II, fo. 408ʳ.
[2] Dean and Chapter Library, Canterbury, *Accounts of Canterbury College*, years 1443-4. The accounts mention him as 'third fellow' for one term. His name does not appear in the 1444-5 accounts.
[3] *Supra*, p. 113.
[4] Lambeth Palace, *Register of Archbishop Stafford*, fo. 197ʳ.
[5] On December 8th, (Stone, op. cit. p. 96).
[6] On his correspondence with Tiptoft cf. *supra*, p. 113. A letter of William Alde to Cranebroke is in MS. (B.M.) Royal, 10. B.IX, fo. 121ᵛ.
[7] Now MS. (B.M.) Royal, 10.B.IX. For a description of the contents of this MS. cf. G. F. Warner and J. P. Gilson, *Catalogue of the Western Manuscripts in the Old Royal and King's Collections*, London, 1921, vol. I, pp. 314-21. This MS. was obtained by Cranebroke from J. Hinder, 'capellanus' (MS. (B.M.) Royal, 10.B.IX, ff. 1ʳ, 201ʳ) in 1452, Hinder being perhaps another Christ Church monk since his name appears in the Christ Church obituary (MS. (B.M.) Arundel no. 68, fo. 18ʳ). But several additions were made to it by Cranebroke after 1452. [8] *Supra*, p. 113.

Cranebroke's handwriting betrays his study of Italian manuscripts,[1] which is confirmed by some of the texts transcribed into his notebook. Neo-classical works collected by him in it include some of Plutarch's minor works latinized by Guarino da Verona, Cencio Romano's Latin version of the pseudo-Platonic *Axiochus*, and several other translations from the Greek, as well as treatises by Poggio, Bruni, and Guarino.[2] All these works suggest an interest in Greek literature as well as in Italian learning, and it would be interesting to know how they reached him: it seems almost certain that they were acquired by him while at Canterbury: if so, it is very likely that the originals of the texts which he transcribed were lent to him by some friend interested in literature, rather than derived from the Christ Church library. The main importance of learned manifestations at Canterbury, such as those of Chart and Cranebroke, is that they form part of the background to the intellectual outlook of William Sellyng.[3] If Sellyng was eventually able to achieve distinction as a classical scholar, he owed it in part to these modest efforts, which probably first acquainted him with the existence of other values than those contained in the teaching of the schools.

Almost parallel with that of Canterbury was the rise of humanism in the University of Oxford, which had enjoyed a particularly close connexion with Christ Church since Archbishop Islip had founded Canterbury College during the second half of the fourteenth century.[4] As a whole Oxford about 1450–60 was still fundamentally medieval. Studies had undergone no radical change in their organization for centuries, and the Latin Aristotle still reigned supreme and infallible as in the days of Chaucer's clerk. The faculties of Divinity and Decrees ruled the University and conditioned its outlook. Peacock's fall had been applauded, and no body in England was more zealous in the apprehension of heretics, and in the upholding of rigid orthodoxy. Since original speculation had ceased with Wycliffe and University training was chiefly appreciated as an avenue to preferment,

---

[1] Cf. for instance MS. (B.M.) Royal, 10.B.IX, fo. 122ᵛ.

[2] Cf. the contents of *Ibid.* The MS. includes two speeches from Livy and three epigrams by Ausonius transcribed by Cranebroke (*Ibid.*, ff. 53ʳ⁻ᵛ, 55ʳ), and two works by Bruni partly copied by Cranebroke himself in 1459 (*Ibid.*, ff. 64ᵛ⁻7ʳ, 68ᵛ). It is possible that we owe to Cranebroke the Greek alphabet and vowels in MS. (B.L.) Selden, *sup.* no. 65, fo. 146ʳ, since this MS. belonged to Canterbury College and has Cranebroke's characteristic mark at fo. 72ʳ.

[3] On Sellyng cf. *infra*, pp. 153–9.

[4] In 1361 or 1362 (H. C. Maxwell-Lyte, *A History of the University of Oxford*, London, 1886, p. 177).

Oxford had reached a stage when a departure from tradition had become pressing. The outward decadence of the University reflected the state of its learning. Endowment and books were grossly insufficient.[1] Buildings were inadequate while colleges were practically close corporations more anxious for their own welfare than for that of the University. University politics, moved by petty intrigue and inspired by time serving, were mainly directed to flatter the great. Denunciations of the state of affairs had no response in an atmosphere where sycophancy was an accomplishment and original thinking savoured of heresy. What Oxford needed was an upheaval in values. With its studies crystallized into jaded and out-of-date formulas, more modern standards were necessary to arouse it from its intellectual stagnation.

If we take one of its most typical members at this time, Thomas Gascoigne,[2] who served as Chancellor more than once, we shall find no interest in polite letters in him. A perusal of the two large volumes of his *Liber de Veritatibus*[3] discloses neither knowledge of nor the use of works connected with Italian culture, nor any attempts towards adapting his Latin to classical models. Still the slow infiltration of neo-classical writings into Oxford is perceptible even in the case of a conservative like Gascoigne, for his library possessed at least one humanistic work, this being one of Ambrogio Traversari's translations of the Greek Fathers.[4] Gascoigne was also the annotator of a manuscript of Seneca's letters and treatises.[5] But it would be idle to deduce any humanistic leanings from his having studied those works, since Seneca had been very popular throughout the Middle Ages, when he was considered to be almost a Church Father because of his supposed correspondence with St. Paul. Still, the presence of Italian texts, about which more will be said later, and other evidence suggests that interest in humanism was growing in Oxford from about 1440 onwards. From this period

---

[1] The state of the University is reflected in several of the letters included in its official letter-books, cf. *Epistolae Academicae*, vol. I, *passim*. There is yet no satisfactory account of the University of Oxford during the fifteenth century. A useful picture of the medieval University is in H. E. Salter, *Medieval Oxford*, (O.H.S.) Oxford, 1936.

[2] On Gascoigne cf. especially Gascoigne, op. cit., and W. A. Pronger, 'Thomas Gascoigne' E.H.R. liii (1938) pp. 606–26, liv (1939) pp. 20–37.

[3] Now MSS. Lincoln Coll. Oxford, nn. 117–8. Extracts from this work are in Gascoigne, op. cit.

[4] Now MS. Lincoln Coll. Oxford, no. 33.

[5] Now MS. Balliol Coll. Oxford, no. 129. On the notes being in Gascoigne's hand cf. Little, op. cit. p. 57, n. 10.

the Latin of the official correspondence of the University begins to show some improvement. References to Plato[1] and Cicero,[1] Greek history and literature,[1] and the learned men of Italy,[1] begin to appear in these letters, and interest in Latin translations from the Greek is also visible in them.[2] Duke Humphrey's books were accepted with enthusiasm,[3] and their popularity is emphasized not only by the wide use of them by members of the University,[4] but also by the transcripts of some of them which were made in Oxford during the century.[4] That Duke Humphrey's books were a fruitful influence in Oxford can hardly be doubted, as it is also certain that the Oxford authorities were very anxious to increase the University stock of classical and neo-classical texts whenever an opportunity arose. Thus after Humphrey's death repeated efforts were made by the University to secure his Latin manuscripts,[5] and similar attempts were made when it became known that Adam de Moleyns had bequeathed books to Oxford.[5] When Tiptoft wrote from Padua in 1460 sending a list of volumes he intended to present to the University with a view to the improvement of Latin standards in England,[6] he received a reply clothed in a graceful humanistic style and sprinkled with classical quotations, betraying both acquaintance with and interest in the achievements of the Italians as well as genuine enthusiasm for his handsome offer.[6]

But humanism would hardly have had a successful start in Oxford had not influential persons in University circles taken some active interest in it. Considering the state of Oxford culture, it was inevitable that the first followers of Italian fashions should be schoolmen looking upon them as a change from the ordinary medieval *curriculum*, and as a means of improving the style of their writings. Such was actually the position of Thomas Chaundler,[7] who may be considered in many ways as one of the principal pioneers of early humanism in Oxford. Although his attempts at writing like a classicist met with mediocre success, his personal influence proved very valuable. Born in Wells about 1418,[8] Chaundler had been educated at Winchester[8] and New

[1] *Epistolae Academicae*, vols. I, II, *passim*.
[2] *Ibid.*, vol. I, pp. 203, 241, 245.
[3] *Supra*, pp. 66–7.
[4] *Epistolae Academicae*, vol. I, pp. 245–6, *supra*, pp. 25, n. 3; 49, n. 2; 61, n. 2.
[5] *Supra*, pp. 67, n. 4; 80, n. 6.   [6] *Supra*, p. 116.
[7] On Chaundler cf. especially James, *The Chaundler MSS.*, Schirmer, op. cit. pp. 73–81, and the article on him in the supplement to the *D.N.B.*
[8] James, *The Chaundler MSS.*, pp. 1–2. Chaundler obtained his D.D. in 1455 (*Ibid.*, p. 1), and presented New College with MSS. New Coll. Oxford, nn. 34, 46, 50, 242.

College, Oxford.[1] Two years of residence at the latter secured him a fellowship there,[1] so that he was enabled to continue his studies in an academic atmosphere doubtless congenial to his learned tastes. His appointment to the Wardenship of his former school[1] in 1450 took him away from Oxford. Nevertheless his new duties enabled him to continue his intellectual pursuits. A degree in Canon Law obtained in 1452[1] testifies to this, just as the bestowal upon him of the Chancellorship of Wells during the same year[1] shows that the road to ecclesiastical preferment was also open to him. Chaundler's absence from Oxford was not to be a very long one. His authority in academic circles was high enough to justify his appointment to the Wardenship of New College in 1454,[1] an office which he filled with distinction until 1475.[1] To his Wardenship of New College were added other dignities, both ecclesiastical and academic, the latter including the Chancellorship of Oxford University from 1457 to 1461 and from 1472 to 1479,[1] and the Vice-Chancellorship from 1463 to 1467.[1] In 1480 Chaundler was made an Apostolic Protonotary,[2] and from 1482 until his death he held the Deanery of Hereford.[2]

As can be seen from this biographical outline, Chaundler spent most of his life in Oxford, where his exalted position was bound to advertise his interest in humane literature within the University. As Chancellor of Wells he was in contact with his Bishop, Thomas Bekynton, to whom he dedicated his *Liber Apologeticus*[3] and his *Collocutiones*[4] and *Allocutiones*,[4] so that it is likely that this connexion, and access to the books given by Gloucester to Oxford, were responsible for introducing him to polite literature.[5] Chaundler's leanings can be detected in his Latin works.[6] Although these are written from a rigidly medieval standpoint, their style displays none the less the influence of Cicero as well as some improvement upon that of most of Chaundler's contemporaries. Cicero appears to have been a great favourite with him: the number of Ciceronian quotations in his writings is large, and

---

[1] Cf. *supra*, p. 133, n. 8.
[2] James, *The Chaundler MSS.*, p. 2, *C.P.R.*, vol. XIII, p. 80.
[3] The MS. of this work given to Bekynton is now MS. Trinity Coll. Cambridge, no. 881. Bekynton presented it to Wells Cathedral where it was seen by Leland, (Leland, *Collectanea*, vol. IV, p. 156). The *Liber Apologeticus* is a kind of mystery play dealing with the position of mankind. For its subject matter cf. Schirmer, op. cit. pp. 77-8.
[4] *Infra*, p. 135, n. 10.
[5] Apart from the actual popularity of Gloucester's donations (*supra*, p. 133), his use of the books presented by the Duke is suggested by his knowledge of Decembrio's Latin *Republic* and Bruni's text of the *Ethics* (*infra*, p. 135).
[6] For a list of Chaundler's writings cf. James, *The Chaundler MSS.*, pp. 7-16.

includes references to the *Tusculanae Disputationes*,[1] and the *Epistulae ad Familiares*.[1] Other Latin authors mentioned by Chaundler are Solinus,[2] Cato,[3] Seneca,[3] Horace,[3] Vergil,[4] and Aulus Gellius.[5] Although it is certain that he knew no Greek, he liked to quote from Greek authors.[6] Such quotations were mainly derived from Cicero, Lactantius, St. Augustine, and John of Salisbury. But besides using secondary sources, he apparently had access to some modern translations from the Greek such as Bruni's *Ethics*[7] and Decembrio's *Republic*,[8] both of which he mentions and probably had seen in the University Library.[9]

Chaundler's literary remains are not very interesting except as evidence of his leanings. The aim of his *Allocutiones*[10] and *Collocutiones*[10] is to prove that William of Wykeham possessed all the Aristotelian virtues, and they have been rightly described as 'a dreary performance.'[11] His dialogue on Bath and Wells[12] resem-

[1] MS. New Coll. Oxford, no. 288, ff. 31ᵛ, 55ᵛ, etc. Chaundler quotes also very often the *De Officiis* (*Ibid.*, ff. 38ᵛ, 39ʳ, etc.). I have been unable to trace any reference to Cicero's speeches in Chaundler's works despite James' statement that Chaundler quotes also from them (James, *The Chaundler MSS.*, p. 5). Chaundler's attitude towards Cicero is clear from his writings. Many of the arguments of his *Allocutiones* are inspired by Cicero. For his attitude towards Cicero cf. also the following passage by him in MS. New Coll. Oxford, no. 288, fo. 38ᵛ: *in opere quidem nostro duos ergo potissime elaboratos in philosophia et oratoria arte secutus sum. Aristotile ui (sic), et Ciceronem e quibus hic latinus extuit ille uero grecus. Sed latinus Cicero noster potior e duobus mea opinione floruit orator.*

[2] *Libellus de Laudibus Duarum Civitatum*, p. 113.

[3] MS. New Coll. Oxford, no. 288, ff. 7ʳ, 23ᵛ; *Official Correspondence of Thomas Beckington*, vol. I, p. 268.

[4] Cf. especially MS. New Coll. Oxford, no. 288, fo. 81ᵛ, where he ends the *Allocutiones* with a quotation fom *Aeneid*, VI, 129–30.

[5] *Ibid.*, ff. 22ᵛ, 23ʳ, 36ᵛ.

[6] *Official Correspondence of Thomas Beckington*, vols. I, p. 267, II, pp. 316–8, 320.

[7] MS. New Coll. Oxford, no. 288, fo. 45ʳ.

[8] *Libellus De Laudibus Duarum Civitatum*, p. 109 has a passage that suggests that Chaundler was acquainted with Decembrio's version of Plato's *Republic*. Plato is also quoted by Chaundler in his dedicatory epistle to Bekynton (*Official Correspondence of Thomas Bekynton*, vol. II, p. 316), but probably from an indirect source. His mention of the *Apologia Socratis* (MS. Trinity Coll. Cambridge, no. 881, fo. 10ᵛ) must equally derive from an indirect source.

[9] To which they had been presented by Gloucester (*Epistolae Academicae*, vol. I, pp. 181, 237).

[10] The *Collocutiones* were originally composed by one of Chaundler's pupils when he was Warden of Winchester (*Official Correspondence of Thomas Beckington*, vol. II, p. 320). Chaundler, however, not only supervised their composition, but also corrected and emended them (*Ibid.*, loc. cit.), so that they may be considered practically as his own work. Both the *Allocutiones* and the *Collocutiones* are in MS. New Coll. Oxford, no. 288. This MS., which is the presentation copy given to Bekynton, must have been written in 1464 or 1465 since it includes a letter of Pius II dated November 1463, and Bekynton died in 1465. The *Allocutiones* were composed after 1461 since they include an allusion to Chaundler's four years' tenure of the Oxford Chancellorship, 1457–61 (MS. New Coll. Oxford, no. 288, fo. 11ᵛ). On these two works cf. James, *The Chaundler MSS*, pp. 7–8. On the MSS. of Chaundler's works cf. *Ibid.*, pp. 17–35. The New College MS. was seen by Leland in Wells Cathedral to which it had been presented by Bekynton (Leland, *Collectanea*, vol. IV, p. 156). On the possible scribe of this MS. cf. *infra*, p. 99.

[11] Leach, *History of Winchester College*, p. 215.

[12] Printed in *Libellus De Laudibus Duarum Civitatum*.

bles the *Allocutiones* and *Collocutiones*: its Latin is similar in quality, and some of the arguments in the discussion are, as in the two other works, based on classical authorities. Closer to the spirit of neo-classicism is Chaundler's dedicatory epistle to Thomas Bekynton,[1] in which the numerous second hand quotations from Greek authors, the examples drawn from classical antiquity, and the general tone, betray an attitude in its author not very different from the humanist's. In his scholarship Chaundler appears to have encountered many of the difficulties which had faced Abbot Whethamstede. Although his aim was to write like a humanist, he was not able to perceive the fundamental difference between the scholastic and modern outlooks, and his attempts at being 'Ciceronian' proved far from successful. His efforts to give a humane character to some of his writings, and his use of neo-classical and ancient texts while pursuing typically scholastic studies, indicate clearly his conception of modern learning merely as a means by which the old learning could be improved. In fact, his appreciation of the antique was subordinated to the help it gave to his more conservative studies, and if he encouraged classicism he did so in order to further the advancement of medieval rather than of Renaissance culture. However, so great was his contemporary reputation that when the Italian scholar Cornelio Vitelli delivered a Latin oration in Oxford about 1491, it was Chaundler who replied to him with a Latin speech which Leland saw at Wells.[1] Chaundler's rôle in the development of humanism in Oxford appears to lie mainly in personal contacts. But his work and his reception of Vitelli are also indicative of an interest in neo-classicism, which is also suggested by his having had his works transcribed in a humanistic script for presentation to Bekynton.[2]

It was very probably through Chaundler's direct influence that the literary interests of John Farley[3] originated and developed. Born in Winchester, Farley had entered Winchester College in 1444,[4] whence he passed to New College where he was elected

---

[1] Printed in *Official Correspondence of Thomas Beckington*, vol. II, pp. 315–20. Leland, *De Scriptoribus*, p. 457.

[2] Now MSS. New Coll. Oxford, no. 288, and Trinity Coll. Cambridge, no. 881. On the writing of these MSS. cf. James, *The Chaundler MSS.*, pp. 29–30. Part of the Trinity College MS. was written by the scribe of the New College one, on whom cf. *infra*, p. 137. Chaundler also presented Bekynton with an illustrated *Bestiary* (*Official Correspondence of Thomas Beckington*, vol. I, pp. 273–4). A Boethius formerly possessed by Chaundler is now MS. (B.M.) Harl. no. 43.

[3] On Farley cf. *The Medieval Archives of the University of Oxford*, vol. II, pp. 284–6.

[4] Kirby, *Winchester Scholars*, p. 64.

to a fellowship on 10 March, 1448.[1] After obtaining his degree of Master of Arts, he secured admission to the Faculty of Theology,[2] and found employment at the same time in the administration of the University, where he succeeded John Mannyngham as scribe, or to use a modern equivalent, Registrar, a post which he occupied in 1458, and which was held by him with his fellowship until his premature death in 1464.[3] But for his early death Farley might have reached some distinction as a scholar. His strong leanings towards Italian learning are disclosed by his handwriting, which was probably influenced by his study of Duke Humphrey's books, one of which is actually mentioned by him in one of his letters.[4] This calligraphic style appears in some of the letters which he wrote for the University,[5] and in one of the Chaundler Manuscripts, the writing of which has been attributed to him.[6] The Latinity and some of the quotations and expressions in Farley's letters are equally suggestive, and make it very probable that it was he who replied on behalf of the University to the Earl of Worcester in 1460,[7] since this letter shows that its writer was able to adopt a humanistic technique when necessary. The interests of Farley were not, however, confined to the imitation of the Latin style and script of the Italian humanists. Besides this, he was probably the first person in fifteenth century Oxford to attempt to learn Greek, but his acquisition of a wide knowledge of this language must remain doubtful.

At his death Robert Grosseteste, Bishop of Lincoln, had bequeathed his books, which included several Greek texts, to the Grey Friars of Oxford.[8] The library of this Franciscan Convent

---

[1] *Register of the University of Oxford*, vol. I, p. 32.

[2] MS. New Coll. Oxford, no. 281, flyleaf.

[3] *Statuta Antiqua Universitatis Oxoniensis*, ed. S. Gibson, Oxford, 1931, p. xx. Farley was already scribe on 11 October, 1458, when he petitioned the University to be allowed to take out a register from the 'four keys chest' for a week (*Munimenta Academica*, vol. II, p. 752). He cannot have been over thirty-four years of age when he died (*The Medieval Archives of the University of Oxford*, vol. II, p. 286).

[4] *Epistolae Academicae*, vol. II, p. 373.

[5] University Archives, Oxford, *Register Ff.4*, ff. 111ᵛ-2ʳ, etc. Italian influence on the handwriting of this register begins in 1459 (*Ibid.*, fo. 108ʳ). Another Englishman writing in an Italian hand at the time was John Pacy, 'capellanus', as it appears from MSS. Pembroke Coll. Cambridge, no. 235, which he wrote in 1464, and Corpus Christi Coll., Cambridge, no. 158.

[6] *The Medieval Archives of the University of Oxford*, vol. II, p. 285.

[7] On this letter cf. *supra*, p. 116. For examples of Farley's letter writing cf. *Epistolae Academicae*, vol. II, pp. 359-61, 366-7, 373-4.

[8] Little, op. cit. pp. 57-8. On the Grey Friars library cf. *Ibid.*, pp. 55-62. This library was widely used by Gascoigne (*Ibid.*, pp. 57-9); at a later date it was apparently used by the Greek scribes Emanuel of Constantinople and John Serbopoulos (*infra*, p. 145, n. 4).

was open to some members of the University during the fifteenth century,[1] so that it is probable that Farley began to learn Greek on these manuscripts, this view being confirmed by his obtaining from the Oxford Franciscans a twelfth century Greek *Psalter* now at Cambridge.[2] The margins of this manuscript contain several transliterations of passages in Farley's hand,[3] which suggest that he began to learn Greek from this *Psalter* with the aid of a Latin *Psalter* by comparing the two texts and transliterating passages into Latin characters.[4] Knowledge of Greek, however elementary, must have appeared something of a distinction to Farley, who did not hesitate to sign his name on some of his official letters in his register in Greek characters, probably in order to display his learning.[5]

John Farley's modest achievement in the field of humanism shows the diffusion of this new form of culture in Oxford academic circles. Such a development is furthermore emphasized by the presence of an Italian scholar teaching Latin eloquence there during some period between 1454 and 1471.

What induced Stefano Surigone[6] to come and teach in Oxford is not known. By birth he was a Milanese,[7] by vocation a member of the order of the Humiliates,[7] and he styled himself Poet Laureate.[7] His teaching of Latin eloquence appears to have influenced William Sellyng considerably,[8] and possibly was the origin of the latter's humane interests. Although we possess no evidence to connect Surigone with either Chaundler or Farley, it is possible that they came into contact with him, while it is certain that his teaching must have added encouragement to the development of polite letters in Oxford. During his visit to England he also wrote a Latin treatise, which he very probably

---

[1] Cf. *supra*, p. 137, n. 8.

[2] Now MS. Corpus Christi Coll. Cambridge, no. 480. On this MS. having belonged to Grosseteste cf. M. R. James, *A Descriptive Catalogue of the Manuscripts in the Library of Corpus Christi College, Cambridge*, Cambridge, 1911, vol. II, p. 422.

[3] MS. Corpus Christi Coll. Cambridge, no. 480, ff. 206ᵛ, 218ʳ, etc. Salter also suggests that these transliterations are by Farley (*The Medieval Archives of the University of Oxford*, vol. II, p. 285). A comparison of these notes with other specimens of Farley's hand confirms Farley's authorship.

[4] This was one of the methods employed by the Italian humanists when learning Greek (Sabbadini, *Il Metodo degli Umanisti*, pp. 18–22).

[5] *Epistolae Academicae*, vol. II, pp. 367–8, 371, 374. Farley's signature in Greek appears also in MSS. Corpus Christi Coll. Cambridge, no. 480, fo. 288ᵛ, (B.L.) Auct. F.5.29, fo. viiʳ.

[6] On Surigone cf. Weiss, *Humanism in Oxford*, p. 28. On his teaching in Oxford at some period between 1454–64 and possibly 1465–71, cf. *Ibid.*, loc. cit. He may have been the *Surygoin* admitted *ad incipiendum in iure canonico* at Cambridge in 1475 (*Grace Book A*, p. 110).

[7] Weiss, *Humanism in Oxford*, p. 28.   [8] *Infra*, pp. 153–4.

dedicated to an English patron,[1] but unfortunately this throws no additional light on his English activities. After leaving Oxford Surigone appears in Cologne in 1471, when he matriculated at that University,[2] being already a Bachelor of Canon Law.[2] About seven years later he reappears in England, where he seems to have established a connexion with William Caxton, whom he had probably met in Cologne.[2] The learning of the Milanese obviously impressed Caxton, who having then an edition of Chaucer's *Boethius* in the press, requested him to compose a Latin elegy in praise of Chaucer to be included in the book. The elegy was printed at the end of the *Boethius*, which Caxton issued in 1478,[3] and it is not to be excluded that he may have availed himself of Surigone's help in editorial activities, as he did later with Carmeliano.[4] The poems by Surigone[5] show him to have been an accomplished Latin poet whose verse could rank favourably with the best of his time. He was apparently one of those wandering scholars who never settled in one place for long, and besides lecturing in Oxford and studying at Cologne, he is known to have taught the humanities at Strassburg[6] and Louvain.[6]

From the various evidence on the development of humanism in fifteenth century Oxford, one can perceive the great influence exercised by Duke Humphrey's donations. It is also apparent that interest in polite letters developed among schoolmen, who accepted them as a complement to their learning rather than as a product of a different cultural outlook. The reasons for what was practically an infiltration of humanistic values into scholastic studies, becomes clear when we remember that by the middle of the fifteenth century scholasticism was in its decline, and that attempts at reforming it by scholastic means were subjected to suspicion, as Peacock's case had proved. Now new standards borrowed from without could at any rate strengthen the crum-

---

[1] The *De Institucionibus boni uiri libellus*, in MS. Trinity Coll. Cambridge, no. 330. On its possible dedication to an English patron cf. Weiss, *Humanism in Oxford*, p. 28.

[2] *Ibid.*, loc. cit.

[3] *The Consolacion of Philosophie*, Westminster, W. Caxton, 1478, ff. 94^r-^v. Surigone's presence in England about 1478 is suggested by his composition of the elegy at Caxton's request for the edition of the *Boethius* (*Ibid.*, fo. 94^v). The elegy was also inscribed on a tablet placed on Chaucer's tomb in Westminster Abbey at Caxton's expense, (*Ibid.*, fo. 93^v).

[4] *Infra*, p. 172.

[5] Preserved in MS. (B.M.) Arundel, no. 249, ff. 94^r-117^v. No references to England or Englishmen occur in these poems.

[6] On his activities in Strassburg and Louvain cf. *Ibid.*, ff. 97^v-8^r, 103^r, 111^r, 112^v, 116^v.

bling façade of scholastic learning. Humanism clearly possessed the required new values. Hence a judicious admission of Italian learning would give new life to the jaded Oxford erudition. This was the opinion of Tiptoft and Flemmyng, whose gifts to Oxford were intended to continue Humphrey's work. That all these efforts, that the work of patrons as well as scholars, proved successful is evident. Surigone's teaching confirms the Oxford appreciation of humanism, and suggests that perhaps further expansion was prevented only by economic difficulties. But the knowledge of Greek which was to be found in Oxford between 1470–80, also indicates that the schemes of Gloucester, Flemmyng, and Tiptoft, were slowly proving fruitful.

Chapter IX

RESIDENCE in Oxford, and contacts with Tiptoft and Chaundler, were probably material in directing the interests of George Neville[1] towards literature. A younger brother of Richard, Earl of Warwick (the Kingmaker), Neville played a rôle of some importance in the perturbed politics of the first period of Edward IV's reign and the Lancastrian restoration of 1470-1. What, however, concerns us are his scholarly rather than his political ventures, as these are particularly interesting in regard to the history of humanism and the beginnings of Greek studies in England.

Neville had been educated at Oxford, where he was Free's contemporary at Balliol College. After following the Arts courses, he had supplicated for the degree of Bachelor of Arts on 15 June, 1450,[2] this being followed by the Mastership of Arts, which he obtained in 1452 without having to submit to all the statutory regulations.[2] Thanks to the great influence of his family, on 9 June, 1453, he was in spite of his youth elected to succeed Gilbert Kymer as Chancellor of Oxford University.[3] The first two years of his Chancellorship were spent in Oxford, but in 1455 he obtained leave to absent himself from the University for some time.[3] On his provision to the Bishopric of Exeter in 1456[4] he tendered his resignation from the Chancellorship,[5] but despite his reluctance to continue in this office he was re-elected to it. Nevertheless he remained firm in his decision, so that his resignation had eventually to be accepted, and a successor elected in the person of Thomas Chaundler.[5] From Exeter Neville was translated to the Archbishopric of York in 1465.[6] But in the meantime he was reappointed Chancellor of Oxford in May 1461, this time holding the office until he was exiled to Calais by Edward IV in 1472.[7]

[1] On Neville cf. F. Godwin, *De Praesulibus Angliae Commentarius*, London, 1616, vols. I, pp. 471-2, II, pp. 63-9, and the article on him in the *D.N.B.*

[2] *Register of the University of Oxford*, vol. I, pp. ix, n. 1, 10.

[3] Le Neve, op. cit. vol. III, p. 467. *Munimenta Academica*, vol. II, pp. 742-3. He was ordained Priest by William Grey, Bishop of Ely, on 21 December, 1454 (MS. (C.U.) Mm. I. 41, fo. 25ʳ).

[4] *C.P.R.* vol. XI, p. 30. Callixtus III had originally intended to give this bishopric to John Halfe (MS. Corpus Christi Coll. Cambridge, no. 170, p. 235).

[5] *Munimenta Academica*, vol. II, p. 758.

[6] *C.P.R.* vol. XII, p. 432.

[7] Le Neve, op. cit. vol. III, p. 467. On Neville's exile to Calais cf. Warkworth, op. cit. p. 25. Besides exiling him, Edward IV made an unsuccessful attempt to deprive him of the Archbishopric of York (*S.P.M.* p. 165).

Already during his stay in Oxford Neville had begun to show himself anxious to encourage learning, and by 1455 he had presented at least one book to the library of his own college.[1] He had also begun to indulge in literary interests, and when we consider his links with Tiptoft[2] and Chaundler,[2] and the advance of humanism in Oxford at the time of his residence there, it seems likely that his leanings towards polite letters were originated while at the University. A person who also undoubtedly exercised a strong intellectual influence over him in that direction was John Shirwood, later Bishop of Durham, who was already closely connected with Neville in 1460 at the latest,[3] and whose first contacts with him probably took place in Oxford. Neville's pursuit of *belles lettres* was testified to by Shirwood,[4] and extant evidence indicates that his intellectual curiosity went out towards Greek learning. The presentation of a Demosthenes and other Greek texts to him by a Greek scribe in 1468[4] points to this; moreover the late Dr. M. R. James suggests that this scribe, Emanuel of Constantinople, was one of the scholars who brought fame to Neville's household.[5] The presentation of this volume is, of course, though suggestive no conclusive proof in itself that Neville attained mastery of the Greek language. Petrarch possessed Greek manuscripts and was in close connexion with the Byzantine Nicholas Sigeros, who gave him a copy of Homer, and with the Greek speaking Calabrians Barlaam and Leontius Pilatus, yet, as is well-known, he never succeeded in learning that tongue, and remained unable to read his Homer and his Plato.[6] But in Neville's case there are some notes in Greek almost certainly written by him,[7] which suggest that he attained to at

---

[1] Now MS. Balliol Coll. Oxford, no. 117. Donor and date of donation of this MS. to Balliol are disclosed by the seventeenth century Donors Book of the library of Balliol College, which reproduces at p. 6 a label formerly on the binding of the MS. bearing the following inscription: *Donum Reuer. in Chro. patris Geo. Neuell epis. Exon. deinde Ebora. Archiep.* 1455.

[2] Neville was Tiptoft's brother-in-law having married his sister Cicely Neville (Mitchell, *John Tiptoft*, p. 19). As Chancellor of Oxford Neville must have been in close touch with Chaundler then a leading Oxford figure.

[3] Cf. *infra*, p. 149.   [4] Cf. *infra*, pp. 144–5.

[5] James, *The Scribe of the Leicester Codex*, p. 446.

[6] On Petrarch's Greek studies cf. De Nolhac, *Petrarque et l'Humanisme*, vol. II, pp. 127–88.

[7] Cf. the note αρχηεπισκόπου in MS. (B.M.) Sloane, no. 278, fo. 1ʳ, and the note αρχηέπισκο ... (the rest of the note is torn off) in MS. Chapter Library, York, XVI.Q.7, fo. 1ʳ. Both these notes are in a fifteenth century hand and doubtless refer to Neville's ownership of the MSS. I learn from the York Chapter Librarian that the late Dr. M. R. James attributed these notes to Emanuel of Constantinople. After comparing them with specimens of Emanuel's handwriting I have reached the conclusion that they are certainly not by him. The writer of these notes shows quite openly his inexperience at writing in Greek, which suggests that they may be by Neville himself.

least an elementary knowledge of that language. Latin learning and especially good Latin writing also attracted Neville, so much so that he chose secretaries capable of composing Latin letters in a style close to that of the humanists.[1] It was probably one of the scholars in his pay who wrote in 1461 the long and interesting letter to the Bishop of Terni, in which news about the battle of Towton is given together with much moralizing upon the evils of civil strife.[2] Still whatever its real authorship, this letter, in which Lucan is aptly quoted, shows that its writer was to some extent under the influence of polite letters, and even if the author was not Neville himself, it displays at any rate the literary spirit in his household.

Yet another instance of Neville's attitude towards learning is to be found in one of the letters written on his behalf to the University of Oxford, a reply to the University's appeal for help in securing the books bequeathed to it by John Tiptoft, Earl of Worcester. On Neville's instructions, the actual writer of the letter stated that in his youth the Archbishop had acquired as many books as possible, had caused others to be copied for his use, and valued nothing so much, as they contained the voice of antiquity, morality, and religion.[3]

A knowledge of the personnel of Neville's household would be of considerable interest. Equally interesting would be the names of those members of it who sought refuge in Cambridge when Neville was exiled to Calais in 1472.[4] Information concerning this has so far been denied to us. On the other hand we are able to identify as having been in Neville's service not only Shirwood,[5] but also a Fellow of Balliol named ' Bulkie',[5] and perhaps the scribe Emanuel of Constantinople.[5] Yet despite this, insufficient evidence has reached us for it to be possible to reconstruct successfully Neville's literary activities. His application to letters, his bibliophily, his probable acquaintance with Greek, are known to us and we are also aware that he was given to patronage. We know too that his household enjoyed the reputation of being a

---

[1] Shirwood and a Fellow of Balliol College named Bulkie wrote Latin letters for Neville (Tait, op. cit. p. 571, n. 5).

[2] This letter was written in London on 7 April, 1461. A contemporary copy of it is in the Archivio di Stato, Venice, and is calendared in *S.P.V.* vol. I, pp. 99–101. A contemporary Italian version of it is in the Archivio di Stato, Milan, and is calendared in *S.P.M.* pp. 60–3. As this letter was both transcribed and translated in Italy, it must have been circularized there as an account of the battle of Towton.

[3] Tait, op. cit. p. 573. The letter is in *Ibid.*, pp. 573–4.

[4] *The Paston Letters*, vol. V, p. 137.

[5] *Supra*, n. 1 and p. 142.

gathering of men of letters, and that Neville's studies ended
with his exile. This last point we owe to John Shirwood, who
after visiting him during his confinement declared that he had
given up all his former interests,[1] and that he had attempted to
teach him his game of *Arithmomachia* in order to distract him.[2]

Evidence about Neville's scholarship discloses little distinction. As in the case of Gloucester, it shows a lively interest in
polite letters but a dearth of actual learning. It is true that as his
extant letters were written by scholars in his pay, we are not in a
position to judge his proficiency in Latin; but the delegation of
his correspondence to secretaries is significant, while the Greek
notes attributed to him give no hint of particular distinction.
The almost total loss of his library prevents us from knowing
what constituted his favourite reading matter. Still the frag-
mentary information that reached us suggests that, like Gloucester and Tiptoft, he was primarily a 'Maecenas' and a connoisseur
of polite letters. It was chiefly as a patron that he contributed to
the advancement of classical studies, since by protecting Emanuel
of Constantinople and Shirwood, he was able to foster the introduction of Greek in England. While Robert Flemmyng's and
John Farley's Greek studies left little, if any, tradition behind
them, it is to Neville that we may trace the beginning of a vigorous revival of Greek in this country, the first since the days of
Robert Grosseteste and Roger Bacon.

Practically nothing is known of the life of Neville's protégé,
the scribe Emanuel of Constantinople. In an interesting essay
Mr. Howard Gray was inclined to identify him with an 'Emanuel
of Constantinople, Knight', who was in England in 1456 when
he was granted a sum of money by the Crown.[3] It is quite
possible that this knight and the scribe were one person: on the
other hand as Emanuel was a name to be found as frequently in
Constantinople as John or William in modern England, it should
be open to doubt as to whether they were actually identical.
Whether the scribe was the Emanuel rewarded by the Crown

---

[1] . . . *et affectus preterea incommoda ualitudine non tantum poterat incumbere leccionibus litterarum
que studiis antea consueuerat.* (MS. (B.L.) Ashmol. no. 344, fo. 24ᵛ) (Shirwood to Cardinal
Barbo on Neville at Calais).

[2] *Ibid.*, fo. 24ʳ. On this game cf. Allen, *Bishop Shirwood of Durham and his Library*, p. 448.

[3] Gray, *Greek Visitors to England in* 1455–6, p. 107. Grants had also been given to three
other Greeks, including the famous Aristotelian scholar John Argyropoulos. But nothing
else is known concerning their visit to England. Probably they came on a diplomatic
mission and departed without giving any appreciable contribution to English learning.
On Argyropoulos in England cf. *Ibid.*, pp. 87–94.

or not, it is possible that he found his way into England with some embassy. Greeks were often employed on diplomatic activities during the fifteenth century on account of their linguistic abilities,[1] and Emanuel settled here for some time. It was in 1468 that he presented Archbishop Neville with one of his transcripts, a Demosthenes,[2] while the presence in this country of various other manuscripts written by him,[3] suggests that he may have found other patrons besides the Archbishop. It is practically certain that he taught Greek to Neville and Shirwood, and it is highly probable that while in England he visited Oxford or its neighbourhood.[4] Thus one might perhaps deduce from this that he was also responsible for teaching Greek to William Grocin while the latter was at New College.[5] In spite of so little evidence, Emanuel's presence here is of great interest, for his activities confirm the supposition that by the second half of the fifteenth century the study of Greek had been taken up in England, and that there was a certain demand for manuscripts in that language.

Greek studies in England during the third quarter of the fifteenth century appear to have been mainly confined to Oxford,[6] Canterbury,[6] and the entourage of George Neville. That not much interest in this language was to be found outside Oxford or Canterbury after the dissolution of Neville's household, is disclosed by the misadventures in London of two famous Greek scholars, Andronicus Callistus[7] and George Hermonymos.[7]

[1] George Hermonymos, to give an instance, was sent to England in 1475 by Pope Sixtus IV on a diplomatic mission. (*Infra*, p. 146.)

[2] Now MS. University Library, Leyden, Voss. Gr. no. 56. On this MS. cf. James, *The Scribe of the Leicester Codex*, pp. 445–7. This MS. contains some *sermones judiciales* of Demosthenes and letters attributed to Aeschines, Plato, and Chion.

[3] The following is a list of the MSS. copied by Emanuel which are still extant: Leicester Town Library, the Codex of the *New Testament*; Cathedral Library, Durham, MSS. C.I.15, (Aristotle), C.IV.1, (Plato); Corpus Christi Coll. Oxford, no. 19, (*Psalter*), nn. 76–7, (Suidas, partly written by John Serbopoulos); (B.M.) Harl. no. 3100, (Suidas, given to Harley by the Durham Chapter); Corpus Christi Coll. Cambridge, no. 81, (Homer); Gonville and Caius Coll. Cambridge, no. 348, (*Psalter*); Trinity Coll. Cambridge, no. 1186, (*Psalter*); University Library, Leyden, Voss. Gr. no. 56, (Demosthenes etc.). Gray, op. cit. p. 112, suggests that the Gonville *Psalter* came to its former owner, the Franciscan Richard Brinkley, from the Oxford Grey Friars, as did MS. Gonville and Caius Coll. Cambridge, no. 403.

[4] This is suggested by Emanuel's transcripts of Suidas which were copied from the Suidas given by Grosseteste to the Oxford Grey Friars, (James, *Greek Manuscripts in England before the Renaissance*, p. 342). This view is corroborated by part of the Corpus Christi MS. being in the hand of Serbopoulos, and by its becoming the possession of William Grocin, and also by Brinkley's probable borrowing of a MS. written by Emanuel from the Oxford Grey Friars. (*Supra*, n. 4.) [5] *Infra*, p. 174.

[6] *Supra*, p. 138, *infra*, p. 157. Of course Flemmyng, Gunthorpe, and Shirwood, pursued the study of Greek in England during the fifteenth century. But theirs were isolated cases which established no tradition of Greek learning in this country.

[7] On Callistus cf. Legrand, op. cit. vol. I, pp. l–lvii. On Hermonymos cf. Omont, *Georges Hermonyme*.

L

The former, after teaching Greek in various towns in Italy, where he met John Free[1] and had Politian[1] among his pupils, had moved first to Paris,[2] and then to London, where he was already in March 1476.[2] Perhaps he was induced to visit this country by recollections of Free: but he failed to find success in London, and he probably died there in 1476.[2] During his short stay in England, he was in touch with his compatriot Hermonymos, whom he helped when the latter was imprisoned and fined, by writing a long appeal from London to a Greek friend in Louis XI's service.[3] From the very little that we know about Callistus's English sojourn, it appears very doubtful that he found opportunities of teaching, or even of introducing Greek texts into this country.

Hardly more fortunate was the visit paid to England by his friend George Hermonymos. This Greek from Sparta had been sent here in 1475 by Pope Sixtus IV to obtain from Edward IV the release of Archbishop Neville from Calais.[4] His mission was successful, and Neville was allowed to return to England.[4] Soon after this, however, Hermonymos was charged with spying on the movements of some Italian merchants, and in spite of his diplomatic character he was imprisoned and fined very heavily.[5] Eventually he succeeded in regaining his freedom, but not until he had surrendered all the money he had brought with him from Rome, all the presents received from the grateful Neville, and had been forced to borrow a large sum for which his friend Callistus stood security.[5] During his visit to England Hermonymos presented Neville, whose tastes appear to have been familiar to him, with an illuminated copy of one of his Latin translations of gnomic sayings ascribed to ancient Greek philosophers,[6] and started a friendship with John Shirwood,

---

[1] *Supra*, p. 109. Legrand, op. cit. vol. I, p. liii. It is possible that also Sellyng was one of his pupils (*Infra*, p. 154).

[2] Legrand, op. cit. vol. I, p. lvi.

[3] Addressed to George Palaeologos Dishipatos, Captain of Touques in Normandy, printed in J. F. Boissonade, *Anedocta Graeca*, Paris, 1829–33, vol. V, pp. 420–6.

[4] Omont, *Georges Hermonyme*, pp. 7, 31. The first indication of Neville's release is his confirmation of an abbot at Westminster in November 1475, (Ramsay, op. cit. vol. II, p. 415, n.).

[5] Omont, *Georges Hermonyme*, p. 8. The alleged amount of his fine, one thousand pounds, is hardly credible when we consider the value of money at the time. Hermonymos had already left England in June 1476, when he was in the Netherlands where he dedicated a work to the Abbot of Dunes (*Ibid.*, p. 35).

[6] The presentation copy to Neville is now MS. (B.M.) Harl. no. 3346. This work was also dedicated by Hermonymos to the Abbot of Dunes (*supra*, n.5). The presentation copy to Shirwood of the *De Virtutibus* is now MS. (B.L.) Auct. G.9.3. The *De Virtutibus* was also dedicated to the Archbishop of Sens by Hermonymos (Omont, *Georges Hermonyme*, pp. 19–20). The versions dedicated to Neville and Shirwood were printed in Paris about 1480

to whom he dedicated some years later his Latin version of the pseudo-Aristotelian *De Virtutibus*.[1] Had Hermonymos found better treatment in this country, it is quite possible that he might have settled here instead of in Paris, and the course of Greek studies in England at the eve of the Reformation might have been very different.

In spite of the scanty success of Callistus and Hermonymos, the pursuit of Greek in this country was advancing slowly. During the same year in which Hermonymos and Callistus were in London, another Greek scholar was to be found there. Unfortunately all we know about the visit to England of Demetrius Cantacuzenus, is that in 1475 he was in London, where he copied a volume of excerpts from Herodotus,[2] possibly for an English patron, a small point yet quite significant. More evidence of a gradual development of interest in Greek in England, is to be found in the presence here of John Serbopoulos of Constantinople.[3] Although the earliest proof of Serbopoulos's residence in England dates from 1484,[4] he was probably already here much earlier. He may have lived at first in Oxford,[5] where we know that at some time he was in touch with Emanuel of Constantinople,[5] and transcribed manuscripts for an academic clientele.[5] These included various copies of the Greek grammar of Theodor Gaza[6] and other texts. Now Gaza's grammar was one of the most fashionable handbooks at the time for learning Greek: hence his frequent transcription of this work indicates the presence of a public anxious to learn Greek, and suggests that he may have alternated his work as a scribe with some teaching.

(*Gesamtkatalog*, no. 2497). The *De Virtutibus* was dedicated to Shirwood after 1484 since he is styled Bishop of Durham.

[1] Cf. *supra*, p. 146, n. 6.

[2] Now MS. (B.N.) Gr. no. 1731. On this MS. cf. Vogel und Gardthausen, op. cit. p. 102.

[3] On Serbopoulos cf. *Ibid.*, pp. 196–7.

[4] When he copied the grammar of Theodor Gaza now MS. Trinity Coll. Dublin, no. 925. The date of this MS. is 1484 and not 1480 as stated in Vogel und Gardthausen, op. cit. p. 196, cf. J. G. Smyly, 'Notes on Greek MSS. in the Library of Trinity College,' *Hermathena*, XXIII (1933), p. 174.

[5] His stay in Oxford is suggested by his having copied ff. 94ʳ–332ᵛ of MS. Corpus Christi Coll. Oxford, no. 77 from a MS. in the library of the Oxford Grey Friars (*supra*, p. 145, n. 3), the rest of the MS. being transcribed by Emanuel of Constantinople. As some of the MSS. copied by Serbopoulos belonged to Grocin (*infra*, p. 148, n. 2), and one of his transcripts of Gaza's grammar was found in Oxford about 1480 (*infra*, n. 6), his having worked for an academic clientele seems likely. He may also have worked for patrons from Reading, where he lived for some years (*infra*, p. 148, n. 1).

[6] Three MSS. of this grammar in Serbopoulos' handwriting are known, and are now MSS. Trinity Coll. Dublin, no. 925, (B.L.) Gr. class.e.96, Trinity Coll. Cambridge, no. 823. According to S. Gibson, *Early Oxford Bindings*, p. 17, the Bodleian MS. was bound in Oxford about 1470; 1480 would be a more probable date.

From 1489 Serbopoulos worked in Reading, where he lived in St. Mary's Abbey, whether as a monk or as a lodger we do not know, and there he copied texts up to the very end of the century.[1] His great industry while in England is perhaps the best proof of the extension of Greek learning which took place during the last quarter of the fifteenth century.[2]

The activities of the group around Archbishop Neville, and of these Greek scribes, start a new range of intellectual action in English learning. With Neville's entourage begins the decline of the supremacy of the Latin translations as means of access to the works of Greek authors, and their replacement by Greek originals. Through the pursuits of Shirwood and Sellyng this was brought to a further stage, and during their time humanism was to attain considerable unofficial recognition. Altogether, it is possible to say that Neville and his friends, and these Greek scribes, were above all responsible for fostering that side of humanism which had up to then been most neglected and disregarded, since it was mainly through their efforts that the study of Greek was established in fifteenth century England.

[1] MS. Trinity Coll. Cambridge, no. 823 was finished by Serbopoulos in St. Mary's Abbey, Reading, on 9 October, 1489. MSS. New Coll. Oxford, no. 254, Corpus Christi Coll. Oxford, no. 106, New Coll. Oxford, nn. 240-1, and Corpus Christi Coll. Oxford, nn. 23-4, were copied in Reading in 1494, 1495, 1497, 1499, and 1500.

[2] The following is a list of the known MSS. copied by Serbopoulos: MSS. (B.L.) Misc. Gr. no. 9, Gr. class.e.96, Selden *sup.* no. 19, Bodl. no. 1864, New Coll. Oxford, nn. 68, 240, 241, 254, Lincoln Coll. Oxford, Gr. no. 18, Corpus Christi Coll. Oxford, nn. 23, 24, 77, 106, 109, Trinity Coll. Cambridge, no. 823, Trinity Coll. Dublin, no. 925. Most of these MSS. are ecclesiastical texts and commentaries on Aristotle. The Corpus MSS. were formerly owned by William Grocin.

CHAPTER X

THE patronage of Neville and the work of Greek scribes in England are evidence of a knowledge of and interest in Greek during the fifteenth century. This is further emphasized by the achievements of Shirwood and Sellyng, both of whom played a very remarkable part in the early history of English humanism.

John Shirwood[1] was a few years senior to Neville and was educated at Cambridge, where he obtained his degrees of Master of Arts and Bachelor of Divinity.[2] The study of theology was apparently his main pursuit there. But a desire for a more advanced study of it brought him to Oxford, where he incorporated as a Cambridge graduate in October 1456,[3] and eventually obtained his Doctorate in Divinity.[4] Possibly Shirwood's taste for the antique was aroused during his stay in Oxford. With access to classical and modern texts rendered easy by Duke Humphrey's generosity, it is likely that Shirwood availed himself of such facilities, thus becoming attracted towards Latin letters. It was probably owing to his proficiency in them that he was able to secure the patronage of George Neville, a link which proved particularly valuable to him.

Shirwood's close connexion with Neville, whom he may have met in Oxford, began at the latest in 1460 when he became Chancellor of Exeter Cathedral:[5] when Neville was translated to York in 1465 he followed him north, becoming Archdeacon of Richmond during the same year.[5] Six years later he added to his preferments the 'golden prebend' of Masham in York Minster,[5] and soon afterwards he probably went to Rome to reside at the Curia.[6] As an associate of Neville, Shirwood was bound to be

---

[1] On Shirwood cf. especially Allen, op. cit., Liddell, *The First Century of the Library of Corpus Christi College, Oxford* (Unpublished Oxford B.Litt. thesis), B. Behrens, 'The Origins of the Office of English Resident Ambassador in Rome,' *E.H.R.* XLIX (1934) pp. 645-53.

[2] As Shirwood describes himself as a D.D. in 1461 (*Allen*, op. cit. p. 446, n.8), he must be identified with the John Shirwood who was licensed to incorporate in Oxford and allowed to proceed D.D. with an M.A. and B.D. from Cambridge on 27 October, 1456, (*Register of the University of Oxford*, vol. I, p. 9).

[3] *Ibid.*, loc. cit.

[4] *Supra*, n. 2.

[5] Le Neve, op. cit. vols. I, p. 419, III, pp. 140, 202.

[6] As MSS. Corpus Christi Coll. Oxford, nn. 60, 92, were copied for Shirwood by an unidentified Italian scribe in 1471 and 1472 and were obviously illuminated in Italy, and Shirwood is known to have been already in Rome on 15 January, 1474, (Allen op. cit. pp. 447-8), it seems very likely that he went to Rome about 1471. Shirwood paid a short visit to England in 1474 or 1475, this being suggested by his visit to George Neville at Calais, which took place during either of these years and on which cf. *Ibid.*, pp. 448-9.

regarded at first with suspicion after the restoration of the
Yorkists: nevertheless he was able to secure a general pardon for
himself from Edward IV in June 1471,[1] and eventually gain the
entire confidence of the Crown. In 1476 Shirwood became an
Apostolic Protonotary,[1] and one year later his services were
rewarded by his appointment as King's Proctor in Rome.[2] But
Edward IV's death probably brought Shirwood back to Eng-
land, where he seems to have enjoyed the confidence of Richard
III, who not only consented to his provision to the vacant
Bishopric of Durham,[3] but even went as far as to write in March
1484 to the Pope, asking him to make Shirwood a cardinal.[4]
After having been favoured by Edward IV and Richard III,
Shirwood also appears to have commanded the respect of Henry
VII, who renewed his appointment as Proctor in Rome on
28 February, 1486,[5] and appointed him in 1487[6] a member of an
embassy to Rome headed by Thomas Mylling, Bishop of Hereford, another member of it being the Prior of Christ Church,
William Sellyng. Shirwood reappears in England in 1490, when he
wrote to John Paston from Aukland, trying to exchange coals of
Durham for Norfolk corn,[7] but in February 1492 he was again
on his way to Rome on royal business,[7] and there he died in the
evening of January 14th, 1493.[7]

As far as we know, Shirwood's literary activities began while he
was with Neville, whom he served for some years as secretary.
It was while in his household that he began to purchase and
collect classical works,[8] this being consonant with his duties,
which appear to have included the composition of Latin letters,[8]
a task doubtless performed to his master's satisfaction, and

---

[1] *P.R.* 1467–77, p. 267, *C.P.R.* vol. XIII, p. 209.
[2] On 12 December, 1477 (*P.R.* 1476–85, p. 60).
[3] Shirwood's bull of provision is dated 29 March, 1484, and is in *Historiae Dunelmensis Scriptores Tres*, ed. J. Raine (Surtees Society no. 9), London, 1839, pp. ccclxviii–ix.
[4] Rymer, op. cit. vol. XII, p. 216.
[5] Allen, op. cit. p. 451. Shirwood was in Rome in May 1484, when he was consecrated Bishop of Durham, and he was also there in 1485; perhaps he returned to England in the summer of 1485 (*Ibid.*, loc. cit.).
[6] *Ibid.*, loc. cit. On this embassy cf. Balzani, *Un' Ambasciata inglese a Roma, passim*, Bur-
chardus, *Diarium*, vol. I, pp. 257–9.
[7] *The Paston Letters*, vol. VI, pp. 131–2. Shirwood heads his letter with IHΣ X$\rho\varsigma$. He
entered Rome on June 14th (Allen, op. cit. p. 452). A letter from Cardinal Francesco Todes-
chini Piccolomini to Pope Alexander VI states that the Bishop of Durham died on the
preceding evening. The letter is undated but the editor of the *Venetian State Papers*, where
it is calendared, has dated it 12 January, 1494 (*S.P.V.* vol. I, p. 216). Burchardus, op. cit.
vol. II, p. 36 gives 14 January, 1493, as the date of Shirwood's death, a date followed by
Allen (Allen, op. cit. p. 452).
[8] *Supra*, p. 143, n. 1, *infra*, p. 152.

perhaps also some teaching as well.[1] It was probably at this time that Shirwood began to learn Greek, and considering the links between Neville and Emanuel of Constantinople,[2] it seems possible that the Greek scribe was his first teacher. It is also very likely that it was through Neville that he came across George Hermonymos, from whom he may have received additional instruction in Greek, and who seems in any case to have been appreciative of Shirwood's patronage. Even after several years had elapsed from the time he left England, Hermonymos appears to have been anxious to retain Shirwood's protection. It was doubtless with such an end in mind that he dedicated to him some time between 1484 and 1493 one of his translations from the Greek,[2] which incidentally he also dedicated to another patron,[2] according to a practice only too common among Renaissance scholars.

Shirwood's intellectual interests strayed beyond mere book-collecting, reading the classics, and composing Latin letters. Besides attaining a knowledge of Greek impressive enough to make Richard III mention it when recommending him to Pope Innocent VIII,[3] he was able to write Latin both well and in conformity with Italian standards. Such a proficiency is proved by his treatise on a mathematical game, which he published in Rome[4] in 1482, and dedicated to his patron, Cardinal Barbo.[4] The introduction to this is so typically a humanistic preface, that it would alone be proof of Shirwood's mastery of Latinity as interpreted by the Italians. Besides this, if Leland is to be relied on, he also composed a Latin poem in praise of England[5] which has not been found, and which would doubtless have told us more about his classical studies. In the absence of more literary remains, one must turn to Shirwood's books to seek more information concerning his tastes.

Shirwood's library[6] is one of the most interesting amongst those collected by an Englishman during the fifteenth century. Begun by him, as we saw, while he was with Neville, its earliest

[1] This is suggested by his being referred to as *magister meus* by someone doubtless closely connected with Neville's household (Tait, op. cit., p. 571, n. 5).

[2] *Supra*, p. 142.

[3] Rymer, op. cit. vol. XII, p. 214.

[4] Where it was printed by S. Plannck (Proctor, no. 3630). A fifteenth century MS. of this work is part of MS. (B.L.) Ashmole, no. 344. The dedication to Barbo is dated 1 April, 1482. Later Barbo recommended Shirwood to Richard III for the Bishopric of Durham (Rymer, op. cit. vol. XII, p. 221).

[5] Leland, *Collectanea*, vol. IV, p. 41.

[6] On which cf. Allen, op. cit., Liddell, op. cit., *passim*.

acquisitions, as far as we know, were Peter Cantor's commentary on the *Psalter*, which he bought in London on 6 June, 1461,[1] a fifteenth century volume containing the *De Viris Illustribus* falsely attributed to Pliny as well as several other texts including some biographies by Bruni, purchased in London in 1464,[1] and a twelfth century Trogus Pompeius acquired in York in 1465.[1] More important additions were made during his visits to Rome, where as early as 1471 and 1472 a Terence[1] and Cicero's *De Finibus*[1] were transcribed for him by an Italian scribe. In Rome he also made large purchases of printed books, particularly from the press of Sweynheim and Pannartz, which at the time of his death included Martial's *Epigrams*, Statius' *Sylvae*, Frontinus' *De Aquaeductibus*, Aeneas Sylvius' *Dialogus de Somnio*, the *Comedies* of Plautus, the modern translations of Plutarch's *Lives*, the *Vitae Pontificum* by Platina, the *Disputationes Camaldulenses* by Cristoforo Landino, George of Trebizond's *Rhetoric*, Polybius, and Dionysius of Halicarnassus in Latin, treatises by Leon Battista Alberti, and probably Festus' *Collectanea*, Bruni's *De Bello Italico*, and a Latin Themistius, besides several copies of the writings of those classical authors who had been known in England throughout the Middle Ages.[2] Shirwood was also the owner of Greek manuscripts,[3] but of these there only survives a grammar of Theodor Gaza now at Cambridge,[4] and the pseudo Aristotelian *De Virtutibus* copied by George Hermonymos,[5] who had included the original text as well as his own Latin translation in his presentation copy.

Shirwood is one among many fifteenth century English prelates who alternated political and ecclesiastical duties with humanistic relaxations, but kept his learning to himself. Unlike Bekynton or Grey, he appears to have become learned in Greek, and he was moreover a better Latin scholar than most of his English contemporaries. His contacts with Neville, Mylling, Sellyng, and others,[6] suggest that he may have both influenced and been influenced by other learned men, while his visits to Rome proved certainly beneficial to his outlook and to his

---

[1] Now MSS. Corpus Christi Coll. Oxford, nn. 49, 60, 81, 84, 92.
[2] A list of the extant remains of Shirwood's collection of printed books is in Allen, op. cit, pp. 455–6.
[3] *Ibid.*, pp. 453–4.
[4] Now MS. (C.U.) Ii.IV.16. On this MS. cf. Allen, op. cit. p. 453.
[5] Now MS. (B.L.) Auct. G.9.3.
[6] According to Leland, *De Scriptoribus*, p. 484, Millyng knew Greek, but this is the only authority for his knowledge of that language.

intellectual pursuits. The fact that Richard III emphasized his Greek learning to the Pope, is particularly interesting not only as a sign that by the end of the Yorkist regime classical learning was officially recognized as a useful qualification for advancement, but also because it shows that Shirwood's erudition impressed his contemporaries. In many ways Shirwood can be compared as a scholar with Robert Flemmyng, whom he probably met in Rome, and about whose contacts with him we unfortunately have no positive information.

The embassy sent by Henry VII to Rome in 1487 included, besides Mylling and John Shirwood, another distinguished ecclesiastic, in whom neo-classical learning doubtless reached the highest standards ever seen in an Englishman since John Free. This was the Prior of Christ Church, William Sellyng,[1] whose literary pursuits, begun when English humanism was still at an elementary stage, had by the time of his death reached a point when but little progress was necessary to attain to the standards set by the Italians. The career of Sellyng had begun with his admission into the Benedictine order when still very young. Professed monk about 1448,[2] he had passed through the mill of the monastery school from which he was sent to Canterbury College, Oxford, where he was already in residence as a student in 1454.[3] Two years later he obtained priest's orders,[4] which, however, did not prevent him from continuing his theological studies at Oxford, where he supplicated for the degree of Bachelor of Divinity on 7 February, 1458.[5] Besides applying himself to the study of theology, Sellyng came under the influence of polite letters while at the University, where he is known to have attended the courses on Latin eloquence which the Italian scholar Stefano Surigone was holding in Oxford.[6] Among

---

[1] On Sellyng cf. especially Schirmer, op. cit. pp. 154-62, 181, Leland, *De Scriptoribus,* p. 482, Tanner, op. cit. pp. 161-2, Gasquet, *The Eve of the Reformation,* pp. 22-6, *Christ Church Letters,* pp. xxxvii-xliii. On the inconclusive evidence that Sellyng's family name was 'Tilly' cf. Gasquet, op. cit. p. 22, n. 1.   [2] Stone, op. cit. p. 189.

[3] Sellyng was already at Canterbury College on 18 April, 1454 (Dean and Chapter Library, Canterbury, *Sede Vacante Books,* vol. II, fo. 39ʳ). He was also at Oxford in 1455, 1457-60, and 1462-4 (Dean and Chapter Library, Canterbury, *Accounts of Canterbury College,* and *Treasurer's Rolls* for the period). The letters written from Canterbury College in *Christ Church Letters,* pp. 13-7, are by another William Sellyng. The statement in Tanner, op. cit. p. 161, that Sellyng was a Fellow of All Souls College, Oxford, is erroneous since no member of the regular clergy was allowed to hold a fellowship at that college.

[4] On September 18th, 1456, (Schirmer, op. cit. p. 181), and celebrated his first mass on September 26th (Stone, op. cit. p. 66). He had become an acolyte in 1448, a subdeacon in 1449, and a deacon in 1450, (Schirmer, op. cit. p. 181).

[5] *Register of Oxford University,* vol. I, p. 31.

[6] Weiss, *Humanism in Oxford,* p. 28.

Sellyng's intellectual activities during this academic period was the composition of Latin orations under the supervision of Surigone,[1] possibly some intercourse with Chaundler,[1] and obviously an intense study of classical authors. Thus the development of Sellyng's interests may be traced to his University days rather than to contacts with monks pursuing literary studies at Christ Church, Canterbury, like Henry Cranebroke, although perhaps association with fellow monks of the Cranebroke type may have first aroused a taste for classicism in him. Sellyng was probably still in Oxford, when he obtained leave in 1464 to go and continue his studies at a University abroad for three years,[2] a privilege which was doubtless accepted with enthusiasm because of the opportunities it offered. Sellyng naturally went to perfect his studies in Italy, a country he had probably been advised to visit also by Surigone, his departure very likely taking place soon after he left Oxford. His movements in Italy are not easy to trace with accuracy: but we know that while there he studied at the Universities of Padua[3] and Bologna, and that he apparently obtained in the latter his Doctorate of Divinity on 22 March, 1466.[4] According to tradition it was in Bologna that Sellyng acquired his knowledge of Greek.[5] If this is true, he was probably taught it by either Andronicus Callistus or Lionorus, who appear as Professors of Greek at Bologna during that period:[6] that he learnt it, as has often been alleged,[7] from Politian is chronologically impossible.[7] Although it is quite probable that Sellyng's knowledge of this language was acquired

[1] *Supra*, p. 153, n. 6. Sellyng corresponded with Chaundler at a later date on Canterbury College business (*Literae Cantuarienses*, vol. III, pp. 260–2, 267–71). It seems, however, likely that Sellyng met Chaundler in Oxford, this being suggested by the latter's contacts with Canterbury College disclosed by the aforementioned correspondence.

[2] *Literae Cantuarienses*, vol. III, pp. 239–40.

[3] *Ibid.*, vol. III, p. 293. In Padua Sellyng was lodged by 'Johannita Bely' an English-woman who was the widow of a Venetian citizen (*Christ Church Letters* pp. xxxviii–ix). About her being English and residing in Padua cf. Archivio Notarile, Padova, MS. iii–31, ff. 360^r–1^r.

[4] S. Mazzetti, *Memorie Storiche sopra l'università e l'istituto delle scienze di Bologna*, Bologna, 1840, p. 308. It is unlikely that Sellyng was the *Gulielmus de Anglia* who took a Doctorate in Canon Law at Bologna in 1468, as is suggested in Mitchell, *English Law Students at Bologna in the Fifteenth Century*, p. 274, since Sellyng was not a Doctor of Canon Law. Sellyng is styled as D.D. of Bologna in *Literae Cantuarienses*, vol. III, p. 291.

[5] *Infra*, n. 7. Sellyng's Greek learning is already mentioned in 1475, (*Literae Cantuarienses*, vol. III, p. 291).

[6] U. Dallari, *Rotuli dei Lettori, Legisti, e Artisti dello Studio Bolognese dal 1384 al 1799*, Bologna, 1888–1919, vol. I, p. 70. Of course it is not to be excluded that Sellyng may have learnt the first rudiments of Greek in Oxford from Surigone or Emanuel of Constantinople.

[7] This was first alleged in Leland, *De Scriptoribus*, p. 482. As Politian was born in 1454 his teaching Sellyng is out of the question. On interest in Greek at Canterbury College during Sellyng's residence there cf. *supra*, p. 131, n. 2.

in Italy, it is nevertheless not out of the question that he may already have had some slight acquaintance with it before he left England. After all some interest in Greek existed in Oxford, both in the University at large and at Canterbury College, at the time of his residence there:[1] thus he may have learnt the first rudiments at Oxford from Surigone or Emanuel of Constantinople. After spending a few years abroad, Sellyng returned to Canterbury where he was already in March 1469, when he publicly charged a heretic.[2] His return to England was, however, only temporary. Christ Church was then anxious to obtain some indulgences for the forthcoming Jubilee of St. Thomas à Becket: hence the monastic authorities sent Sellyng and another monk, Reginald Goldstone, to Rome to supplicate Pope Paul II for them.[3] Doubtless the choice of Sellyng for this mission was mainly dictated by his previous experience of Italy, but besides this his skill in Latin oratory may also have been material in determining his appointment. Both envoys reached Rome safely, and throughout their visit they were befriended and lodged by Pietro Mellini, an ecclesiastical lawyer well known in English monastic circles.[4] Additional help came to them from an influential prelate, the Bishop of Urbino,[5] thanks chiefly to whose kindly assistance the desired privileges were secured for the monastery.[5] It is not known how long Sellyng remained in Rome, or whether he was given to any pursuits of a learned nature while there. But in all probability in 1470 he returned to his monastery, of which he was appointed Chancellor in the following year.[6] Some entries in a fine Italian hand in one of the Canterbury Registers written during his Chancellorship,[7] suggest that humanistic influence already extended to his handwriting. Moreover it was probably then that he began to teach Greek in his monastery,[8] thus continuing the traditions of Theodore of Tarsus. In 1472 the Prior-

---

[1] Cf. *supra*, p. 154, n. 7.   [2] Stone, op. cit. p. 108.

[3] A letter recommending Sellyng and his companion Goldstone was issued by the Prior of Christ Church on 3 October, 1469, and is in *Literae Cantuarienses*, vol. III, pp. 244-5.

[4] Mellini's kindness to Sellyng and Goldstone is disclosed by the fraternity letter granted by Christ Church to him and printed in Balzani, op. cit. p. 208. On Mellini's relations with England cf. *Ibid.*, p. 187, n. 2.

[5] A fraternity letter granted by Christ Church to the Bishop on 13 January, 1470, mentions the help he gave to Sellyng in Rome (Dean and Chapter Library, Canterbury, *Register S*, fo. 245ᵛ). The bull granting special indulgences for St. Thomas' jubilee was issued on 4 June, 1470, and is in *Literae Cantuarienses*, vol. III, pp. 253-5.

[6] *Christ Church Letters*, p. xli.

[7] W. A. Pantin, 'English Monastic Letter Books', *Historical Essays in Honour of James Tait*, Manchester, 1933, p. 209. The handwriting of Sellyng's autograph orations in MS. (B.M.) Cotton, Cleop. E. III, also shows Italian influence.

[8] On his teaching of Greek cf. *infra*, p. 157.

ship of Christ Church fell vacant, and on September 10th of that year Sellyng was elected to it by the Chapter.[1] The period of his rule over the monastery appears to have been divided by him between ecclesiastical duties, diplomatic activities, and literary studies. Already in 1473 he was in correspondence on business connected with Canterbury College with Thomas Chaundler,[2] whom he had probably met in his Oxford days, and although we lack direct evidence, it is perhaps not unreasonable to infer that some learned intercourse may also have taken place between them.

Meanwhile his reputation as an accomplished scholar, and especially as a fine Latin orator, was growing. During the short reign of Edward V he appears to have intended to deliver a Latin oration to the Convocation of the Clergy on 19 April, 1483,[3] and during the reign of Richard III or Henry VII he is known to have introduced proposals in Convocation accompanied by speeches in choice Latin.[4] With the advent of the Tudors Sellyng's accomplishments still found favour with the Crown. Thus in 1487 he was sent on a mission to Rome with the Bishops of Durham and Hereford,[5] both of whom must have proved congenial companions to him because of their favourable attitude towards humane learning. The embassy reached Rome on 8 May, 1487,[5] and when the English envoys appeared before Pope Innocent VIII, it was Sellyng who delivered an elegant Latin speech in the King's name.[5] This mission was followed by other important diplomatic activities. In 1490 he was one of the envoys sent over to France to negotiate for peace with Charles VIII,[6] which occasioned a meeting with the French scholar

---

[1] Stone, op. cit. p. 146.

[2] *Supra*, p. 154, n. 1. Sellyng was also in correspondence with the Papal Collector Gigli (*Christ Church Letters*, pp. 35–6). Gigli had humane interests, but it is not known whether Sellyng's relations with him were solely connected with official business, or whether they embraced other fields as well. As Gigli's activities as a humanist do not appear to begin before 1485 no account of him is given in this work. For a similar reason no account of Robert Widow will be found.

[3] The autograph draft of this oration is in MS. (B.M.) Cotton, Cleop. E.III, ff. 106ʳ–16ʳ, and is printed in E. Fueter, *Religion und Kirche in England im Fünfzehnten Jahrhundert*, Tübingen, 1904, pp. 68–78. That this oration was not delivered is shown by the following note at fo. 106ʳ: *Oraciuncula ordinata ut diceretur in conuocacione cleri die 19 Aprilis 1483 pro Edwardo V non tamen est dicta hoc tempore.*

[4] These speeches are in *Ibid.*, ff. 117ʳ–22ᵛ, and are entitled *Proposiciones in conuocacione cleri circa tempore Ricardi III uel Henrici VII.*

[5] Burchardus, op. cit. vol. I, pp. 257, 259; Sellyng's oration is in Balzani, op. cit. pp. 198–206. On this embassy cf. *supra*, p. 150.

[6] Gaguin, *Epistolae et Orationes*, vol. I, p. 95. On 20 March, 1490, Gaguin wrote that he was waiting for Sellyng (*Ibid.*, vol. I, p. 334). The letter accompanying Gaguin's presents is in *Ibid.*, vol. I, pp. 383–4, and was written in Paris on 22 June, 1492. The gifts consisted of copies of Gaguin's *De Intemeratae Virginis Conceptu*, and *De Misera Hominis Conditione*.

Robert Gaguin, who was one of the French King's commissioners.[1] As a result of it a friendship started between Sellyng and Gaguin, who on his return to France began a correspondence with the Prior of Christ Church, to whom he later, in 1492, sent two of his works as presents.[1] Just when his political and literary ability was at its highest, Sellyng died in 1494,[2] leaving behind him the reputation of being a capable administrator, a skilled diplomat, and a very learned scholar.[3]

Sellyng's orations[4] enable us to perceive his command of Latin uncontaminated by barbarisms, and his acquaintance with the canons of oratory as interpreted by Italian humanists. Apparently he composed his orations surrounded by books, his fluent prose being actually the outcome of patient study.[5] His restrained use of allusions to ancient history or the classics was obviously intentional, in order to emphasize the few which he employed, and in this he also conformed with the best traditions of Renaissance oratory, the end of which was the shape of the speech as a whole rather than its stock of quotation or information. Besides being perhaps the foremost Latin scholar of his times in England, Sellyng occupies an important place among the promoters of Greek studies in this country. Some often quoted notes by William of Worcester prove with certainty that Sellyng taught Greek at Canterbury.[6] But besides this, we have evident proof of his proficiency in that language in his Latin translation of a sermon of St. John Crysostomus, which he finished in 1488.[7] Of course if we compare this work with

[1] Cf. *supra*, p. 156, n. 6.   [2] On December 29th, (Stone, op. cit. p. 146).
[3] Sellyng's obituaries mention his learning and his able administration. The longest of these is in Wharton, *Anglia Sacra*, vol. I, pp. 145–6, another one is in Dean and Chapter Library, Canterbury, MS. D.12, and is given in Balzani, op. cit. p. 188, n. 1. The long inscription placed on Sellyng's tomb is in E. Hasted, *The History and Topographical Survey of the County of Kent*, Canterbury, 1778–99, vol. IV, p. 556.
[4] Preserved in MS. (B.M.) Cotton, Cleop. E.III.
[5] This may be inferred from his marginal notes to one of his autograph orations, in which he states that the composition of the oration took him four days, and that he wrote it notwithstanding the scarcity of books around him at the time (MS. (B.M.) Cotton, Cleop. E.III, fo. 122ᵛ). His use of books in the composition of his orations is also disclosed by another note by him (*Ibid.*, fo. 125ʳ).
[6] Cf. the following note in MS. (B.M.) Cotton, Julium, F.VII, fo. 118ʳ: *Nothe de certis terminis grecorum declaratis per doctorem sellyng ecclesie xpi Cantuar.* This note is followed by short notes on Greek accents and diphthongs and some scribbles in Greek, all these showing that Worcester either attended one of Sellyng's lectures or had access to the notes of someone who had attended them. Besides this, these notes show that Sellyng actually taught Greek at Christ Church. As Sellyng is not styled prior in these notes, it is possible that the lesson which inspired the aforementioned annotations was delivered before his election to that office, but about this there can be no certainty.
[7] A fifteenth century MS. of this is in MS. (B.M.) Add. no. 15673. Date and authorship of the version are disclosed by the following colophon at fo. 28ᵛ: *Finit sermo sancti Crisostomi*

Free's Latin Synesius, we can but recognize the superiority of Free's work. Still Sellyng's translation is competently done, and shows a fine knowledge of Greek and a far greater ability in rendering the text into Latin than that displayed by the medieval translators of Crysostomus. As a whole his is a sober version aiming above all at a clear rendering of the meaning of the original. It is neither as painfully close to its original as most medieval translations were, nor does it fall into those excesses of translating licence committed by famous humanists. His interpretation of the text is close without being *ad verbum*, and conveys a satisfactory idea of the original Greek text. Sellyng's Greek learning fired the imagination of his monks to such an extent that his distinction in that language was duly recorded on his tomb,[1] and in the obituary book of the Monastery of Christ Church, Canterbury.[1]

It is much to be regretted that only very little is known about Sellyng's library.[1] No doubt part of it was brought by him from Italy, but besides this he probably acquired some books from Lombard merchants,[2] and had some transcribed for him by professional scribes. According to Leland his collection, which was partly destroyed by fire during the reign of Henry VIII,[3] included Greek manuscripts[3] and apparently Cicero's *De Republica*,[4] although it seems very unlikely that he should have owned that treatise. Among the Greek manuscripts collected by Sellyng there were possibly the Homer and Euripides now at Corpus Christi College, Cambridge,[5] and as the Homer was copied by Emanuel of Constantinople it is possible that, if it belonged to Sellyng, it may have been acquired from that scribe in England. Of contemporaries we only know for certain that

quam pulcerrimus. quem e Greco in Latinum Traduxit Reuerendus in xp̄o pater Willelmus Sellyng prior ecclesie Christi Cant. Sacre pagine professor. Anno domini 1488.

[1] For his obituaries cf. *supra*, p. 157, n. 3. Sellyng's obituary published by Wharton mentions his building of a library at Christ Church over the prior's chapel, and his stocking of it with books mainly of literary subjects. On this library cf. also James, *The Ancient Libraries of Canterbury and Dover*, pp. l–li.

[2] His letter to the Lombard merchant 'Humphrey Gentyll' in Schirmer, op. cit. p. 181, in which he asks him to show a Livy to a friend, suggests that Sellyng himself may have acquired books from Italian merchants.

[3] Leland, *De Scriptoribus*, p. 483. For a description of the fire which destroyed Sellyng's library cf. *Letters and Papers Foreign and Domestic of the Reign of Henry VIII*, ed. J. Gairdner, vol. IX, London, 1886, p. 226. Leland states also that the Greek texts in Sellyng's library included Cyril on the Prophets, Basil on Isaiah, and Synesius.

[4] Leland, *De Scriptoribus*, p. 483.

[5] Now MSS. Corpus Christi Coll. Cambridge, nn. 81, 403. About the view that these MSS. belonged to Sellyng cf. M. R. James, 'The Sources of the Library of Archbishop Parker,' *Cambridge Antiquarian Society, Octavo Publications*, no. 32, Cambridge, 1899, p. 9.

he possessed Gaguin's *De Intemeratae*[1] *Virginis Conceptu*, and *De Misera Hominis Conditione*,[1] which were presented to him by their author, but knowledge of Sellyng's outlook and studies makes it certain that he must have owned other modern literary writings as well.

The place occupied by Sellyng is obviously one of very considerable importance in the history of classical scholarship in England. As a Greek scholar he translated at least one work into Latin, collected manuscripts, and, most important of all, imparted his knowledge of that language by teaching it in his monastery. In the sphere of Latin he contributed in improving the standards practised in Christ Church, where he was also instrumental in spreading humane culture. His own example doubtless proved of much inspiration to others, and whether or not he was Thomas Linacre's teacher,[2] he certainly played an important part in moulding the outlook of English humanists in the generation after him. Thus when compared with previous exponents of classicism in England, Sellyng appears to have exercised a position of greater importance, since besides leaving behind him a collection of important texts, he also bequeathed through his teaching a vigorous impetus that was not lost after his death.

[1] *Supra*, p. 156 n. 6. There is no extant MS. which is known to have certainly belonged to Sellyng. MS. (B.L.) Laud, F.120, which is described as formerly his property in the article on Sellyng in the *D.N.B.*, was actually owned by the William Sellyng who was Abbot of St. Augustine's, Canterbury.

[2] Schirmer following others states that Linacre had been Sellyng's pupil at Canterbury and that he went to Italy with him (Schirmer, op. cit. p. 163). This may have been so; on the other hand we do not possess any contemporary evidence stating that Linacre was taught by Sellyng. The earliest authority on Linacre going to Italy with Sellyng in 1487 is Leland, *De Scriptoribus*, p. 483.

CHAPTER XI

CAMBRIDGE in the fifteenth century did not differ much from Oxford. As in Oxford theology and Canon Law conditioned the general outlook. Classical pursuits were conducted on traditional lines, while the medieval *curriculum* remained the subject matter of liberal studies. But unlike Oxford Cambridge had had no Duke Humphrey as protector. Its benefactors, like King Henry VI or John Somerset, usually focussed their generosity upon the colleges, and viewed modern learning with little enthusiasm. Hence when interest in neo-classicism was aroused there it was not due to the zeal of patrons. Through the seizure of Glouce-ster's property at his death a part of his library came to Cam-bridge.[1] But these books went to King's College[1] and not to the University library, so that they were not generally available as the Duke's Oxford donations were. Altogether if we compare Cambridge with Oxford from the standpoint of *belles lettres* we can but realize its inferiority. We do not find there that taste for Italian learning already present in Oxford by the middle of the century. All we find are scholastic studies continuing un-changed. Such an apathy towards the New Learning was due to several causes. Without a Gloucester as patron, no initial stimulus had been received. Without a Canterbury College, contacts with Canterbury were less direct. It is true that Tiptoft had not been forgetful of Cambridge scholarship,[2] but it is doubtful that he succeeded in bringing any influence there. The decay of Cam-bridge learning, as well as that of Oxford and England in general, is echoed in the considerations which moved William Bingham to found Clare Hall. Above all one can see in them the anxiety at the decay of Latin letters, a state of affairs in his view 'whereby not merely was the knowledge of sacred scripture and the Latin requisite for the pursuit of the law and the affairs of the realm likely to perish, but also the power of communicating with foreigners.'[3]

As far as the presence of literary interests in Cambridge is concerned, the contents of some of its libraries during the fifteenth century are rather enlightening. The University Library cata-

[1] *Supra*, p. 67, n. 4.   [2] *Supra*, p. 118.
[3] Kingsford, op. cit. p. 195.

logue compiled in 1473[1] registers only one humanistic work, the *De Remediis* by Petrarch, and some texts of classical authors well known during the Middle Ages. Peterhouse had only one neo-classical manuscript, Petrarch's *Letters*,[2] the St. Catharine's Hall catalogue, drawn up in 1475,[3] includes four modern Italian entries, these being two copies of Petrarch's *De Remediis*, Bruni's *Ethics*, and Decembrio's *Republic*, while that of Pembroke College could display only one, a copy of Leonardo Bruni's *Letters*.[4] The only place in Cambridge where a collection of valuable Renaissance texts could be found was King's College, where, as we saw, a part of Duke Humphrey's library had been placed after his tragic death at Bury St. Edmund's in 1447.[5] Manuscripts in this library included Bruni's translations of the *Ethics*[5] and of the *Phaedrus*,[5] some latinized Plutarch's *Lives*,[5] two copies of Decembrio's Latin text of Plato's *Republic*,[5] the *De Avaritia* by Poggio,[5] and a translation of St. Athanasius made by Beccaria for his English patron.[5] Apart from these no neo-classical volumes appear in fifteenth century Cambridge library lists, nor are any entered in the extant University lists of pledges.[6] Additional evidence for the little taste for polite letters in Cambridge may be perceived in some University correspondence written during the second half of the century, in which the Latin style, construction, and vocabulary, as well as the script, are still traditionally medieval and suggest no contacts with Italy.[7] As head of King's Hall, John Gunthorpe does not appear to have brought modern influences to bear on Cambridge scholarship, while the settling of part of Archbishop Neville's household in this town in 1472[8] has not left any perceptible traces on its learning.

And yet it seems impossible that such an important academic

[1] Printed in H. Bradshaw, 'Two lists of Books in the University Library,' *Cambridge Antiquarian Society, Communications*, II (1864) pp. 239-78.
[2] James, *A Descriptive Catalogue of the Manuscripts in the Library of Peterhouse, Cambridge*, p. 20.
[3] Printed in 'A Catalogue of the Books which were given to the Library of St. Catharine's Hall, Cambridge, by Dr. Woodlark the founder of the College,' ed. G. E. Corrie, *Publications of the Cambridge Antiquarian Society*, vol. I, (1840-6) pp. 1-11.
[4] M. R. James, *A Descriptive Catalogue of the Manuscripts in the Library of Pembroke College, Cambridge*, Cambridge, 1905, p. xvii.
[5] *Supra*, pp. 57, n. 4; 64, nn. 3, 4, 7; 65, n. 8; 67, n. 4.
[6] Cf. the lists of books deposited as pledges in *Grace Book A*, pp. x-xvi, and *Grace Book B*, pt. I., pp. viii-xiii.
[7] Cf. for instance the University correspondence in MS. (C.U.) Gg. V.37, and *Grace Book A, passim*.
[8] *Supra*, p. 143.

M

centre as Cambridge should have remained entirely uninfluenced, when neo-classicism was flourishing both at Oxford and at Canterbury.Was it that humane studies were pursued so privately by members of the University that evidence concerning them failed to reach us? Or was there just lack of curiosity? Tiptoft bequeathed part of his library to Cambridge: whether these books reached the legatee is doubtful, yet his gift is indicative of an intention on his part to further classical scholarship there as well as in Oxford. Whatever the case, the earliest signs of contacts with Italian culture to be detected in Cambridge appear about 1478, when the presence there of an Italian Franciscan, Lorenzo Traversagni, better known as Lorenzo da Savona,[1] is suggestive of the introduction of new values.

During his youth Lorenzo had studied for five years, both at Padua and Bologna, under Master Francesco da Savona, later Pope Sixtus IV.[2] After lecturing at Bologna,[2] and perhaps at Oxford,[2] he had gone to Cambridge where he lectured on theology and obtained his Doctorate of Divinity.[3] Divinity was obviously not his sole pursuit at Cambridge, for he completed there on 6 July, 1478, a *Rhetorica*, which enjoyed enough popularity to be printed twice in England during the fifteenth century.[3]

This treatise is constructed on modern lines and was obviously inspired by classical models. Although some of the examples in it derive from Holy Scripture, one can detect in it a strong Ciceronian influence, and a certain independence of the dogmatism of medieval handbooks. Although Lorenzo was fundamentally a schoolman, this book indicates his appreciation of modern values, which is furthermore disclosed by a Latin poem which he dedicated in 1485 to William of Waynfleet, Bishop of Winchester. This work, which he entitled *Triumphus Amoris Jesus Christi*,[4] is hardly outstanding in its verse, which conforms with prehumanist prosody. But the dedicatory epistle,[5] apart from its interesting allusions to Magdalen College, Oxford, is strikingly neo-classical in its prose. Besides, the script of the

---

[1] On Traversagni cf. Wadding, *Scriptores Ordinis Minorum*, pp. 160–1, Little, op. cit. pp. 265–6, and the article on him in the *D.N.B.*
[2] Little, op. cit. p. 266.
[3] Venn, *Alumni Cantabrigienses*, pt. I, vol. IV, p. 23. The *Rhetorica* was printed by Caxton in 1479 (Gordon Duff, no. 368), and by the '*St. Albans scholemayster*' in 1480 (*Ibid.*, no. 369). For the date of its completion cf. the '1480' edition, sig z5v.
[4] This poem was finished in the London Grey Friars in 1485 (Wharton, op. cit. vol. I, p. 326), and is in MS. Lambeth Palace, no. 450.
[5] Printed in Wharton, op. cit. vol. I, p. 326.

doubtless autograph presentation volume is so typically modern that it can but suggest its author's association with Renaissance scholarship.[1] Alongside with these writings, Traversagni also composed a handbook on letter-writing now at Munich,[2] which gives additional information as to the nature of his interests. In the light of such evidence it seems probable that he was able to attract the attention of part of academic Cambridge to polite letters. Perhaps it was partly this disclosure of new standards of taste that induced the University to engage an Italian, Caius Auberinus, who begins to appear in Cambridge records as early as 1483–4.[3] The employment of this scholar by the University as lecturer and letter writer suggests no doubt a desire to improve current Latin standards, and as such it hints at an awakened consciousness of classical values. Auberinus was first employed solely as a letter writer, but after a few years he combined these duties with those of a lecturer,[4] his teaching including the *Comedies* of Terence.[5] Payments made by the University to the writers of its official correspondence disclose that Auberinus's work was better paid than that of his colleagues,[6] an obvious sign that it was more appreciated. Though all his letters are now lost, and only fragments of his career are disclosed by the extant Cambridge accounts, we possess enough information about him to be fairly certain that he brought a valuable contribution to the development of *belles lettres* in Cambridge.

It is possible to infer from our scanty information that

[1] The appearance of the Lambeth MS. shows that it must have been a presentation copy, doubtless in the author's autograph.

[2] This is the *Arenga Fratris Gulielmi Sauonensis de epistolis faciendis* in MS. Bayerisches Staatsbibliothek, Munich, no. 5238. A religious treatise composed by him at Savona is now MS. Biblioteca Marciana, Venice, Class. X. cod. 246. For a list of Traversagni's literary remains cf. Wadding, op. cit. p. 161.

[3] The earliest mention of Auberinus in Cambridge is in the Senior Proctor's accounts for 1483–4, according to which he was paid 6s. 8d. for letters written on the University's behalf (*Grace Book A*, p. 185). On Auberinus cf. C. H. Cooper, *Athenae Cantabrigienses*, Cambridge, 1858–1913, vol. I, p. 9. Auberinus must have lectured on classical subjects, this being suggested by his being styled *poeta* (*Grace Book A*, p. 202), an appellative this generally given to humanists lecturing at the Universities, and he must have been the graduate of another University since in 1491 he was allowed to hold the rank of any degree he obtained elsewhere (*Grace Book B*, pt. I, p. 30). *Grace Books A* and *B* contain records of payments made to Auberinus for letters written for the University between 1483–4 and 1503.

[4] The earliest recorded payment to him for lecturing was made in 1492 (*Grace Book B*, pt. I, p. 44). Some payments for unspecified services made to him in 1486 (*Grace Book A*, p. 202) suggest that they were remuneration for lectures, this being also hinted by other payments as stipend made to him in 1487–8 (*Ibid.*, pp. 219–20).

[5] J. B. Mullinger, *The University of Cambridge from the Earliest Times to the Royal Injunctions of* 1535, Cambridge, 1873, p. 434.

[6] Cf. for instance the payments to the Vicar of Trumpington for letters written for the University in *Grace Book B*, pt. I, pp. 10, 69, etc.

Cambridge humanism was still in its infancy when the Tudors came to the throne. It is only its very beginnings that may be traced to the Yorkist period. Yet despite the state of Cambridge classical scholarship, what is perhaps the most typical production of early English humanism was the work of a Cambridge scholar who had studied in Italy. Although the achievement of John Doget is inferior in quality to that of Free, or Sellyng, or Flemmyng, his work none the less embodies more than theirs the main characteristics of English fifteenth century learning. His was the work of an average English scholar, and as such it is more representative of contemporary culture than the production of humanists endowed with more brilliant gifts and more under the influence of the Italians.

Doget[1] came from Dorset, and was a nephew of Cardinal Bourchier in whose household he probably received his early education.[2] From there he went to Eton,[3] and then to King's College, Cambridge,[3] where he was admitted in 1451, and where he obtained the degree of Bachelor of Arts in 1455,[3] this being followed by that of Master of Arts in 1459.[3] It is possible that the beginnings of Doget's leanings towards humane letters originated in Cambridge. Several books formerly owned by Humphrey, Duke of Gloucester, were, as we saw, to be found in Doget's college, and included Decembrio's translation of the *Republic*[4] and Bruni's latinized *Phaedrus*.[4] Consequently it does not appear improbable that Doget's Platonic interests were excited by the study of these volumes. In 1460 Doget obtained Priest's orders,[5] yet he continued to reside at Cambridge, where he was granted leave to read in the Divinity Faculty in 1464.[6] But during this year he resolved to go and continue his studies in Italy, and accordingly he made the necessary arrangements for this journey

[1] On Doget cf. Scofield, *The Life and Reign of Edward IV*, vol. II, pp. 448–9, Mitchell, *English Students at Padua*, 1460–75, pp. 113–4, Venn, op. cit. pt. I, vol. II, p. 53, the article on him in the *D.N.B.*, and especially Hurnard, *Studies in Intellectual Life in England from the Middle of the Fifteenth Century till the Time of Colet* (Unpublished Oxford D.Phil. thesis). An abstract of this thesis is in *Abstracts of Dissertations for the Degree of Doctor of Philosophy*, vol. VIII, Oxford, 1936, pp. 36–40.

[2] This is suggested by a passage in his letter of dedication of his commentary on Plato's *Phaedo* to Cardinal Bourchier (MS. (B.M.) Add. no. 10344, fo. 7ᵛ).

[3] Venn, op. cit., pt. I, vol. II, p. 53. In 1459 Doget was made an acolyte, this being followed by his ordination to the priesthood in 1460 (*Ibid.*, loc. cit.).

[4] *Supra*, pp. 57, n. 4, 64, n. 3.

[5] *Supra*, n. 3.

[6] *Grace Book A*, p. 50. Some impediment to his inception must, however, have taken place, since leave to incept was again granted to him in 1471–2 (*Ibid.*, p. 89). Later he must have gone to study theology in Oxford, since in 1489 he was incorporated in Cambridge as D.D. Oxon (*Ibid.*, p. 139).

on 5 June, 1464.[1] In these he was the victim of unpleasant swindling,[1] so that his studying at Padua was rendered less agreeable by money worries.[1] This did not, however, prevent him from moving eventually to Bologna, where he has been tentatively identified with the recipient of a Doctorate in Canon Law on 23 November, 1469.[2] After completing his studies there, Doget returned once more to Cambridge to take up again his theological pursuits.[3] His return to England coincided with the beginning of his remarkable collection of benefices.[4] Diplomatic appointments also came to him, including missions to Pope Sixtus IV and the Kings of Sicily and Hungary in 1479 and 1480.[5] Richard III continued to display the same benevolent attitude towards him that Edward IV had shown, and appointed him his Domestic Chaplain in 1483.[6] More benefices were acquired by him under Henry VII,[7] as well as the office of Provost of his Cambridge college, to which he was appointed in 1499, and which he only vacated on his death in 1501.[7]

Doget's interest in classical learning is revealed to us by his commentary on Plato's *Phaedo*,[8] which he dedicated to his uncle, Cardinal Bourchier. As Bourchier is styled 'cardinal' in the preface, the treatise must have been presented to him between 1473, when he received his 'red hat,' and 1486, when he died. The only extant manuscript of this work, a presentation copy to judge from the care with which it was prepared, is written in an Italian script and has English illuminations, which suggests that it is in Doget's own hand, as his handwriting had probably been influenced by the calligraphic style fashionable in Italy. The

[1] Scofield, op. cit. vol. II, pp. 448–9.

[2] Mitchell, *English Law Students at Bologna in the Fifteenth Century*, p. 275. Doget was incorporated at Cambridge as D.Can. Law of Bologna in 1489 (*Grace Book B*, pt. I, p. 17, *Grace Book A*, p. 139). He is already described as Doctor of Canon Law in 1479 (*C.P.R.* vol. XIII, p. 245).

[3] *Supra*, p. 164, n. 6.

[4] On his ecclesiastical dignities etc., which included the Treasurership of Chichester and the Chancellorship of Salisbury, cf. the article on him in the *D.N.B.* In 1479 Doget was licensed to take for life the fruits of all his benefices as if resident on condition that he resided in one of them, or was in the service of Edward IV, or at the Roman Court, or studying letters at a University (*C.P.R.* vol. XIII, p. 249).

[5] Rymer, op. cit., vol. XII, p. 108. He had been sent to Rome to treat a peace between the Pope and Florence (*C.P.R.* vol. XIII, p. 245). On 15 July, 1479, he was about to return to England (*Ibid.*, vol. XIII, p. 247). In 1480 he was also appointed to an embassy to the King of Denmark (Rymer, op. cit., vol. XII, p. 121).

[6] Le Neve, op. cit. vol. I, p. 585.

[7] *Supra*, n. 4. Doget was appointed Provost of King's College on 10 April, 1499 (*Ibid.*, vol. III, p. 683), and died in April 1501. His will preserved at Somerset House, PCC 16 *Moone*, is dated 4 March, 1501, and was proved on the following May 22nd.

[8] In MS. (B.M.) Add. no. 10344.

commentary is dependent on Bruni's latinized *Phaedo*,[1] while other modern translations of Plato, including Decembrio's *Republic*,[1] were also employed. Doget was not an original thinker; hence he approached the *Phaedo* from the standpoint of Christian piety rather than rational speculation. A useful introduction to Platonic mysticism was available in Hermetic and Neoplatonic writings. This was also Doget's view. As a result his work as a commentator was chiefly inspired by them.[1] His aim appears to have been an interpretation of some of Plato's passages as Christian maxims. Because of this he deals principally with an explanation of obscure passages in the *Phaedo*, which are presented so as to emphasize their common points with Christian doctrine. Therefore, as Miss Hurnard has already pointed out, Plato's sayings become in his hands the texts of short homilies hardly connected at all with the subject matter of the *Phaedo*. The resemblance between Platonism and Christianity was not Doget's discovery. In emphasizing this he was following a tradition dating from the earliest centuries of the Church, which humanists like Bruni and Ficino had merely re-examined and developed. But unlike the Italians, Doget strove to prove his thesis with the methods of the schoolman rather than those of the humanist. As his aim was nothing less than the enlistment of Plato among the apologists of Christianity, he disregards logic and metaphysics in favour of cosmology, is more anxious to establish points of contact rather than to examine the Platonic system, and refuses to deal with any other problem arising from the text of Plato. His choice of the *Phaedo* was obviously dictated by its being the Platonic dialogue which appeared closest to Christian doctrine, and he accepted it as a form of poetry, which if not literally true yet held an immanent truth which it was his object to explain.[2] Also the angle from which Doget regarded Plato is typically medieval. A humanist would not have referred to the religion of ancient Greece as *Superstitiosa demonum religione*,[3] and would have dwelt less on Plato's allegorical method. Although the

---

[1] MS. (B.M.) Add. no. 10344, ff. 6ʳ, 29ʳ, 52ʳ, 53ʳ, 66ᵛ. Doget quotes Plotinus from St. Augustine's *De Civitate Dei*, Bk., X, ch. XXX, (*Ibid.*, fo. 54ᵛ). He also quotes Porphiry's *Isagoge* (*Ibid.*, fo. 36ʳ), Apuleius' *De Deo Socratis* (*Ibid.*, fo. 85ᵛ), the *De Divinis Nominibus* by the Pseudo Dionysius (*Ibid.*, fo. 8ᵛ), and Ficino's version of the *Pimander* (*Ibid.*, ff. 32ᵛ, 74ʳ, etc.). On his having employed Ficino's translation cf. Hurnard, op. cit. pp. 364-5.

[2] This conception of Plato's work by Doget was first pointed out in *Ibid.*, p. 584.

[3] MS. (B.M.) Add. no. 10344, fo. 8ʳ.

ultimate ideals behind his treatise approach in some way those of Marsilio Ficino, both his methods and outlook make the gap between him and the Italian Platonist very wide. Perhaps the main interest of Doget's commentary is his handling of antique materials with scholastic methods towards the fulfilment of a scholastic ideal, for in this he embodied that compromise between medieval and modern learning which was typical of the earlier stages of English humanism.

It is apparent from the state of Cambridge scholarship at the close of Edward IV's reign that the University was starting by then to consider the humanities from a less rigidly medieval standpoint than it had hitherto. It is true that any appreciation of Italian humanism there had been fostered mainly by practical considerations, such as an improvement in official epistolography. Nevertheless it must be recognized that whatever its utilitarian motives, the introduction of humanistic standards had been fundamentally a recognition of the superiority of modern Latinity over the Latin style practised until then. The way in which Cambridge began to react to humanism is reminiscent of the first approach of Petrarch's contemporaries to it. Like them Cambridge started by appreciating neo-classicism from what was purely a formal standpoint. What it accepted at first was what might be called the 'surface' of humanism, its views on style rather than its wider and deeper issues. The latter, and in fact everything in humanism except its trimmings, was passed over and will not appear in Cambridge culture until the sixteenth century.

CHAPTER XII

HUMANISM had continued to develop steadily in Oxford since the days of Chaundler's Wardenship of New College, and already towards the close of the reign of Edward IV it was beginning to show greater independence from medieval culture. Gloucester's books had continued to stimulate curiosity in neo-classicism, the transcription of works presented by the Duke by fellows of Oxford colleges[1] being clearly indicative that those volumes still aroused much interest. The donations of Flemmyng, Grey, and Tiptoft,[2] had also played an important rôle which, linked to the activities of Surigone and Greek scribes, had brought about a change in the intellectual atmosphere. It is no exaggeration to say that the period 1475–80 witnessed the conditioning of part of the University outlook by Italian values. It was their ascendancy that brought an improvement in the style of the *Epistolae Academicae*,[3] the prose of which during this period discloses an endeavour to write better Latin.

Some valuable evidence on the change in values in Oxford may also be found in the study of Latin grammar there. Medieval conceptions of grammar had been dominated by the treatises of Donatus and Priscian, and it was only during the fifteenth century that methodical innovations were contributed to Latin grammar by the Italians.[4] Among the grammatical productions of humanism, Valla's *Elegantiae* and Perotti's *Rudimenta Gramaticae* soon became popular both in Italy and abroad, and already during the second half of the fifteenth century their popularity appears to have extended to Oxford. Valla's treatise was among Flemmyng's books in Lincoln College;[5] but other copies of it were doubtless circulating in Oxford by then, and the use of it by an Oxford grammarian is doubtless quite suggestive of its acceptance as an authority in scholastic circles. The popularity of

[1] Robert Sherborne, Fellow of New College, has been suggested as the scribe of MS. (B.L.) Lat. misc. d. 34, which is a copy of one of the MSS. given by Gloucester to Oxford (Craster, *Duke Humphrey's Dante, Petrarch, and Boccaccio MSS.*, p. 303). For other copies by fellows of Oxford colleges cf. *infra*, p. 175, n. 3.

[2] Provided Tiptoft's MSS. reached their legatees.

[3] Cf. the letters in the second volume of the *Epistolae Academicae*.

[4] On humanistic innovations in grammatical studies cf. Sabbadini, *Il Metodo degli Umanisti*, pp. 3–15.

[5] Now MS. Lincoln Coll. Oxford, no. 60.

Valla's work in England was shared by that of Perotti. An edition of the *Rudimenta Gramaticae* with English passages replacing the Italian ones was printed at Louvain in 1486,[1] doubtless for the English book market, a sign this of the demand for it.

But perhaps the best proof of the acceptance in English academic circles of the treatises of Perotti and Valla during the last quarter of the century is furnished by the *Compendium Totius Gramaticae* printed in Oxford in 1483.[2] The *Compendium* was the work of John Anwykyll,[3] a schoolmaster appointed grammar master of Magdalen College School, Oxford, about 1481.[4] The teaching of 'poems, elegances, and the art of humanity' was among Anwykyll's duties,[4] in the course of which he must soon have revealed himself a capable as well as a modern minded teacher. Otherwise why should William of Waynfleet have asked him to compose a treatise incorporating the most up-to-date grammatical methods?[5] The *Compendium Totius Gramaticae* was the outcome of this suggestion, and consisted of an abridgement of Perotti and Valla's works blended with the *Doctrinale* of Alexander of Villedieu, so as to unite the medieval and modern grammatical systems. Like the grammar of Donatus and Perotti's *Rudimenta*, the *Compendium* was in the form of questions and answers, and prose was alternated with didactic verse. The various quotations in this work show how Anwykyll, in spite of his modest post, was fairly well read and attached special value to the usual array of classical works used by medieval teachers. His quotations include Quintilian's *Institutiones*,[6] Ovid,[6] Cicero,[6]

---

[1] By Egidius Van der Heerstraten, Gordon Duff, no. 346.

[2] Two editions of Anwykyll's treatise were issued in Oxford in 1483, Gordon Duff, nn. 28–9. No complete copy of either has survived. Fragments of them are preserved in the Bodleian Library, the Cambridge University Library, and the Library of Magdalen College, Oxford.

[3] On Anwykyll cf. *The Magdalen College Register*, vol. III, pp. 7–10, A. E. Shaw, 'The Earliest Latin Grammars in English,' *Transactions of the Bibliographical Society*, V (1898–1900) pp. 51–2. Perhaps he was the *Magister Anwykyll* who was allowed to incept at Cambridge in two years' time in 1474–5, and who was fined 13s. 4d. in 1475–6 for not incepting in Grammar (*Grace Book A*, pp. 106, 111). He does not appear in the Magdalen College accounts before 1483–4 (*The Magdalen College Register*, vol. III, p. 7). But it seems fairly certain that he was the *informator grammaticorum* to whom a payment was made in 1481 (*Ibid.*, loc. cit.).

[4] *Ibid.*, loc. cit.

[5] That Anwykyll was asked to compose his treatise by Waynfleet is suggested by Carmeliano's poem for the Oxford edition of the *Compendium* (*Infra*, p. 171). Anwykyll composed also a *Vulgaria quedam abs Terencio in anglica lingua traducta*, this being a collection of passages illustrating the Latin syntax. The *Vulgaria* was printed in Oxford in 1483, and reprinted three other times at least during the fifteenth century, Gordon Duff, nn. 392–5. Anwykyll died in 1487 (*The Magdalen College Register*, vol. III, p. 7).

[6] *Compendium Totius Gramaticae*, sigg. f4^v, k2^v, 3^v, l1^v, 4^r, 5^r, m3^v, n2^r–3^r.

Plautus,[1] Horace,[1] Sallust,[1] Priscian,[1] Donatus,[1] Terence,[1] and naturally Valla and Perotti, to both of whom he acknowledges his debt.[1] The constant mention of the names of these scholars, and the way in which he refers to them, also shows that Perotti and Valla's reputations as grammarians were well established in Oxford; also that mention of them would advertise a work favourably. And indeed the *Compendium* enjoyed a certain amount of popularity both in England and on the Continent. In 1483 two editions of it, to which were prefixed two introductory Latin poems by the Italian Pietro Carmeliano,[2] were issued in Oxford,[2] these being followed by editions abroad, one at Deventer in 1489,[3] which suggests the adoption of the *Compendium* as a textbook by the schools of the Brethren of the Common Life, and another at Cologne in 1493.[3]

The comparative success enjoyed by Anwykyll's teaching,[4] as well as by his treatise, is valuable in showing us that grammatical teaching on medieval lines was beginning to be considered out-of-date, and that even conservative citadels like Oxford were accepting newer systems of grammar. It is also obvious from the *Compendium* that despite the limitations of his scholarship, Anwykyll was able to play some part in the development of English humanism through his compromise between medieval and modern teaching of grammar.

Perhaps the *Compendium* had been revised by Pietro Carmeliano,[5] whose activities in England command attention since they are of importance as far as the spread of Italian culture in this country is concerned. The real family name of Carmeliano was 'Fava',[6] and he had been born in Brescia or its neighbourhood in 1451.[6] Nothing definite is known about him until his arrival in England in 1481,[6] except that he had been wandering through Europe for several years in quest of fortune.[7] As 'Rolls House' appears to have been his residence in 1482,[7] it is probable that he had already secured by this time some minor administrative

---

[1] Cf. *supra*, p. 169, n. 6. [2] *Supra*, p. 169, n. 2. *Infra*, p. 171. [3] Gordon Duff, nn. 30–1.

[4] A grant by Magdalen College to Anwykyll dated 18 June, 1487, praises him for his innovations in the teaching of grammar: '*consideratis multimodis uigiliis et laboribus quos idem Magister Johannes perpessus est circa nouam et perutilem formam docendi pro eadem schola conceptam et prescriptam per eundem . . .*' (*The Magdalen College Register*, vol. III, pp. 7–8).

[5] On Carmeliano cf. especially Guerrini, *Pietro Carmeliano da Brescia Segretario Reale d'Inghilterra*, Tanner, op. cit., pp. 154–5, and the article on him in the *D.N.B.*

[6] Guerrini, op. cit. p. 6. The date of Carmeliano's arrival in England is disclosed by his stating in 1482 that he had already spent one year in this country (MS. (B.M.) Royal, 12.A.XXIX, fo. 2ʳ).

[7] *Ibid.*, ff. 2ʳ–ᵛ. Both the poem and its dedication are in *Ibid.*, which is the autograph presentation copy to Edward, Prince of Wales.

appointment, but about this we possess no details. Carmeliano was obviously anxious to make a career for himself in this country, and as his humanistic qualifications constituted his main, and probably his only asset, he deemed it imperative to secure valuable patrons through his literary activities. With this end in mind he wrote a Latin poem on 'Spring', which once completed he sent in 1482, accompanied by a flattering dedication, to Edward, Prince of Wales.[1] Besides attempting to gain the patronage of the heir to the throne, he tried to attract the King's attention as well, and for this reason he presented him with a Venetian edition of Cicero's *De Oratore* with a commentary penned on its margins and a dedicatory poem, both composed by him.[2] The persistence shown by Carmeliano in dedicating works to royalty, suggests that such homage brought him remuneration, as it certainly did under the Tudors. The death of Edward IV and the usurpation of Richard III deprived Carmeliano of two potential or actual patrons; but he did not despair of gaining the favour of the new Sovereign. He therefore dedicated a Latin poem on St. Catherine of Egypt, which he had already offered to Edward V's Chancellor, John Russell,[3] to Sir Robert Brackenbury, Constable of the Tower of London, and a favourite of the new King.[3] The dedication included a short panegyric of King Richard, but we have no evidence as to whether Carmeliano was rewarded for his pains. During 1483 he may possibly have moved from London to Oxford,[4] if so, obviously in search of work. The printing press which had been introduced into England but a few years earlier by William Caxton, was flourishing in Oxford by this time, and in this new device Carmeliano may have found a source of profit. The publication of Anwykyll's *Compendium* gave him an opportunity to contribute two Latin poems[5] in praise of Anwykyll and his work as well as courting

[1] Cf. *supra*, p. 170, n. 7.

[2] This copy was seen by Tanner, who described it, in the Ely Cathedral Library (Tanner, op. cit. p. 155), and must have been the edition printed by Andrea de Paltasichis in 1478, *Gesamtkatalog*, no. 6749. Mr. Reginald Gibbon, the Ely librarian, informs me that this book is no longer there, and that it does not appear in the library catalogue compiled in 1796.

[3] The copy dedicated to Russell, who is addressed as Chancellor, is now MS. Gonville and Caius Coll. Cambridge, no. 196. In the preface Carmeliano states to have dedicated a *principale opus* to the King, this being possibly the *De Vere*. The copy dedicated to Brackenbury is in MS. (B.L.) Laud. misc. no. 501, which is in Carmeliano's autograph. The *D.N.B.* describes this work as the life of St. Mary of Egypt.

[4] Carmeliano's presence in Oxford is suggested not only by his contacts with Anwykyll, but also by his connexion with the Oxford printer Theodoric Rood, for whom he edited two works.

[5] These poems are in the Deventer edition of Anwykyll's *Compendium* at sig a1v. Although

the favour of William of Waynfleet, to whom one of the poems was addressed.[1] It seems likely that while in Oxford Carmeliano may have added to his income by alternating editorial activities with teaching. Direct evidence on this point is lacking; yet it seems probable that like Surigone before him he was able to lecture on humane subjects in that University. His efforts at improving the standard of Oxford scholarship were not confined to editing Anwykyll's handbook and possibly teaching. Even after the issue of the *Compendium* he had kept in touch with its printer, the German Theodorick Rood, and two years later, in 1485, he edited for him the *Epistles* of the Pseudo Phalaris in the Latin version by Francesco Griffolini,[2] to which he had added a Latin poem in which both the alleged author and the translator were commended to the reader.[2] In 1485 Carmeliano probably returned to London, where he continued his editorial activities. He had by now come into contact with William Caxton, at whose request he prepared for the press some diplomatic correspondence on the war between Pope Sixtus IV and Venice over Ferrara.[3]

With the beginning of the reign of Henry VII we find that Carmeliano soon established himself in the favour of the new monarch.[4] But as far as our study is concerned, it is his activities up to 1485 which are of interest. From these we can perceive that by the end of the reign of Edward IV it was possible for an Italian scholar to make a living in England, and to be able to exert some intellectual influence through editing for the printers. It is Carmeliano's editorial work that forms his real contribution to early English humanism, as by this means he was able to popularize some choice examples of neo-classical epistolography.

If the careers of Anwykyll and Carmeliano disclose the Oxford attitude towards humanism, this approach is confirmed furthermore by the steady progress of Greek in that University. Interest

the extant fragments of the two Oxford issues do not include the first pages, it is none the less certain that the two poems appeared in them, since both Anwykyll and Waynfleet were dead when the Deventer edition appeared. Moreover Carmeliano had no connexions with the Deventer printer, who doubtless reproduced the former edition.

[1] Cf. *supra*, p. 171, n. 5.
[2] Gordon Duff, no. 348. Carmeliano's poem is at sig aiv.
[3] Gordon Duff, no. 371. The title of this publication suggests that it was issued in order to furnish models of polite diplomatic literature rather than news.
[4] Already in 1486 he was in receipt of a Crown pension (W. Campbell, *Materials for a History of the Reign of Henry VII*, (R.S.) London, 1873–7, vol. II, p. 38), probably obtained as reward for his Latin poems celebrating the birth of Prince Arthur preserved in MS. (B.M.) Add. no. 33736. In 1488 Carmeliano obtained letters of denization (P.R. 1485–94, p. 189), and in 1496 he is described as Latin Secretary to the King (J. Gairdner, *Letters and Papers Illustrative of the Reigns of Richard III and Henry VII*, (R.S.) London, 1861–3, vol. I, p. 102).

in Greek had, as we saw, already been present in Farley[1] and some of the monks at Canterbury College earlier in the century.[1] Nor had other students of it been lacking. The various copies of Gaza's grammar[2] and other texts transcribed by John Serbopoulos in England,[2] are sufficiently indicative concerning this point. Instead so far historians have traced the beginning of Greek studies in Oxford to the coming of Cornelio Vitelli in 1475. As Vitelli's coming must be postponed of some fifteen years,[3] his rôle in the evolution of Greek studies in Oxford changes its aspect. However, a further confirmation of the already manifested view that Greek was known in Oxford from Neville's times is given by the early career of a man who became one of the recognized leaders of the New Learning, William Grocin.[4]

Like many other promoters of neo-classicism in this country, Grocin was educated at Winchester College, which he entered in 1463.[5] Already while there he appears to have distinguished himself in Latin, for on the visit of a French ambassador to the College he is reputed to have replied to the visitor's challenge with an impromptu Latin verse.[6] This episode and his graceful Latin epigram 'To Julia when she pelted him with snowballs',[7] indicate that he could, when still very young, compose Latin verse both classically inspired and metrically sound. After two years at Winchester, Grocin entered New College in 1465;[8] two years later he was admitted to a fellowship,[8] which he kept until 1481, when he vacated it for the college living of Newton Longueville in Buckinghamshire.[8] After two years' absence he returned to Oxford in 1483 on his appointment as Reader in Divinity in Magdalen College,[9] and it was as such that he successfully opposed a Master John Taylor in a disputation held when Richard III visited the college.[9] Grocin's departure for Italy took place about the year 1488:[10] still apparently already before

---

[1] *Supra*, pp. 131, n. 2; 138.
[2] *Supra*, pp. 147–8.
[3] Weiss, *Cornelio Vitelli in France and England*, p. 223.
[4] On Grocin cf. especially Burrows, *Memoir of William Grocin*, Schirmer, op. cit., pp. 170–5.
[5] Burrows, op. cit. p. 335.
[6] Bale, op. cit. p. 707.
[7] Printed in Schirmer, op. cit. p. 146.
[8] Burrows, op. cit. pp. 334, 336.
[9] Grocin appears as Reader in Divinity in the Magdalen College accounts for 1483–4 (*The Register of Magdalen College, Oxford*, New Series, vol. I, p. 15). The disputation before Richard III took place on 25 July, 1483, and is described in *Ibid.*, vol. I, p. 12.
[10] Burrows, op. cit. p. 337. It is, however, possible that Grocin had already left for Italy at the end of 1487, since he had already resigned his readership for some time on 23 March, 1488, (*The Register of Magdalen College, Oxford*, New Series, vol. I, p. 20). Grocin was

going abroad he had acquired some knowledge of Greek.[1] Our source for this is Erasmus, who stated explicitly that Grocin acquired his first rudiments of Greek in this country.[1] Perhaps additional evidence of this is furnished by *Register Ff4* of the Oxford University Archives, in which the signature Βιλελμος Γροκιν appears at the top of fo. 127ᵛ, which contains official University correspondence written in 1476. As the handwriting changes with this letter, this seems suggestive that Grocin, then a Fellow of New College, had taken charge of the University correspondence just as Farley, also a Fellow of New College, had before, and that he was following Farley's fashion of signing in Greek. Of course this may not be so, and the signature may have been added by someone else:[2] yet when we connect this with Erasmus' statement and other available evidence, it seems reasonable to infer that Grocin was acting as University Registrar in 1476, and that he learnt some Greek in Oxford before going to Italy. Chronology is against Vitelli having been his first master, though he might have influenced him at a later date; but John Serbopoulos or perhaps Emanuel of Constantinople, both of whom were the scribes of manuscripts owned by Grocin,[3] may have been very likely his earliest teachers of Greek.[4] A statement that knowledge of Greek was widespread in Oxford at the time would of course be erroneous: nevertheless Grocin's early career confirms the existence of Greek studies there, a fact already hinted at by the scribal pursuits of Emanuel of Constantinople and Serbopoulos.

The Oxford interest in things Greek was far from being restricted to a study of the language and original texts. Humanistic versions of Greek authors had been popular in Oxford since the time of Duke Humphrey, so that copies of them were plentiful. References to Plato and Plutarch are frequent occurrences in the *Epistolae Academicae*,[5] and the translations by Bruni,

already back in Oxford, where he went to reside in Exeter College (Burrows, op. cit. p. 337), on 4 June, 1491, when he held a theological disputation with the Warden of Merton College (*Registrum Annalium Collegii Mertonensis*, ed. H. E. Salter, (O.H.S.) Oxford, 1921, p. 147).

[1] Burrows, op. cit. p. 337.

[2] The signature is in a fifteenth century hand.

[3] *Supra*, p. 148, n. 2. The considerable number of MSS. written by Serbopoulos in Grocin's possession does especially suggest that he was in contact with this scribe.

[4] Late sixteenth century tradition credited William of Waynfleet with having introduced the study of Greek into Magdalen College (Gray, op. cit. pp. 110–1). Available evidence must, however, discredit this tradition.

[5] *Epistolae Academicae*, vols. I, pp. 123–4, 203, II, pp. 355, 476.

Guarino, and others, were eagerly collected in academic circles.[1] Bruni's Latin text of the *Ethics* gradually replaced the medieval versions of that work. Transcripts of it were available in the University Library[2] and the libraries of Lincoln,[2] Balliol,[2] and Magdalen[3] Colleges, while individual members of the University were anxious to own it. Thus John Goolde, a Fellow of Magdalen College, transcribed it in 1471–2,[3] and quite possibly others did the same. So much had the popularity of Bruni's version grown by the last quarter of the century, that a printed edition of it was issued in Oxford by Theodorick Rood,[4] doubtless in order to meet with the large demand for this text.

The productions of the Oxford press, and some foreign printed books to be found in Oxford during the fifteenth century, are also particularly valuable as witnesses of the spread of Italian values in the University. The publication of Bruni's *Ethics*, of Cicero's *Pro Milone* about 1483,[4] of Anwykyll's *Compendium* in 1483, and of Francesco Griffolini's latinized Phalaris in 1485, speak for themselves. Besides this a list of books valued in Oxford in 1483,[5] and one of the Oxford bookseller Thomas Hunt compiled during the same year,[5] include among their entries Valla's *De Vero Bono*, Perotti's *Rudimenta*, and Donatus on Terence, while Vergerio's *De Ingenuis Moribus* and Poggio's *Facetiae* were bound in Oxford during this same period.[6] All this indicates beyond doubt the growing demand for humane literature, and the change in taste which was taking place in Oxford during the later part of the century. Moreover, the productions of other English presses similarly witness the growth of a taste for polite letters in this country. The *De Tullianis Elegantiis* by Agostino Dati, and the *Nova Rhetorica* by Lorenzo da Savona were published by the '*St. Albans Scholemayster*' in 1479 and 1480,[7] and the *Rhetorica* had proved popular enough to be issued also by Caxton in 1479.[8] On the other hand the great

---

[1] *Supra, passim.*

[2] *Epistolae Academicae*, vol. I, p. 181, Weiss, *The Earliest Catalogues of the Library of Lincoln College*, p. 349, MS. Balliol Coll. Oxford, no. 242, given to Balliol by Grey.

[3] The MS. of Bruni's *Ethics* now Magdalen Coll. Oxford, no. 49 was presented to the college by its scribe John Goolde, who finished it on 1 February, 1472. This MS. also includes the *Politics*, which were probably transcribed at a later date, and were also presented by Goolde to the College.

[4] Gordon Duff, nn. 32, 104.

[5] Both lists are in *Collectanea*, (O.H.S.) vol. I, pp. 141–3.

[6] Gibson, op. cit. pp. 21, 26. Printed copies of Agostino Dati and of Perotti's *Rudimenta* were also bound in Oxford during this period (*Ibid.*, pp. 21, 26).

[7] Gordon Duff, nn. 111, 369.

[8] *Supra*, p. 162, n. 3.

majority of Caxton's productions suggest no connexion with Italian learning. Yet he was by no means unacquainted with it, as is shown by his contacts with Surigone[1] and Carmeliano,[1] and by his appreciation of the loss to scholarship caused by the death of John Tiptoft:[2] he also knew some of Boccaccio's Latin writings,[2] and refers in one of his prefaces to the library of Poggio.[2]

In addition to these productions of English printers, the book trade was increasingly importing books from the Continent, both printed and in manuscript, which naturally included a fair number of neo-classical texts. This coupled with the origin of some classical and modern manuscripts, which were to be found in England during the fifteenth century and are still extant, makes it obvious that such writings could easily be found in stationers' shops, both in London and in Oxford, during the later part of the century. Some passages in the *Vite* of Vespasiano[3] and in the letters of Flavio Biondo,[3] actually confirm the exportation of humanistic texts from Italy into England, and we know that these manuscripts were often transcribed again in this country,[4] so that specimens soon multiplied. These manuscripts appear to have been particularly popular among high prelates. Some of these, like Shirwood and Grey, took advantage of their journeys to Italy to purchase books, and are known to have received gifts of manuscripts from Italian scholars; for instance John Chedworth, Archdeacon of Lincoln, had dedicated to him during his term of office as Rector of the Jurists of the University of Padua[5] some Latin poems by Ludovico Lazzarelli,[6] and had a Latin oration in praise of England addressed to him by Giusto de Giusti.[7] James Goldwell, who became Bishop of Norwich in

---

[1] *Supra*, pp. 139, 172.

[2] *The Prologues and Epilogues of William Caxton*, pp. 34–5, 47, 78.

[3] Da Bisticci, op. cit. p. 505, Nogara, op. cit. pp. 208, 212.

[4] *Supra, passim.* On the importation of books into England during the fifteenth century cf. H. R. Plomer, 'The importation of books into England during the Fifteenth and Sixteenth Centuries,' *The Library*, IV (1923) pp. 146–50. A MS. containing the treatise by Agostino Dati and Valla's *Elegantiae* in a small hand based on the Italian model but probably English is now MS. Trinity Coll. Cambridge, no. 1123. A copy of Petrarch's *Secretum* and Cencio Romano's version of the pseudo-Platonic *Axiochus*, written in England about the middle of the fifteenth century, is now MS. National Library of Wales, Peniarth, no. 336A. The *Axiochus* has a preface by an anonymous author addressed to Reginald Butler, Bishop of Hereford, (1451–3), (*Ibid.*, pp. 208–10).

[5] Chedworth's rectorship lasted from 1467–8 (Mitchell, *English Students in Padua*, 1460–75, p. 109). On Chedworth cf. *Ibid.*, pp. 109–12.

[6] These form the *Liber de Apparatu Patauini Astiludii* (copies of which are in MSS. (B.M.) Arundel, no. 212, Durham Cathedral Library, Hunter, no. 123), which was printed in Padua by G. B. Martini in 1629.

[7] In MS. (B.M.) Cotton, Nero, A.X. ff. 1ʳ–38ʳ. A letter of Giusti to Chedworth written from Verona on 16 July, 1468, is in *Ibid.*, ff. 38ᵛ–40ʳ.

1472[1], was similarly a collector of neo-classical manuscripts, and his library, which he left to All Souls College, Oxford,[2] included Petrarch's *De Remediis*,[2] Valla's *Elegantiae*,[2] and *Invectivae*,[2] which he purchased in Rome in 1467, versions of Xenophon's *Hiero*[2] and St. Basil[2] by Bruni, and a volume containing the *Exhordia* by Barzizza and letters by Guarino, Poggio, Francesco Barbaro, Richard Petworth, and others,[2] which almost certainly came to him from Christ Church, Canterbury. John Russell, whom Sir Thomas More described as one of the most learned men of his time,[3] and who became Bishop of Lincoln in 1480,[3] also possessed several humanistic texts. Amongst these were Petrarch's *Epistulae Seniles*,[4] Boccaccio's *De Casibus*,[5] an *Aeneid* with the thirteenth book by Maffeo Vegio,[5] and perhaps treatises by Aeneas Sylvius.[6]

The possession of neo-classical texts was not, however, the monopoly of the higher ranks of the Church. It was a Dr. Gavin Blenkensop who presented Pembroke College, Cambridge, with a collection of examples from the letters of Bruni in 1470,[7] and a Fellow of Magdalen College was the donor of a copy of Bruni's *Ethics* to his college.[7] This abundance of humanistic manuscripts in Yorkist England is also disclosed by the notebooks of William of Worcester. It is apparent from them that he had in his hands the Latin Diogenes Laertius by Ambrogio Traversari,[8] Cristoforo Buondelmonti on the Islands of Greece,[8] the *Cicero Novus*[8] by Bruni, and Guarino's *Regulae*,[8] as well as some books formerly owned by Free, a Greek manuscript now

[1] Stone, op. cit. p. 118.

[2] Now MSS. All Souls Coll. Oxford, nn. 38, 61, 64, 91, 93, (B.L.) Rawlinson, G.47, Imperial University Library, Tokyo, A.100.1300. Goldwell also owned MSS. Gonville and Caius Coll. Cambridge, nn. 66, 70, 246, 482. Perhaps he was the *Jacobus Norwych* who wrote his name in some of the humanistic treatises in MS. Trinity Coll. Cambridge, no. 1420.

[3] Sir. T. More, *History of King Richard III*, ed. J. Rawson Lumby, Cambridge, 1924, p. 23. Russell received the Lincoln temporalities on 9 September, 1480, (Rymer, op. cit. vol. XII, p. 136). On Russell cf. especially *Propositio Johannis Russell*, ed. H. Guppy, Manchester, 1909.   [4] Now MS. New Coll. Oxford, no. 267.

[5] Now MSS. New Coll. Oxford, nn. 263, 271.

[6] This is suggested by a quotation from this author in one of the drafts of speeches prepared by Russell for the intended Parliament of Edward V, printed in *Grants etc. from the Crown During the Reign of Edward the Fifth*, ed. J. G. Nichols, (C.S.) London, 1854, pp. xxxix–l. These speeches include quotations from Solinus, Valerius Maximus, Sallust, Boccaccio, Aeneas Sylvius, and the Odyssey. Russell's Pliny is now MS. New Coll. Oxford, no. 274. It is interesting to note that he also owned two copies of Cicero's *De Officiis*, Mainz, Fust and Schoeffer, 1465, *Gesamtkatalog*, no. 6921, now in the University Library, Cambridge, and at Lambeth Palace. The Cambridge copy was bought by him in Bruges in 1467.

[7] *Supra*, pp. 161, n. 4, 175.

[8] MSS. (B.M.) Cotton, Julius, F.VII, ff. 67ᵛ–8ʳ, 93ʳ, 105ʳ; Corpus Christi Coll. Cambridge, no. 210, p. 279, Balliol Coll. Oxford, no. 124, fo. 242ᵛ.

N

in the Bodleian Library,[1] a volume of excerpts,[1] and some auto-graph lecture notes,[1] amongst them. Despite his access to Renais-sance literature, William of Worcester remained, however, un-affected by modern values. He was only a dilettante without qualifications for scholarship whose accomplishments lay rather in the direction of antiquarianism, as his voluminous compilations testify.

The presence of many works of Italian humanists in this country, suggests strongly that by the last quarter of the century the writings of the most famous Italian men of letters had be-come accepted here as what one might call, to use a modern expression, 'standard authors.' Besides Petrarch and Boccaccio, scholars like Bruni, Poggio, and Aeneas Sylvius, came to be considered writers of authority, and passages from their works are to be found quoted alongside with those of medieval authors.[2] This indicates plainly the value attached to their writings, which is also emphasized by the products of English printing during the century.

This appreciation of humanistic authors, the establishment of humane learning in Oxford, the beginnings of it in Cambridge, make it manifest that, as had been the case in Italy a century earlier, the various individual efforts of scholars had furthered the development of humanism sufficiently to secure its recog-nition in some University circles by the end of the Yorkist period. That this was so is perhaps enough to refute the charge of intellectual barrenness, which has been brought against fifteenth century England.

[1] *Supra*, pp. 108, n. 1; 110, n. 5; 111, n. 2. On Worcester cf. especially F. A. Gasquet, *The Old English Bible and Other Essays*, London, 1908, pp. 247–75, Worcester, *Itinerarium*, *The Paston Letters*, *passim*, and the article on him in the *D.N.B.*

[2] *Epistolae Academicae*, vol. II, p. 568, *supra*, p. 177, n. 6, etc. Even a conservative like Sir John Fortescue is found quoting Bruni's *Isagogicon* and Poggio's version of Diodorus in his *De Natura Legis Naturae*, and *De Laudibus Legum Angliae* (*The Works of Sir John Fortescue, Knight*, ed. Lord Clermont, London, 1869, vol. I, pp. 70, 137, 151, 340, 347).

CONCLUSION

ENGLISH humanism in the fifteenth century was very different in its manifestations from contemporary Italian humanism. Whereas in Italy the cult of the antique had completely transformed cultural values, in England we find neo-classicism absorbed into the sphere of scholasticism and used for the furtherance of scholastic ends. Moreover, in Italy humanism had been considered as a new intellectual system displacing or revising all the conceptions of the Middle Ages; but in England humanism was conceived not as a new cultural manifestation or a refinement in taste, but rather as a means of improving some aspects of scholasticism. This fundamental difference was due to several reasons. As it was observed by the Venetian author of the *Italian Relation of England*, English learning during the fifteenth century was practically the monopoly of ecclesiastics.[1] Ecclesiastics ruled the Universities. Besides this they occupied several places of great importance in the administration of the state. The Civil Service was practically in their hands, and diplomacy was to some extent under their control. The average layman of the fifteenth century had little time for learning. Politics, trade, or war, absorbed his energies to the exclusion of intellectual pursuits. Laymen devoting part of their time to letters were only exceptions. In the history of English classical studies during the fifteenth century Humphrey of Gloucester and Tiptoft typified a small minority. The majority were men like Flemmyng, Free, Gunthorpe, and Sellyng, each of whom was in holy orders, and most of whom had played a considerable rôle in academic affairs before being absorbed into ecclesiastical and political activities. As a result of this, if humanism was to obtain admission into the orbit of English culture it could only secure it through schoolmen, who would obviously be influenced by their particular outlook, and would consider it as subsidiary to their formal studies. As schoolmen their main interest was theology. Moreover, many of them took a 'dilettante' interest in Latin style. It was consequently unavoidable that when in contact with Italian learning they would approach it with a view to the improvement of their favourite pursuits. As it was pointed out in one of the early chapters of this book, a powerful reason for the first acceptance of neo-classicism in this country was the attitude towards Latin style prevalent in

[1] *Italian Relation of England*, ed. C. A. Sneyd, (C.S.) London, 1847, p. 22.

some English literary circles during the first half of the fifteenth century. This attitude alone would not, however, have proved strong enough to secure the establishment of new values in England. Style has seldom been an end in itself, and had humane learning not offered potentialities in other fields it would probably have exerted little influence on English intellectual life. But those schoolmen who came into contact with it were quick to perceive its practical potentialities.

Already during the earlier decades of the century Latin treatises and translations from the Greek by the Italians had begun to reach England. Now by this time English scholasticism had stopped producing original speculation. Neither the opponents of Wycliffe nor his followers brought any valuable contribution to scholastic thought, so that it was only natural that some English schoolmen should regard those productions of Italian learning as means for the improvement of their studies. It is perhaps incorrect to say that the English schoolmen were attracted by neo-classicism as a whole. The evidence that has reached us suggests that very few, if any, perceived the fundamental difference between scholasticism and humanism. All they saw was that the Italians were particularly proficient in Greek and Latin letters, but this they regarded as a normal development of medieval scholarship rather than as a result of a reaction against those cultural canons for which their learning stood. The wider intellectual issues raised by Italian humanism evaded them, and beyond its mechanical side they failed as a whole to understand it.

The value of Greek in philosophy and Divinity was already appreciated in the days of Humphrey of Gloucester. The translations made expressly for him were chiefly of works of theology and philosophy which would prove useful to the studies of schoolmen. The superiority of these translations over those made in the days of Robert Grosseteste was obvious to Gloucester and his contemporaries, and their value fully realized. Hence a tendency to apply Greek learning to theological and philosophical studies becomes increasingly evident as the century draws on.[1] The extant Greek manuscripts possessed by Robert Flemmyng contain only religious literature. Sellyng translated a

---

[1] A similar application of the humanities to the furtherance of philosophy and theology could be found at Chartres during the twelfth century (A. Clerval, Les Écoles de Chartres au Moyen Age du Ve au XVIe Siècle, Chartres, 1895, p. 230), and in France and Germany during the last quarter of the fifteenth century.

work of St. John Crysostomus. The majority of the texts copied
by Emanuel of Constantinople and John Serbopoulos were
religious works or treatises connected with the study of Aristotle
and his philosophy. Altogether, it was the study of Plato,
Aristotle, and the Fathers of the Church, rather than of Greek
literary authors, which was pursued in fifteenth century England.
Among Italian humanists the one whose writings proved most
popular here, and whose authority was most quoted, was
Leonardo Bruni, who was known in this country chiefly as the
translator of Aristotle. To sum up, it is the elements in Greek
studies which were deemed suitable for the furtherance of scholasticism that were accepted here. The others were disregarded,
and we do not find any real study of Greek secular literature in
England before the sixteenth century.

The Greek side of humanism was not the only one which
attracted the attention of English schoolmen. The Latin side
was similarly channelled to the pursuit of ends not exactly conforming with humane ideals. It is true that in several cases the
study of modern Latinity was prompted by an interest in rhetoric
or by intellectual curiosity, and that persons like Duke Humphrey,
Flemmyng, Tiptoft, and Gunthorpe, were fundamentally eclectic
in their attitude to learning. Nevertheless the angle from which
this aspect of neo-classicism was approached by the majority
was perhaps as a whole more utilitarian. Its value in diplomacy
was already realized by Thomas Bekynton, and it was very probably his appreciation and innovations in the language of diplomacy that led to its becoming a recognized part of the armoury
of statecraft. It is difficult to establish exactly the criteria govern-
ing the selection of civil servants during the fifteenth century.
Still, if we examine the careers of the great majority of the
exponents of classicism in England from about 1440, we shall
find that they were often employed by the Crown, in embassies
or as Proctors in Rome, as King's Clerks, or very often in such
exalted positions as Keeper of the Privy Seal or King's Secretary.
The conclusion forced on us by this is that a high standard of
classical Latin constituted a sure avenue to a brilliant political or
diplomatic career, and eventually to high preferment in the
Church. As we have seen, two important passages in contemporary documents confirm this view. In his funeral oration of
Guarino da Verona, Ludovico Carbone on mentioning Robert
Flemmyng states quite explicitly that it was because of his pro-

ficiency in the humanities that he was appointed Henry VI's Proctor in the Court of Rome. Richard III when recommending John Shirwood to Pope Innocent VIII, emphasized especially Shirwood's learning in Greek and Latin as grounds for advancement.

A utilitarian conception of the humanities is the main feature of humanism in England during the fifteenth century. Above all it consisted in drawing from Italy those elements which were of value in theology, philosophy or diplomacy. It is true that the influence of humane learning is also to be felt in Latin rhetoric, prosody, and even in calligraphy as well as in Latin prose. But its influence in these fields was partly an outcome of the reasons which had made the study of modern Latin popular.

The utilitarian ideals of early English humanism are reflected in some of the libraries assembled by leading English scholars and patrons. The books collected by Flemmyng, Tiptoft, and Gunthorpe, suggest an eclectic outlook. But those of Humphrey, Duke of Gloucester, and Grey show plainly these utilitarian features. Books of poetry are very scarce in them. On the other hand their libraries abounded in grammatical treatises, epistolaries, translations from the Greek, and collections of orations.

The utilitarian attitude of Gloucester is furthermore emphasized by his requests for books from Decembrio. Practically all these texts were related to medicine, philosophy, agriculture, and other branches of science; none of them belonged to pure literature.

All this indicates that humanism was adopted in England during the fifteenth century as a means rather than an end. It was seldom pursued for its own sake; but the various fields in which it brought its influence to bear were soon able to display its beneficial action. In theology it disclosed new horizons through its introduction of Greek and Platonism. Philosophy also became richer with a more accurate knowledge of Aristotle and with a wider acquaintance with Plato. It raised the standard of diplomatic language to one not very distant from that attained in Italy, and certainly not inferior to that of other European countries. Grammar and rhetoric were revised and brought into closer conformity with Renaissance ideals.

Unlike the case of Italy, all these changes were brought about through compromise and without a concerted effort. Economic difficulties, the principal of which was that the Universities had little provision for humanistic teaching because of lack of endowed lectureships in such studies, the difficulty of obtaining manuscripts and of making contacts with foreign scholars and of travelling to Italy, restricted at first the pursuit of neo-classicism to a limited yet influential number of persons. These scholars pursued it mainly as a hobby, and only influenced its development through personal contacts rather than through actual teaching, and through donations of books to learned institutions.

Because humanism was hardly considered more than a medium this was also a decisive factor against the setting up of a humanistic society. Pure humanists did not exist in England: there were only some schoolmen who pursued modern as well as scholastic studies. If this co-operation of classical learning with scholasticism prevented humanism from developing independently, it also prevented hostility between classicists and schoolmen during the fifteenth century. As both aimed at similar ideals there were not to be found here, as in Italy, schoolmen attacking literature and humanists mocking scholasticism. No works like Giovanni Dominici's *Lucula Noctis*[1] were written in England. No preachers denounced humanism from the pulpits. Instead we find the humanities at the service of scholasticism and attempting to further its development.

The difference in its ideals compared with humanism as practised in Italy, its compromise and subordination to medieval culture rather than antagonism with it, were above all instrumental in shaping the characteristics of the New Learning as conceived by Grocin, Colet, Linacre, and More. An examination of the achievements of these great scholars will disclose alongside with strong humanistic elements some very solid scholastic foundations. Indeed, it may be stated that the English learning of the eve of the Reformation included the best characteristics of humanism and scholasticism. The reasons which brought about this compromise between the culture of the Middle Ages and that of the Renaissance, can only be explained by the early history of humanism in this country. And when reviewing the features of the New Learning of the early decades of the sixteenth century, it is impossible not to recognize them as the natural evolution of the modest and amateurish activities of the English humanists of the fifteenth century.

[1] Dominici's *Lucula Noctis* was composed at the beginning of the fifteenth century, and is an attack on the spreading of humanistic studies. It was published in *Beati Johannis Dominici Lucula Noctis*, ed. R. Coulon, Paris, 1908.

INDEX OF NAMES